THE SHAW
POCKET BIBLE HANDBOOK

THE SHAW
POCKET BIBLE HANDBOOK

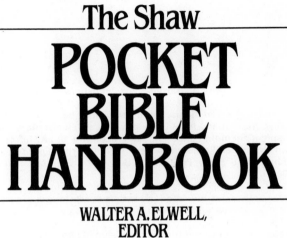

The Shaw
POCKET
BIBLE
HANDBOOK

WALTER A. ELWELL,
EDITOR

Harold Shaw Publishers
Wheaton, Illinois

Unless otherwise indicated, all Scripture references are from the *New International Version*.

Prepared under the editorial supervision of Miriam Mindeman

ISBN 0-87788-683-0

Printed in the United States of America

Library of Congress Cataloging in Publication Data
Main entry under title:

The Shaw pocket Bible handbook.

   Bibliography: p.
   Includes index.
   1. Bible—Handbooks, manuals, etc.
I. Elwell, Walter A.
BS417.S44 1984   220.6′l   84-5455
ISBN 0-87788-683-0

---

12 11 10 9 8 7 6 5 4 3 2

94 93 92 91 90 89 88 87 86 85 84

Contents

The Bible: A Book Set in History

Culture of Bible Times

Archaeology & the Bible

A Brief Chronology of Biblical Events

2 What the Bible Teaches about Christ & Christian Faith

◯ The Life of Christ

◯ The Teachings of Christ

◯ What Christians Believe

3 The Bible: A Book for People Today

◯ How the Bible Came to Us

◯ How to Read the Bible More Effectively

❹ Concise Summaries of the Books of the Bible

◯ Old Testament

◯ Apocrypha

◯ New Testament

❺ Exploring the Bible

◯ Key Verses for the Christian Life

Contributors

Walter A. Elwell, Ph.D. (Edinburgh), is Professor of Bible at Wheaton Graduate School, and an author, lecturer, and editor (*Evangelical Dictionary of Theology*). He is the general editor of this handbook and his contributions include the articles, "The Life of Christ," "The Teachings of Christ," "How to Read the Bible More Effectively," and "Concise Summaries of the Books of the Bible."

R.K. Harrison, Ph.D. (London), is a well-known author, lecturer, and O.T. scholar. His *Introduction to the O.T.* is regarded as the best conservative work on the O.T. His contributions to this handbook are the articles, "Archaeology & the Bible," and "A Brief Chronology of Biblical Events."

H.D. McDonald, Ph.D. (London), B.D. (London), is Vice Principal Emeritus of London Bible College (London, England), and an author, teacher, and N.T. scholar. He has traveled widely, and taught in North American schools and seminaries, in addition to writing numerous books, including *Salvation* and *Theories of Revelation*. His contribution to this handbook is the article, "How the Bible Came to Us."

Leon Morris, Ph.D. (Cambridge), is an internationally known lecturer, teacher, author, and N.T. scholar. Formerly Vice Principal of Ridley College (Melbourne, Australia), he is best known for his works on the Gospel of John and the theme of love in the N.T. His contribution to this handbook is the "Glossary of Important Biblical Words."

Hazel Perkin, M.S. (McGill), is a biblical researcher and Principal of St. Clement's School (Toronto, Ontario). Her contribution to this handbook is the article, "Culture of Bible Times."

R.E.O. White, M.A. (Liverpool), B.D. (London), has been a pastor, author, and lecturer in Greek N.T. and Ethics. He has written over 30 books, including *Christian Ethics,* a major work on Christian behavior. His contribution to this handbook is the article, "What Christians Believe."

Introduction to this Handbook

The Bible is one of God's greatest gifts to the world. Its remarkable power to affect lives is acknowledged even by those who don't believe it. The Bible can be found in virtually every literate home and has been the world's overall best-seller. Year by year it is the best-selling book. The Bible exists in more versions and editions than any other book and has been translated into more languages than any other written item. Millions of people live by it, and others try to destroy it.

The reason why the Bible is so important to the world is that it contains the word and will of God for us. In it we find out who God is, how the world came to be, how the world will end, what our problems consist of, God's solution to human sin in Jesus' death and resurrection, how to live our lives, and much more. All we need to know about spiritual matters can be found here. It is a complete spiritual guide. Besides that, the Bible is a wonderful companion. In it we can find comfort, hope, encouragement, strength, and joy.

If all of that is true, why do most people know so little about the Bible? Part of the answer might be that at times we don't really want to know what is there, but that is not the whole story. Many times we *do* want to know what is there, but we get lost in unfamiliar wording, obscure customs, strange places, and complex ideas. The ancient world seems foreign to us who live in modern technological society. That fact should not surprise us. It *is* a foreign world; the writers of the Bible would feel just as out of place in our world.

If we want to know more about the Bible, how should we begin? What we need is a guide to get us going in the right direction. The book you have in your hands is designed to be that. It was written by scholars who are committed to the Bible's full inspiration, and who want to open up its pages to anyone interested in making the most important journey of their lives.

This little guidebook has five sections. The first section describes customs and cultures of Bible times and provides a brief look at significant archaeological discoveries in the last hundred years.

The second section takes up the life and teachings of Jesus, which is the heart of what the Bible is about. It also includes a summary of Christian doctrine.

The third section begins with a short discussion of how the Bible has been transmitted down through the ages. After that, ideas for meaningful Bible reading are offered.

The fourth section deals with the Bible's contents. Here we go through the entire Bible book by book, giving an overview of events and teaching.

The fifth section includes a glossary of important biblical words and ideas, key verses for memorization, interesting Bible facts, and a suggested reading list.

This guidebook is written as short pieces that are grouped together in larger sections, allowing for easy reading. The smaller pieces, along with the Bible verses mentioned, may be read one at a time or in larger chunks. Or a person may skip around for variety's sake, looking at a book a day, say Matthew or Mark, along with a key Bible word such as *gospel*. Or one could simply go through this book from beginning to end, taking everything as it comes. Do whatever seems best to you. The result will be the same: God's word will come alive as we read it. God's will becomes more evident to us as we open our hearts to him. Nothing is more important in life than our relationship with God. It is the sincere desire and prayer of those who offer this book to you that God will be more a part of your life because you have taken time to work through the pages of the Bible with an open heart and mind.

Walter A. Elwell

Index to Maps & Figures

List of Abbreviations

Old Testament

Genesis	Gen.
Exodus	Exod.
Leviticus	Lev.
Numbers	Num.
Deuteronomy	Deut.
Joshua	Josh.
Judges	Judg.
Ruth	Ruth
1 Samuel	1 Sam.
2 Samuel	2 Sam.
1 Kings	1 Kings
2 Kings	2 Kings
1 Chronicles	1 Chron.
2 Chronicles	2 Chron.
Ezra	Ezra
Nehemiah	Neh.
Esther	Esther
Job	Job
Psalms	Ps.
Proverbs	Prov.
Ecclesiastes	Eccles.
Song of Solomon	Song of Sol.
Isaiah	Isa.
Jeremiah	Jer.
Lamentations	Lam.
Ezekiel	Ezek.
Daniel	Dan.
Hosea	Hos.
Joel	Joel
Amos	Amos
Obadiah	Obad.
Jonah	Jon.
Micah	Mic.
Nahum	Nah.
Habakkuk	Hab.
Zephaniah	Zeph.
Haggai	Hag.
Zechariah	Zech.
Malachi	Mal.

New Testament

Matthew	Matt.
Mark	Mark
Luke	Luke
John	John
Acts of the Apostles	Acts
Romans	Rom.
1 Corinthians	1 Cor.
2 Corinthians	2 Cor.
Galatians	Gal.
Ephesians	Eph.
Philippians	Phil.
Colossians	Col.
1 Thessalonians	1 Thess.
2 Thessalonians	2 Thess.
1 Timothy	1 Tim.
2 Timothy	2 Tim.
Titus	Titus
Philemon	Philem.
Hebrews	Heb.
James	James
1 Peter	1 Pet.
2 Peter	2 Pet.
1 John	1 John
2 John	2 John
3 John	3 John
Jude	Jude
Revelation	Rev.

The Bible:
A Book
Set in History

1 / The Bible: A Book Set in History

Culture of Bible Times
by Hazel Perkin

Archaeology & the Bible
by R.K. Harrison

A Brief Chronology of Biblical Events
by R.K. Harrison

Culture of Bible Times
by Hazel Perkin

The word culture refers to the ideas, customs, skills, arts, etc., of a particular group of people at a particular time. We begin having our society's culture instilled in us from infancy onward, first of all, by the family into which we are born or adopted. This process of acculturation continues

A Jew in Jerusalem blows a "shofar" or ram's horn, used in ancient Israel to summon the people on military and religious occasions. (R. Nowitz)

as we are exposed to our environment, schooling, religious education, and friends or peers, though we are generally unaware it is happening.

In our Western culture we may be accustomed to eating three meals a day, living in small nuclear families, and listening to recorded music in offices, stores, homes, and even cars. We may understand certain words and actions to be unkind or impolite and others to be cordial and friendly. However, a person in another culture may be unfamiliar with these and other aspects of our culture that are so familiar to us we rarely think about them.

People in the ancient world of the Bible were influenced just as strongly by their cultures as we are by ours, and each biblical writer wrote from his own cultural perspective. This means that some of the terms and concepts in the Bible may be rather unfamiliar to many of us because of our separation from Bible lands and times by long distance and many centuries. However, we can

Babylonian clay tablet with a stylus held in the correct position for writing cuneiform, a wedge-shaped script. (ORINST)

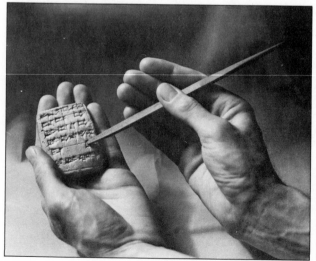

bridge that gap and understand more fully the intent of the biblical writers by studying the way they lived and how they viewed the world.

For example, a study of patriarchal customs shows that for people in Bible times, to be born a male was far more significant than to be born a female. Boys had more privileges and freedom than girls, a higher status that continued through adulthood. Knowing this we can see that Jesus treated women in a revolutionary way, considering the customs of the times. We begin to understand why Jesus' disciples were so amazed that he would even be "talking with a woman" other than a relative (John 4:27), to say nothing of discussing important spiritual issues with her. We also understand what a shock it must have been that, in a culture which did not recognize a woman's testimony in a court of law, God allowed women to be the first witnesses of Jesus' resurrection (Luke 24:1–12; cf. Acts 2:17–18).

The following discussion is only a partial coverage of the large amount of resource material available on the culture of Bible times. See the suggested reading list on page 390 if you'd like to study the subject more deeply.

Childhood
Childhood was brief in Old Testament times. Children, frequently seven in number, generally grew up in loving families. The younger ones would sit on the mother's lap (cf. Isa. 66:12–13) and would play with a variety of toys, some of which have been recovered from excavations. Although there were no team sports, children devised their own games, and boys wrestled. At an early age each child would be allotted some task such as gathering fuel (Jer. 7:18), bringing water from the well, tending flocks (Gen. 29:6), and caring for cattle.

The father was the provider for the family, working in the fields or at a trade or occupation. One of his duties was to instruct his sons in a trade or profession. Boys

Three young girls in modern Bethlehem. (D. Birkey)

would follow their father to the fields or workshop and watch him as he did his work. As the son grew older he would help increasingly, and so master that trade or profession. In the same way a girl learned household skills from her mother.

Adolescence as such was unknown in Bible times. The child soon became a young adult and was encouraged to participate as fully as possible in family life. When religious festivals were held, children often accompanied their parents to the sanctuary, as Jesus did when he was twelve (Luke 2:42). Young girls were not veiled or secluded, but visited freely with friends and neighbors when they had finished their tasks.

In the early patriarchal period a son or daughter could be put to death for disobeying their father, but with the advent of the Mosaic legislation a father had to refer the case to the elders (Deut. 21:18–21). Children convicted of disobedience, gluttony, or drunkenness could be stoned to death. The authority of the father also extended to a married son living in the household.

Education

Education has always been a high priority for the Jewish people. A child was taught to understand the Jews' special relationship with God and how important it was to serve the Lord (Exod. 12:26–27; Deut. 4:9). Of special importance was the history of the Jewish people; this knowledge helped to sustain the ideal of a homeland through periods of servitude and exile. As children's early teaching occurred within the family, so their understanding of faith was enriched by family practices, particularly meals connected with religious festivals like the Passover. When the boys in the family grew older, they would be taught more of their religious heritage and traditions by the father.

By New Testament times elementary schools were provided by the community, often in the synagogue or the teacher's house. Boys began school about seven years of age and sat at the feet of the teacher, who expounded the Law and other Scriptures. Education beyond the elementary level was the responsibility of the rabbis, scribes, and Pharisees. A boy was expected to have a thorough knowledge of Hebrew history and the Law, and was also instructed in reading, writing, arithmetic, as well as in other subjects, which may have included herbal knowledge (cf. 1 Kings 4:33).

Marriage

Marriage, a relationship that by Christian times had become a sacrament, was originally a binding exchange of vows between bride and groom as a result of negotiation by their parents. Many Israelite men married only one wife; others in Old Testament times had two wives (Deut. 21:15) or one or more concubines. David had more than one wife; Solomon had 700 (2 Sam. 5:13; 1 Kings 11:3; Song of Sol. 6:8–9). Herod the Great had nine wives.

Marriages were frequently arranged with near relatives

or members of the clan or tribe. As the bride was to become a member of her husband's family, it was important for the groom's parents to know whether she was suitable and likely to be compatible with her relatives. The consent of the bride and groom was sometimes obtained, but was not required. Although marriage was expected to be for life, a wife could be divorced by a simple statement to that effect by her husband; she could not divorce him. Jewish law later required a written document for divorce, but in any case divorce was rare in Old Testament times.

The betrothal, which occurred about a year before the marriage, was a formal binding agreement (Matt. 1:18; Luke 1:27; 2:5). After it, the betrothed woman was considered to belong to her future husband, and he was then regarded as a son-in-law by the bride's family. In the interests of establishing proper family relationships, the man was exempt from military service during the first year after the formal marriage ceremony (Deut. 24:5).

The bride-price was one reason for the frequency of monogamy. Few men could afford to provide such a substantial sum more than once. The bride-price was a purchase price paid to the bride's father to compensate him for the loss of his daughter's work in the home or fields. The price was sometimes paid in the form of work, as when Jacob served Laban for fourteen years to obtain Leah and Rachel (Gen. 29:15–28). Some of the dowry was customarily given to the bride herself, often in the form of jewelry that she wore as part of her adornment at the wedding.

The groom was lavishly attired for the wedding in sumptuous scented garments and with a garland of flowers on his head. Preparations for the bride included bringing a translucent quality to her skin and braiding her hair, if possible with gold and pearls. Her adornment included the finest clothing, along with a veil. Thus prepared, she and her bridesmaids awaited the arrival at her parents' home of the bridegroom's procession. As it

This Yemenite Jewish bride is arrayed for her wedding day. (R. Nowitz)

wound its way through the village or town, the torchlight wedding procession of the groom and his friends was the setting for music (Jer. 7:34) and merriment. The procession then returned with the bride and her entourage to the home of the groom's family where wedding feasts often continued for seven days, sometimes even for fourteen. A specially prepared bridal chamber awaited the young couple. The young bride immediately began hoping to fulfill her special duty, namely, the provision of sons.

Figure 1 The Jewish Calendar *(See also Jewish Feast Days, p. 256)*

Order of civil year	Order of religious year	Hebrew month	Western equivalent	Days of celebration
1	7	Tishri	Sept/Oct	1st, Rosh Hashanah 10th, Yom Kippur 15th–21st, Sukkot
2	8	Marchesvan	Oct/Nov	
3	9	Kislev	Nov/Dec	25th, Hanukah
4	10	Tebet	Dec/Jan	
5	11	Shebat	Jan/Feb	
6	12	Adar	Feb/Mar	14th–15th, Purim
7	1	Nisan	Mar/Apr	14th–21st, Passover & Unleavened Bread
8	2	Iyyar	Apr/May	
9	3	Sivan	May/June	6th, Pentecost
10	4	Tammuz	June/July	
11	5	Ab	July/Aug	9th, Destruction of the Temple
12	6	Elul	Aug/Sept	
		Adar Sheni	Intercalary month*	

* Each year that the barley was not ripe on the 16th of Nisan this month was to be added, but never to be added for two years in a row.

The young woman's role was to be responsible for the household cooking, cleaning, spinning, weaving, sewing, and also to provide occasional help in the fields or vineyards. She was expected to give the early stages of education to her children (Prov. 1:8; 6:20; 31:10-31).

As head of the household, the father made all decisions. Even a promise made by a wife was invalid without her husband's consent (Num. 30). Nevertheless, the status of the wife was superior to that of many Arab women who, with their children, were considered working property. A wife and her sons could not be sold into slavery, although a daughter could be. But as late as New Testament times an entire family could be sold for debt incurred by one of its members (Matt. 18:25).

Although a wife could not leave her husband, she might have to be subordinate to a new wife or concubine and be denied the right to inherit property. Yet even in those circumstances she would not be segregated, but would participate in feasts and family activities. A wife had the affection and respect of her children, especially when she was the mother of sons. Nevertheless a man's possessions were listed as his wife, servants, slaves, and animals (Exod. 20:17; Deut. 5:21). The subservient status of the wife is seen in her designation of her husband as lord or master (Gen. 18:12).

Females in a family were allegedly under the protection of a male. As a child, a girl's father was her master; as a bride, her husband; as a widow, her husband's closest male relative. The perfect wife in biblical times was expected to be discreet, quiet, sensitive, and charming (Prov. 9:13; 11:16, 22; 21:9). She also needed to possess organizational and management skills for the household and the family's finances (Prov. 31:10-31). Strong, dominant women, with public roles like Deborah, Jael, and Judith, were rare. By Roman times, however, women were highly respected and often helped their husbands in business. The attitude of Jesus toward women also helped to enhance their status in the early Christian era. By New

Testament times it was hoped that the women would be loving, holy, reverent (Titus 2:4; 1 Pet. 3:2-6).

Courtyard in the ruins of a house in ancient Corinth. (L. Shaw)

Buildings

Many families lived in towns or cities surrounded by thick, defensible walls. Sometimes a city would have three concentric walls with heavily fortified gates frequently constructed with six large pillars. Architecturally the buildings were practical and plain in design, but often showed precision and good engineering.

Solomon's temple was designed in the Syro-Phoenician style, which was artistic and elegant. The use of white limestone added to the sparkling appearance of the building in sunshine and moonlight. The use of bronze and wood overlaid with gold, the wooden floor, sculpture, and sunlight shining through the high windows made the temple unique in its magnificence.

The homes of the common people were in sharp contrast. Many were built of stone, some of lath and plaster. They generally consisted of one main room, although larger houses were built around a central courtyard. All houses had flat roofs, which could sometimes be covered with an awning to provide a relaxing, peaceful place (Acts 10:9). Brushwood, earth, and clay were used to make the flat roof, which was frequently not waterproof. It sometimes sprouted grass, and often had to be rolled flat after a rainstorm. Rooms with beaten mud floors provided living and sleeping quarters for the family members and their animals. Open slits in walls served as windows, which might be covered by a lattice at night. The fewer the windows, the less sun could penetrate, and thus the house would remain cool and comfortable during the day. After sunset the dull mud walls would be illumined by the small light of flickering oil lamps.

Politics

The culture of a people—social attitudes, mores, family life, and leisure—are affected both by the political framework and by commercial interaction with

Statue of Augustus Caesar, who was emperor of Rome at Jesus' birth. (H. Vos)

SPQR
IMP·CAESARI·DIVI·F·
AVGVSTO
PATRI·PATRIAE

neighboring civilizations. Politics, or matters relating to the city-state (Greek *polis,* "city"), necessarily influences the lives and activities of the citizens. The first city-states were organized in southern Mesopotamia. Their politics consisted of managing, or mismanaging, city affairs and trying to avoid being conquered by powerful neighbors. A king or queen normally ruled a city-state, which consisted of the city itself and the lands just outside its walls. Such rulers had priests and court officials as advisers, and occasionally sent ambassadors to the courts of other city-states.

In Egypt a ruler would often make decisions at his accession about relations with nearby peoples. Thus a pharaoh might decide to invade Nubia or conquer Palestine and Syria just to establish his own power there. Kings were not always popular with their subjects, however, and periodically a ruler would be killed following a conspiracy among his officials or his palace women.

On rare occasions two nations would be fighting one another when a third would try to attack them. That happened in 583 B.C. when Syria and Israel were at war and suddenly the Assyrians threatened to destroy both armies. Israel and Syria promptly joined forces to defeat the Assyrians. At times nations also co-existed in peace, making treaties with one another for trading purposes.

A conquering nation always took goods and tribute from the conquered people, and sometimes would tax them heavily for years. In such cases a governor-in-residence would be appointed to make sure that the conquered city officials and other aides collected the tribute. Any attempt to avoid payment usually resulted in severe punishment. The Hebrews paid heavy taxes to the Assyrians and Romans, and, needless to say, the tax collector was always an unpopular person. The political life of the Jews in Christ's time was made difficult by the presence of a Roman governor who strictly controlled the amount of political freedom the Jews could enjoy and saw that taxes were collected.

Trade

Although essentially a poor country, Israel was situated on main trading routes, particularly the north-south route. Egypt exported corn and manufactured goods, as did Ebla. Phoenicia expanded manufacturing activities along with its shipping trade. Israel, mainly an agricultural country, was able to sell oil, wine, as well as wool in bulk, linen cloth, and metal. Wheat was the major commodity traded along the east-west route that crossed Galilee. Trade was at its greatest during the reigns of David and Solomon, the latter building up a vast fortune by taxing the trading-caravans that passed through his land. Solomon also constructed a fleet of merchant ships for Red Sea commerce, which extended his commercial interests. Generally speaking, however, Israel normally traded with Phoenicia and Egypt, only occasionally sending goods to Syria. By the Roman period, trade with more distant areas had been built up, to the advantage of the Jewish people.

Arts & Leisure
Literature was a well-developed art form, as is evidenced by the Hebrew and Greek Scriptures. The cultivation of the mind was enhanced by composing and memorizing proverbs. Although leisure time was scarce, lyre and flute music were popular. Instrumental and vocal music, as well as dancing by men or women in separate groups, formed an integral part of Israelite social life and religious function (Exod. 15:20; 1 Sam. 18:6; 2 Sam. 6:14, 21, etc.).

Meals
It is doubtful if families in Bible times had any meal comparable to our breakfast either for children or parents. If the father worked in the fields, he would probably take a light lunch, as would children who tended herds or flocks. Such a meal would include flat cakes or loaves, olives, figs, and curds or cheese from goats' milk. The young children would help to prepare an early dinner, the main daily meal. This mealtime was essentially a family occasion, and probably started in time to take

Grain storage pits at the house of Caiaphas in Jerusalem. (L. Shaw)

advantage of whatever daylight remained. Conversation would continue into the evening by the light of small oil lamps. The evening meal would include bread or cakes from hand-grown grain, often barley, goats' cheese or curds, along with vegetables such as lentils, beans, peas, and leeks. Although vegetables were not always available, they added variety to the meal when present. Salt, garlic, and possibly vinegar were used for flavoring. Wine, frequently well watered, was drunk with the meal.

Food was cooked in olive oil, with honey used as a sweetener. The problem with these meals, in other than wealthy families, was that they were extremely monotonous despite the wife's cooking skills. However, the exhausted and hungry family members were probably less concerned with variety than with the fact that there was food on the table. Meat was rarely eaten except after a sacrifice, since at other times the animals were too valuable for the poor to consider slaughtering for food. The wealthy fared better in enjoying kid's meat or venison (Gen. 27:3–33; 2 Sam. 12:2–3; Luke 15:29) or a fatted calf for special feasts (1 Sam. 28:24; Matt. 22:4). Pheasants, turtledoves, quails, pigeons, and partridges were also eaten (Exod. 16:13; Deut. 14:4–19), and several varieties of fish were available.

Lavish feasts were frequent in the days of King Solomon. Women wearing finely woven gowns and decked in elaborate jewels would sit or lounge with their hosts at large tables, where food of all kinds including meat, fowl, and sweets would be washed down with large quantities of wine and beer. In New Testament times the main course consisted of a bowl of meat and/or vegetable stew placed in the center of the table. Family and guests would then break off small pieces of bread and dip them in the communal bowl. Visitors at mealtimes were quite frequent, as it was the Hebrew custom to extend hospitality to travelers. This was also a means of discovering information of a political, commercial, or social nature from other towns or villages.

Clothing

Merchants bringing silk and finely woven fabrics would travel in caravans over vast distances from as far away as India. Fine linen was imported from Egypt. In Palestine clothing was frequently made of linen from locally grown flax. Everyday clothes were made from an ordinary quality linen; priests wore more expensive linen (Exod. 39:27). Wool could easily be made into clothing by semi-nomadic people, but flax for linen could be cultivated only by a settled community.

The poor often wore coarse clothing made from goat or camel hair, which was rough and very uncomfortable. Also known as sackcloth, it was often worn as a sign of penitence. It also served as a blanket for warding off the cold at night. Cotton was known in Egypt and elsewhere, and in Roman times a form of local wild silk was obtainable. Fine gold wire gave luxury to garments, while different colors were obtained from plant or animal sources: red from an insect, yellow from a flower, saffron from the stigma of a crocus, and purple from the Murex mollusk. Purple dye from Tyre (Ezek. 27:16), renowned for its color, became a symbol of royalty and wealth.

Olive presses such as this produced the cooking oil for people in Bible times.
(J. Jennings)

The clothing of most people was simple in style. The loin cloth was worn by men of all social levels from an early period, with the later addition of an outer and inner garment. The inner garment of wool or linen had an opening for the neck and arms, and generally had long sleeves. Often belted at the waist, it fell either to the knees or ankles. The outer garment, cloak or mantle, generally made of animal skin or wool, was almost square, with openings for the arms, and was worn draped over one or both shoulders. As a man was considered naked unless he was wearing his cloak, he was forbidden to lend or pledge it. At night he removed it for use as a blanket (Exod. 22:26–27; Deut. 24:13). Jesus' undergarment was woven without seam (John 19:23) and would have been worthless if cut into pieces. That was why Roman soldiers at his crucifixion decided to cast lots to see who should have it.

Fine linen with elaborate embroidery was used for outer clothing by the wealthy. Kings sometimes wore an additional garment similar to the priest's vest-like tunic or

A modern-day weaver at work in northern Transjordan. (J. Jennings)

ephod. Both kings and priests wore an elaborate headdress to symbolize their status. The adornment of such garments contrasted sharply with the simplicity of most people's dress.

Most women in biblical times wore simple white clothing, although blue or black homespun was sometimes seen. Wealthy women wore garments of brightly dyed fine linen, often in scarlet or purple, and elaborately decorated with embroidery, jewels, and gold or silver detail (2 Sam. 13:18). Such garments were also worn on festive occasions and at weddings (2 Sam. 1:24; Ezek. 16:10, 13). The undergarment worn by a woman was similar to a man's except that it was higher at the neck and normally fell to the ankles. Headwear, although rarely mentioned in the Bible, was probably like the prayer-shawl sometimes seen today, and was held in place by a cord. Women often wore a veil that was held in place by a circlet of coins that may have formed part of their dowry. Jewelry was normally designed in gold, sometimes with semi-precious stones inset. As early as 2700 B.C. the royal graves at Ur give evidence of a high qualilty of design and craftsmanship in jewelry. Gold chains were popular, as were circlets, anklets, bracelets, and pins for clothing or hair. Footwear generally consisted of open leather sandals.

Hair & Cosmetics

In the Old Testament a man's long hair was a sign of virility, but in Greek and Roman times shoulder-length or even shorter hair became fashionable. Women took pride in long hair, which was often braided, but in early Christian times women were warned against spending excessive time on the new elaborate styles with massed curls obtained by using curling irons and ointments. Although grey hair earned respect for age and wisdom, some women preferred to use red or black hair dyes. Herod the Great is said to have dyed his hair with henna. Hebrew men often wore beards, which by Roman times might have been trimmed by the newly discovered and expensive razors of tempered steel.

Among the most popular cosmetics was eye makeup (2 Kings 9:30), made from kohl, green malachite, or stibium, and mixed with gum arabic. Those substances served a medical as well as cosmetic purpose, providing a useful antiseptic for eye infections (frequent in lands abounding with flies). Eyes were often outlined in black to give the appearance of increased size, and eyebrows were darkened with a black paste. Some Bible references associate eye makeup with prostitutes or loose women (metaphorically in Jer. 4:30 and Ezek. 23:40). Lipstick was favored by women in Greek and Roman times, and some face powder, rouge, and paint for toe and finger nails was also used. Perfumes, oils, and ointments were popular for gifts (Wis. Sol. 2:7), for personal wear (Song of Sol. 1:13), and especially for ritual occasions, weddings, and feasts.

Figure 2 Money in the Bible

Measure	System equivalent	Approx. weight	Approx. U.S. value
gerah	1/10 beka 1/20 shekel		$ .02
beka	10 gerahs 1/2 shekel		$ .25
shekel*	2 bekas 20 gerahs	10 g 1/2 oz.	$ .50
mina	50 shekels 100 bekas	500 g 1 lb.	$ 25.00
talent	60 minas 3000 shekels	30 kg 66 lbs.	$ 1,500.00
gold shekel			$ 8.00
gold mina			$ 400.00
gold talent			$24,000.00

* ordinary working day's wage

Figure 3 Weights & Measures in the Bible

Liquid Capacity

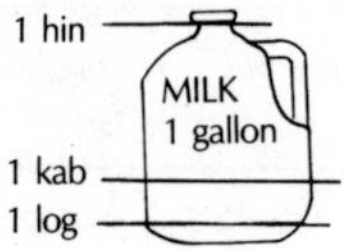

Measure	System equivalent	Approximate equivalents	
		Metric	U.S.
log	1/12 hin	0.33 ℓ	1/12 gal.
kab	4 logs 1/3 hin	1.3 ℓ	1/3 gal.
hin	12 logs 3 kabs	3.67 ℓ	1 gal.
seah	6 kabs 2 hins	7.33 ℓ	2 gal.
bath	3 seahs 6 hins	22 ℓ	6 gal.
homer	10 baths 60 hins	220 ℓ	60 gal.

Dry Capacity

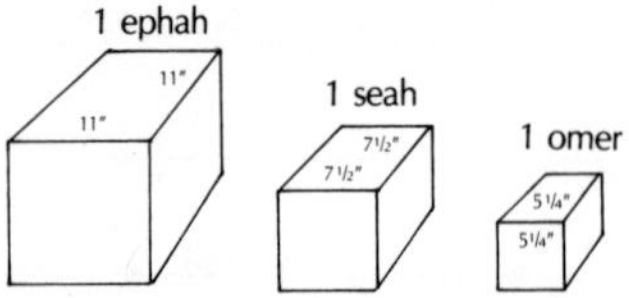

Measure	System Equivalent	Approximate equivalents	
		Metric	U.S.
log	1/4 kab	0.33 ℓ	20½ cu. in.
kab	4 logs	1.2 ℓ	73 cu. in.
omer	7 logs 1⅘ kabs	2.4 ℓ	146½ cu. in.
seah	3⅓ omers 6 kabs	7.3 ℓ	¼ cu. ft.
ephah	10 omers 3 seahs	22 ℓ	¾ cu. ft.
lethech	15 seahs 5 ephahs	110 ℓ	3¾ cu. ft.
homer	10 ephahs 2 lethech	220 ℓ	7¾ cu. ft.

Weight

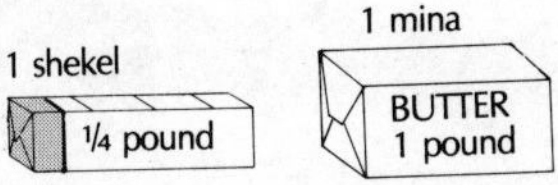
1 mina
1 shekel
1/4 pound
BUTTER
1 pound

Measure	System equivalent	Approximate equivalents Metric	U.S.
gerah	1/20 shekel	0.5 g	1/50 oz.
beka	10 gerahs 1/2 shekel	5 g	3/16 oz.
pim	1 1/2 bekas 3/4 shekel	7 g	1/4 oz.
shekel	2 bekas 1 1/2 pims	10 g	1/2 oz.
mina	75 pims 50 shekels	500 g	1 lb.
talent	60 minas 3000 shekels	30 kg	66 lbs.

Length

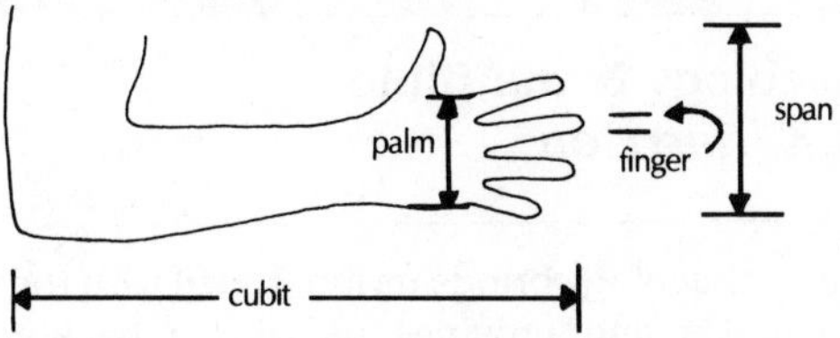
palm
finger
span
cubit

Measure	System equivalent	Approximate equivalents Metric	U.S.
finger (digit)	1/12 span	2 cm	3/4 in.
palm (handbreadth)	4 fingers 1/3 span	7.5 cm	3 in.
span	12 fingers 3 palms	22.25 cm	9 in.
gomedh	3 3/4 palms 1 1/4 spans	30 cm	12 in.
cubit	6–7 palms 2 spans	44.5 cm	17 1/2 in.
fathom	4 cubits 8 spans	2 m	2 yds.

A corner of the Parthenon on the Acropolis at Athens. (L. Shaw)

Archaeology & the Bible
by R.K. Harrison

Biblical archaeology brings us into touch with the world of Bible peoples and provides us with a background of knowledge against which we can begin to understand the biblical narratives better. Archaeology reveals to us the conditions of life in past centuries, and in some cases recovers for us material objects that people used—from pieces of pottery to elegant gold vessels and jewelry, from clay tablets dealing with the business accounts of a long-dead Babylonian family to papyrus scrolls recording the diseases of ancient Egyptians and the medicines that they took.

Archaeology is not meant to "prove" the truth of the Scriptures, because this revelation from God, being basically spiritual, has to be evaluated spiritually (see 1 Cor. 2:14). Yet our understanding of that revelation as something from God that was experienced by real people helps us see that our faith is not the result of myth, magic, or folklore, but instead is rooted deeply in history.

Sometimes the discoveries seem to have a direct bearing on the Bible itself. For example, in 1983 after three seasons of work on Mt. Ebal in central Palestine, Israeli archaeologists announced the discovery of a rectangular structure made of stone blocks, that was most probably the stone altar Joshua built on Mt. Ebal (Josh. 8:30–31) following Moses' command. All around the structure were ashes and the remains of sheep bones, signs that the area was important religiously. As part of their research, the archaeologists dated the bones to the twelfth century B.C.

When we learn through archaeology about some of the great cities mentioned in Scripture, and the splendid place they occupied in past centuries, we begin to see how time passed as people lived and died, governments rose and fell until the time came when Christ was revealed as the Savior of mankind. We learn also that what the Bible has to say about some of these famous places was in fact the sober truth. While Jerusalem came to be known in history as the "holy city" because God's temple was there, other places were notorious for their wickedness. The Jews regarded proud Babylon as the home of all wickedness, and it was left in ruins by divine judgment, as prophesied by Isaiah. Archaeology has also shown how Nineveh, the capital of Assyria, struck terror in the minds of people because of the brutality of the Assyrian armies, but even that fell to a stronger power, as prophesied by Nahum. Proud Athens, the intellectual center of ancient Greece, was dedicated to the service of the pagan goddess Athena, and ruins of her temples may still be seen there today. Corinth, a Greek city that had an evil reputation in Paul's day, contains the earliest known Christian cemetery, showing that the gospel light was able to shine through the pagan darkness of that corrupt place. Archaeologists have even uncovered the site where Paul stood in judgment before Gallio (Acts 18:12–17).

Map 1 Nine Key Archaeological Sites Today

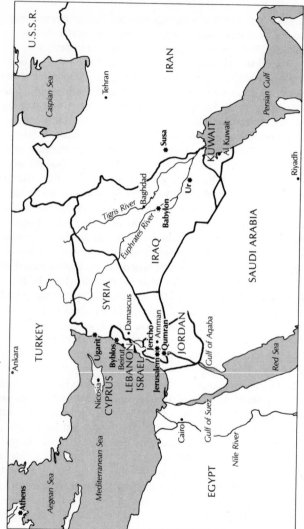

While archaeology helps us to understand ancient life and times, many of the ruins carry a stern reminder of God's direct judgment upon human wickedness and disobedience. In this sense, therefore, the stones still cry out as witnesses to God's revelation through the Law, the Prophets, and Jesus.

We have chosen nine sites for a brief study here (see Map 1). All of them have been excavated to varying degrees, and all were important places at one time or other. Some of them are already well known to us through records of ancient history as well as what Scripture has to say, but others are not so familiar, since they are not mentioned in the Bible, and they occur only occasionally in ancient historical records. Also included are some sites discovered only through archaeological excavations, showing that archaeology does in fact fill out the picture of ancient life by recovering places of great importance that had disappeared from history. The familiar sites discussed here are Athens, Babylon, Jericho, Jerusalem, Susa, and Ur. The unfamiliar ones are Byblos, Qumran, and Ras Shamra (Ugarit).

Athens

This celebrated Greek city was named after its patron goddess Athena, and was a very ancient site. The hill known as the Acropolis was settled first, perhaps c. 6000 B.C., but only many centuries later did the city become famous for its learning and democratic institutions. Athens was the principal city of Attica in ancient Greece and was at its height in the fifth century B.C. under Pericles. It enjoyed revival under Philip of Macedon, father of Alexander the Great, and was a renowned center of philosophy. Athens was a busy cosmopolitan city, and the temples on the Acropolis were marvels of engineering and sculpture. Excavations in Athens have done much to recapture its splendor in the biblical period.

The city was visited by Paul on his second missionary

journey. Of special interest is the Agora (marketplace), which figured prominently in both commercial and civic activities. It was located NW of the Acropolis. Paul spent some time in this area endeavoring to convert Jews and other Athenians to faith in Christ (Acts 17:17). Little has survived of the Agora except the foundations of buildings and the Stoa, or porch, which has been reconstructed. The Stoa was a narrow, lengthy building with a colonnade along one side, opposite which was a blank wall. It was the setting for lectures, conversations, and philosophical discussions (see photo below).

The Areopagus from which Paul addressed the assembled philosophers (Acts 17:22–32) was a rocky hill about 400 feet high, situated S of the Agora. The Acropolis lay to the SE within sight of the Areopagus, so that as Paul was criticizing superstition and worship in temples made with human hands he could see the Parthenon, along with its associated temples that were decorated with pagan deities. The altar "to the unknown god" was one of many in

Facing the ruins of the Agora, the marketplace Paul visited at Athens, is a reconstruction of the Stoa, a portico where philosophical discussions took place. (H. Vos)

Greece. An altar recovered from Pergamum in 1909 was similarly inscribed. The synagogue where Paul preached (Acts 17:17) has not been identified, although some ancient Jewish graves have been discovered in Athens. Paul's efforts to present the Christian faith philosophically unfortunately won few converts.

Bible book: Acts

Babylon

This ancient city, located in the plain of Shinar (Gen. 11:2), was named Bab-ilu (Gate of God). A capital city in Mesopotamia, it was first mentioned by name about 2200 B.C. It was one of the oldest human habitations and was apparently built on or near the site of the Tower of Babel (Gen. 11:3–9). Famous as the capital of Hammurabi (1792–1750 B.C.), it lost its power after 1300 B.C. The city became famous again under Nebuchadnezzar II (605–562 B.C.), who spent 40 years laboring to make it the most splendid capital known.

Excavations at the site have uncovered the huge brick outer wall of the city. This barrier was 87 feet thick and 350 feet high, with the top forming a road on which four chariots could drive side by side to block attacks. Twenty-five beautiful avenues intersected with 25 others, dividing the city into squares. The royal palace was a magnificent structure, surrounded by a triple wall with huge bronze gates. Nearby were the terraced Hanging Gardens, made by Nebuchadnezzar for his Median queen Amyitis. Irrigation canals and pumps brought water into the heart of the city for the gardens, orchards, and parklands that covered much of Babylon. Small wonder that Nebuchadnezzar would boast as he did (Dan. 4:30).

The Hebrew captives deported to Babylon (Jer. 52:28–30) would have helped to beautify and enlarge the city, but its splendor was not to last. Isaiah foretold its destruction (Isa. 13:19), Jeremiah predicted that it would become a desolate ruin (Jer. 51:37), and Daniel stated that the

Ruins of the "Summer Palace" built by Nebuchadnezzar (605–562 B.C.) at Babylon. (J. Jennings)

Medes and Persians would conquer it (Dan. 5:26–28). This prophecy was fulfilled in 538 B.C.

Excavations near the city's great Ishtar Gate have uncovered a series of tablets written in Babylonian, listing the rations of oil and grain supplied to captives in Babylonia between 595 and 570 B.C. Jehoiachin of Judah was mentioned, thus confirming the historicity of the captivity as described in Kings (2 Kings 24:15).

Bible books: Genesis, 2 Kings, Isaiah, Jeremiah, Daniel.

Byblos

Known to the ancient Phoenicians as Gebal, this seaport N of Beirut was first identified and excavated in 1860. It was occupied almost continuously from 5000 B.C. to the Crusades period. The Greeks who traded in this city knew it as Byblos ("book") because it was the center for papyrus manufacture, and this name is the origin of our word "Bible." In OT times it was an important locale for the Canaanite religion and was famous for its artisans and craftsmen, many of whom were hired by Solomon to construct the temple in Jerusalem (1 Kings 5:18). Because Gebal was a port, it employed carpenters and shipbuilders who constructed trading vessels for the merchants of Tyre (Ezek. 27:9).

In about 1115 B.C. Gebal was visited by an Egyptian ambassador named Wen-Amun, who was sent to many places by Rameses XII to purchase cedar for a ceremonial boat dedicated to an Egyptian god. The trading relations that Gebal had were typical of Palestinian maritime life in the time of Solomon, and the account of Wen-Amun's travels and adventures confirms this.

Ruins of a sanctuary for worship of pagan gods at Byblos. (J. Jennings)

An interesting discovery made in 1925 by Montet was that of the sarcophagus of Ahiram, king of Gebal. Dated about 1250 B.C., this stone coffin was made by the dead king's son. On it the king was depicted sitting on a throne of sphinx-like design in front of a table spread with sacrificial offerings. The sarcophagus lid carried an engraved inscription which identified the ruler, his son, and the nature of the contents. This inscription is very important

because it is one of the earliest examples of the ancien
Phoenician script. Other inscriptions, tombs, coins, and
buildings have been uncovered at the Byblos site, some
artifacts going back to nearly 3000 B.C.

A new hieroglyphic script was discovered in 1930 at Ge
bal, written on copper as well as stone. The inscriptions
were done later than 2200 B.C. but to date they have not
been deciphered. Their discovery demonstrated how early
the people of Palestine set down words in written form.

Bible books: 1 Kings, Ezekiel

Jericho

This ancient Palestinian settlement was first occupied
about 8000 B.C., and was an impressive walled city two
thousand years later. It was important in antiquity because it stood at the intersection of two ancient highways,
overlooking the pass from the plain up to Jerusalem. After
Joshua's victory over Jericho (Josh. 6), the city was rebuilt
as a village, but only became important again by New Testament times. It was in this elegant city that Jesus healed
a blind man (Luke 18:35–43) and dined with the wealthy
Zacchaeus (Luke 19:1–10).

There are three related sites in the Jordan valley known
as Jericho. The OT city, Tell es-Sultan, is about 1 1/2 miles
NW of the modern city (er-Riha), and is located beside
Elisha's Fountain (2 Kings 2:19–22), the only perennial
spring in the area. NT Jericho was situated almost a mile S
of its OT counterpart.

Sir Warren sank an unproductive shaft at Tell es-Sultan
in 1868, but better results were obtained by archaeologists Sellin and Watzinger (1907–09). Garstang's excavation of the eight-acre mound (1930–36) led him to identify
four successive cities of Jericho dating from c. 3000 B.C.
He concluded that Jericho had collapsed under Joshua
c.1400 B.C. More precise excavating techniques employed
by Kathleen Kenyon (1952–58) have revised Garstang's
conclusions radically. The city walls he attributed to the

Late Bronze Age (Joshua's time) actually belonged to the Early Bronze Age, more than a thousand years before Joshua's period.

Kenyon was unable to recover any significant traces of the Jericho that Joshua attacked, due to severe erosion at

Excavations in the mound of Canaanite Jericho facing the Mount of Temptation in the west. (H. Vos)

the site, but she succeeded in tracing the occupational history of the mound back to c. 9000 B.C. A thousand years later Jericho was a town surrounded by a stone wall that was surmounted by at least one massive tower to guard the ten-acre site.

Middle Bronze Age (c. 1900–1550 B.C.) tombs have preserved a remarkable collection of pottery, metal daggers, ornaments, wooden stools, tables, beds, jewelry, inlaid trinket boxes, and Egyptian scarabs. Excavations at er-Riha have uncovered the winter capital of Herod the Great and Archelaus, with its citadel, courts, villas, palace, public buildings, and large private homes.

Bible books: Joshua, 2 Kings, Matthew, Luke

Jerusalem

This place may have been settled by 3000 B.C. on the lowest areas of the present city. Originally a Jebusite fortress, it became David's capital, housing the royal palace and later the Temple. Jerusalem was the scene of some of Christ's works, and the place of His death and resurrection.

This ancient site is mentioned in the nineteenth century B.C. Egyptian Execration Texts and in the fourteenth century B.C. Amarna tablets, records kept during the time when the Jebusites controlled Jerusalem. The Jebusites constructed underground watershafts which tapped the spring of Gihon, bringing water within the city walls. This system was augmented under Hezekiah (2 Kings 20:20; 2 Chron. 32:3), who had a tunnel built ending in the Pool of Siloam. An inscription near the entrance of the pool, written in eighth century B.C. Hebrew script, and first found in 1880, commemorated this event. Another pool, Bethesda (Bethzatha), has also been located in Jerusalem underneath the church of St. Anne. One of its walls bears a faint representation of an angel disturbing the waters (John 5:2–9).

Tracing the ancient city walls has presented problems

ecause Jerusalem has shifted N during its history. Warren
nd Wilson found that the lowest levels of the W wall were
Ierodian, though some archaeologists have considered
hem the work of Nehemiah. Warren uncovered David's
vall on Mount Ophel and revealed parts of the old Jebu-
ite foundations. Attempts to find David's tomb have
ailed, due largely to the destruction of buildings on the
E hill area, but the ruins of a large tower have been un-
overed, perhaps the one mentioned by Jesus (Luke 13:4).

The location of Golgotha in relation to the W wall in
Christ's time has been much debated. Some hold that the
>resent day Church of the Holy Sepulchre marks the site
of Christ's crucifixion and burial, and others favor the site
near the Damascus Gate known as the Garden Tomb. The
ock sepulchre there is dated between 100 B.C. and A.D. 100
and could have held Christ's body.

In addition to the layers of rubble that have built up
over the centuries in Jerusalem, archaeologists face an-
ther problem as they seek out the city's significant bibli-

Excavations south of the temple mount in Jerusalem. (J. Jennings)

Caves at Qumran where the Dead Sea Scrolls were found. (L. Shaw)

cal sites: Jerusalem has been inhabited continuously and remains so today. This means that excavations can only take place in carefully chosen sites, and these often are not the ones considered most promising. Nevertheless, valuable discoveries continue to be made. In 1983, Wheaton College students excavating at the base of St. Andrew's Church on the south side of the Hinnom Valley recovered from a tomb a seventh century B.C. silver amulet inscribed in ancient letters with YHWH, the divine name of the Lord. This is the earliest mention of God's name ever found in Jerusalem.

Bible books: 2 Samuel, 1 & 2 Kings, 2 Chronicles, Matthew, John, Hebrews

Qumran

This site in a deserted area about eight miles S of Jericho became settled about 130 B.C. by a religious group that had broken away from contemporary Judaism. Their writings, the Dead Sea scrolls, have proven extremely important for a study of the intertestamental and early Christian periods.

In 1947 a young Bedouin shepherd was searching for a lost animal on the steep slopes of the Wadi Qumran at the NW end of the Dead Sea when he encountered a cave containing several jars filled with ancient rolls of leather, along with other manuscript fragments. Attempts were made to sell the scrolls to an antique dealer in Bethlehem, and at some stage the scrolls became separated into two groups, to be reunited only after several years had passed. Meanwhile Jewish and American scholars had discovered that the manuscripts, the celebrated Dead Sea scrolls, were at least 1000 years older than the earliest known manuscripts of the Hebrew Bible.

The scrolls formed the library of the religious community living at Qumran. Extensive searching in eleven caves and other places near the site has recovered about 500 documents, most of them fragmentary. Approximately

100 of the scrolls are books of the Old Testament in Hebrew, including one copy of Isaiah, which is the oldest manuscript of a complete book of the Old Testament and can be dated c.100 B.C. The biblical scrolls have demonstrated the accuracy of transmission of previously known Hebrew texts.

Other scrolls help give us a picture of life at the Qumran community. These include a community rule, a hymn collection, biblical commentaries, and other writings. A "temple scroll," acquired by the Israelis in 1967, supports the strict teachings of the more conservative elements of Pharisaism. A commentary on Habakkuk illumines the objectives of the Qumran community. The group may have arisen about 200 B.C. as a protest against contemporary Judaism, with its members settling in the Judean wilderness to study Scripture under a Righteous Teacher. The community thought of itself as the faithful Israelite remnant destined to prepare for the day of the Lord, and the members looked for a prophet like Moses (Deut. 18:18), a Davidic Messiah, and an Aaronic priest. The Messiah would defeat the remnant's enemies and the priest would govern the state.

The Qumran settlement was first excavated in 1953. Archaeologists have uncovered the community's living quarters, cisterns for ritual baptisms, an aqueduct system, the room where the scrolls were actually written, and a cemetery.

Ras Shamra (Ugarit)

A large mound, Ras Shamra, on the Syrian coast about 25 miles S of the mouth of the Orontes river marks the site of an ancient Canaanite cultural center known as Ugarit. Perhaps the most important finding there for biblical archaeologists has been the writings in Ugaritic, a language closely related to biblical Hebrew and fundamentally important for Old Testament study.

Ugarit's culture reached a peak in the fourteenth century B.C., and then declined and disappeared. It was redis-

Pottery in an excavation trench at Ras Shamra. (J. Jennings)

covered in 1928 when a Syrian farmer struck the top of a rich tomb while plowing. The mound was then excavated systematically, yielding gold objects, a surprising range of Greek pottery, a set of weights, and several bronze images. Some bronze tools and weapons were also recovered in excellent condition.

The discovery of the Ugaritic language came about when archaeologists uncovered many clay tablets written in a strange cuneiform script of alphabetic rather than syllabic character. When deciphered, the tablets showed a close linguistic relationship to Phoenician and biblical Hebrew, but also indicated that the people of Ugarit used an alphabetic script long before the Phoenicians, who probably inherited the idea.

The Ugaritic language contains literary forms that occur also in Hebrew poetry, and study and comparison have helped clarify a number of difficult Hebrew passages. Now such expressions as "rider of the heavens" (Ps. 68:33) are seen to be Canaanite in origin, indicating that Ugaritic and OT Hebrew are somewhat variant dialects.

The recovered writings have revealed that at Ugarit similar ceremonies to those of the Hebrews were observed, such as the wave (Exod. 29:24), trespass (Lev. 5:15), whole burnt sacrifice (Lev. 6:15), peace (Lev. 22:21), and tribute (Deut. 6:10) offerings. While it is illuminating to compare similar references in written records of the two cultures, the languages are not identical, so we can not automatically equate the terms or references being compared. For example, the legislation in Exodus 23:19 prohibiting the boiling of a young goat in its mother's milk was thought to have been illumined by a similar offering recorded in the Ugaritic texts. This is now uncertain, since the Ugaritic word rendered "cook" actually means "slaughter," and there are other problems with the text as well.

The tablets at Ugarit record the depraved and lewd forms of ritual worship indulged in by the Canaanites, showing the threat these practices posed to traditional Hebrew faith and indicating that the O.T. condemnation of such religion was justified.

Bible books: Exodus, Leviticus, Deuteronomy, 1 & 2 Kings, Isaiah, Jeremiah

Susa

This ancient city, now represented by four mounds in southwest Iran, was the place (called Shushan) where the events took place that are described in the book of Esther. In addition, Nehemiah and possibly Daniel resided in Susa for a part of their lives.

Pleasantly situated in ancient Persia about 200 miles E of Babylon, Susa was the winter capital of the Elamite rulers as far back as 2200 B.C. Its real prosperity began in 538 B.C. when Cyrus made Susa one of the richest cities of the east. Darius I (521–485 B.C.) extended the Persian empire from the Nile to the Indus, and the splendor of the period is reflected even now in the ruins of his palace and throneroom.

Griffins, relief from the palace at Susa. (H. Vos)

Daniel, along with other Jews in Babylonia, may have been taken to Susa after 539 B.C. (Dan. 8:2), and it is possible that his encounter with the lions occurred there. According to local tradition, Susa was the site of his death and burial. As the book of Esther relates, Persian king Xerxes I (485–465 B.C.) banished his wife Vashti from his presence early in his reign at Shushan and subsequently married Esther, an attractive and resourceful Jewess who was able to deliver her people from persecution (Esther 8–9). Nehemiah, a high official at the royal court of Susa, was appointed civil governor of Judea in 445 B.C. by Arta-

xerxes I (464–423 B.C.), and he helped bring stability to th
returned exiles in the Jerusalem area (Neh. 2–7).

Excavations beginning in 1851 reveal that the city co
ered nearly 5000 acres, and was divided in four parts: th
citadel mound, the palace area, the business and resider
tial district, and the flat land W of the river. The palace co
ered 123 acres, and was comprised of the splendi
throneroom, the royal residence, and the abode of th
harem. There were numerous courtyards, gardens, stai
ways, and arched gateways, as described in the book c
Esther. From the ruins a cube engraved with numbers wa
recovered and this proved to be a "pur" or lot, after whic
the Jewish festival of Purim was named (Esther 9:26
Clearly the writer of Esther knew Persian court life int
mately, and the book presents an authentic account of th
period.

Bible books: Daniel, Nehemiah, Esther

Ur

This city was the center of a brilliant pagan culture i
southern Mesopotamia. Probably founded c. 2800 B.C., U
was already at its height in the days of Abraham (perhap

*Restored ziggurat, center of worship of the Mesopotamian moon deity, at Ur.
(J. Jennings)*

about 1980 B.C.). It exerted a tremendous social, religious, and commercial influence in the Mesopotamian region and beyond, nevertheless Abraham and Terah were prepared to leave in obedience to God's instructions (Gen. 11:31; 12:1; 15:7). Some years after Abraham left, the city was sacked by Elamite raiders and was lost to history for many centuries.

Today a 150-acre mound is all that remains of Ur. Excavations by Woolley (1922–1934) at the site (Tell Mugheir) revealed the grandeur of the ancient city as seen in the burial places of two important persons, possibly a ruler and his wife. Their attendants had been buried with them, ceremonially attired for the occasion, and included with the bodies were a magnificent golden helmet, a splendid harp decorated with mosaic work, elaborately-designed gold and silver articles, and other beautiful objects of the period.

Woolley also excavated parts of the business district of Ur, and the streets leading to a residential area. The houses there were two-story mud brick and plaster structures built around three sides of a paved courtyard. They contained about a dozen rooms and had toilets and sunken baths, fireplaces, and fountains. Ruined school buildings contained tablets inscribed with student exercises in arithmetic, literature, and other subjects. Small chapels were found throughout Ur, some of them in private homes. The great ziggurat (tiered temple) of Nanna, the moon deity, overshadowed all other buildings in the city.

Deep in the mound, Woolley discovered an eight foot thick layer of water-laid clay, which he attributed to the flood of Noah, but which may have represented the original river-bed. Traces of flood deposits at other Mesopotamian sites varied somewhat from Wooley's date of the Ur stratum, making it difficult to support his claims and impossible to use his findings in debating whether Noah's flood was local or global.

Bible books: Genesis

Figure 4 Ancient False Deities

Deity	Country	Position	Scripture
Molech (Malcam) (Milcom)	Ammon	national god	Zeph. 1:5 Jer. 49:1, 3 1 Kings 11:5, 7, 33
Marduk (Bel)	Babylon	young storm god; chief god	Jer. 50:2 Isa. 46:1 Jer. 51:44
Nebo (Nabu)	Babylon	son of Marduk	Isa. 46:1
Baal	Canaan	young storm god	1 Kings 16:31–32; 18:18–46
Ashtoreth (Astarte) (Queen of Heaven)	Canaan	mother-goddess; love; fertility	Judg. 2:13; 10:6 1 Sam. 12:10 1 Kings 11:5, 33 Jer. 7:18; 44:17–25
Asherah	Canaan	goddess of the sea	Judg. 3:7 1 Kings 18:19 2 Kings 22:4 2 Chron. 15:16
El	Canaan	head of pantheon	
Osiris	Egypt	death	
Isis	Egypt	life	
Hathor	Egypt	mother-goddess	
Chemosh	Moab	national god of war	Num. 21:29 Judg. 11:24 1 Kings 11:7, 33 Jer. 48:7
Dagon	Philistia	national god of grain	Judg. 16:23 1 Sam. 5:2–7

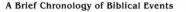

Satellite photo of the Sinai region. (NASA)

A Brief Chronology of Biblical Events
by R.K. Harrison

The various books of the Bible, written over a period of at least 1,200 years, recount the history of a particular people and their interactions with many other cultures. Since all ancient peoples had more than one way of counting time, and since the biblical writers had an interest in the timing of events often quite different from the events that interest us, it is no wonder that Near Eastern scholars have difficulty establishing a firm chronology of biblical events.

The early periods of biblical history present the greatest difficulties, as one might expect. Archaeological evidence of human habitation in ancient Jericho and elsewhere in the Near East goes back to 8000–5000 B.C., called the *Prepottery Neolithic Period,* before metal was used (*-lithic* coming from the Greek word for stone). The transition from stone for tools and weapons to easily smelted metal took place around 4000–3000 B.C., the *Chalcolithic Period* (*chalco* from the Greek word for copper or brass). That transition is seen in some excavations in Egypt and Mesopotamia. The Sumerian culture, evidently growing during that period, was prominent in the *Early Bronze Period* (3000–2000 B.C.), which also marked the rise of an early Semitic people, the Akkadians. Many Near Eastern archaeological sites date back to the *Middle Bronze Period* (2000–1500 B.C.). The *Late Bronze Period* (1500–1200 B.C.), just before the introduction of iron tools and weapons, saw the fall of Hittite and Ugaritic cultures and the rise of Philistine power.

In what period did Abraham and the other Hebrew patriarchs of the Book of Genesis live? Archaeological evidence for some of the customs described in Genesis 11–50 could be used to argue for each of the bronze periods. Since such indirect evidence can be interpreted in different ways, it is best to remain open on possible dates, at least up to the time of Israel's united kingdom under Saul, David, and Solomon. The following tables (pp. 67–75) show that scholarly opinion is divided on the dates of biblical events up to that time, the period when historical documentation from extrabiblical sources becomes relatively firm.

In these tables the central column gives the biblical events associated with the dates in the lefthand column and also the parts of the Bible that were being written at approximately that time. The righthand column mentions some of the archaeological or historical evidence for assigning the biblical event to that particular date. Material in the righthand column appearing in parentheses means that for the time span under consideration the items mentioned may have some bearing on the period, but fail to provide the kind of firm historical documentation possible in later periods. All dates shown should be regarded as approximate, especially those preceded by **c.** (for the Latin **circa,** "about"). (Refer to maps 2 and 3 to locate archaeological sites. Also see pp. 76-77 for O.T. and N.T. time lines.)

Map 2 Archaeological Sites in Ancient Palestine

Map 3 Archaeological Sites in the Ancient Near East

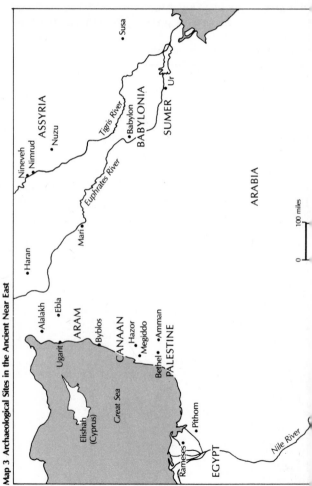

Chronological Table

Date B.C.	Biblical Event	Documented Historical Fact
The Patriarchal Period: Four Suggested Dates		
2166–1805	Hebrew Patriarchs (Gen. 11–50). These dates fit a 15th-century B.C. Exodus and the Hebrew text of Exodus 12:40, which gives 430 years for the time of the Israelites in Egypt.	(Some adoption tablets exist from this period: Sumerian, 2100 B.C., and Old Babylonian, 2000 B.C. Other support comes from 20th-century B.C. texts found at Alalakh, and possibly from Ebla material.)
1952–1589	Hebrew Patriarchs. These dates also fit an early Exodus but are based on the early Greek translation (Septuagint) of Exodus 12:40, which says the Israelites spent 430 years "in Egypt and in the land of Canaan," making the stay in Egypt only 215 years.	(Some support for these dates comes from 18th-century B.C. texts found at Mari, 15th-century B.C. texts from Nuzu, and 16th-century texts from Alalakh.)
1950–1650	Hebrew Patriarchs. These dates fit a later, 13th-century B.C. Exodus and represent a Middle Bronze Period culture.	(Texts from Mari, Nuzu, and Alalakh indicate the historicity of such customs mentioned in Genesis as adoption, selling of a birthright, deathbed wills, marriage contracts, and choice of heirs.)

Cuneiform text on a clay tablet from ancient Ebla. (J. Jennings)

1500–1300	Hebrew Patriarchs. These dates fit a 13th-century B.C. Exodus and represent a Late Amarna Age culture of the 14th-century B.C.	(Hebrew conquest of Canaan would have been proceeding when the Egyptian Pharaoh Meneptah, son of Rameses II, invaded Palestine about 1225 B.C.)

Statue of Rameses II (pharaoh of the Exodus according to the later date) at Luxor Temple. (H. Vos)

The Exodus: Two Suggested Dates

c. 1446	Exodus (Exod., Lev., Num.). This date is indicated by 1 Kings 6:1, which says Solomon began his Temple 480 years after the Exodus, and is supported by Judges 11:26.	(Some Mycenean IIIB pottery from the Judges period found at Hazor, a city destroyed in the conquest of Canaan, suggests by its date an Exodus as early as this.)
c. 1280	Exodus. This date is suggested by Exodus 1:11, which says the Hebrew slaves built the cities of Pithom and Rameses. (*The Pentateuch was written in this period.*)	(Rebuilding of Pithom and Rameses occurred in the 13th century B.C.; Israel is regarded as a nation on the triumphal stele, or monument, of the Egyptian pharaoh Meneptah, c. 1200 B.C.)

The Wilderness Wanderings: Two Suggested Dates

c. 1446–1406	Wanderings (Num., Deut.).	(No external documentation.)
c. 1270–1230	Wanderings. The dates depend on the dates chosen for the Exodus and conquest of Canaan.	(No external documentation.)

Conquest and Judges Period: Two Suggested Dates

c. 1406–1050	Conquest (Josh.) and Judges (Judg.). These dates are based on the idea that the Judges period must have required several centuries.	(The city of Hazor was destroyed in the conquest of Canaan, and the Mycenean IIIB pottery found there suggests a conquest date shortly after 1400 B.C.)
c. 1230–1025	Conquest and Judges. These dates are possible if the Judges narratives overlap.	(Some evidence suggests that Bethel and Hazor were not conquered until the 13th century B.C., when Philistine cities were strong.)

Israel's United Kingdom (c. 1050-931 B.C.)

1050	Saul reigns as king (1 Sam. 8–31).	An iron plow-point found at Gibeah, probably Saul's headquarters, has been dated at about 1010 B.C.
1010–970	David reigns as king (2 Sam.; 1 Kings 1–2; 1 Chron. 11–29). (*Joshua, Judges, some Psalms written.*)	What may be David's walls found on top of earlier Jebusite walls on Ophel in Jerusalem. Millo built by David (2 Sam. 5:9).
970–930	Solomon (*1 & 2 Samuel, Ruth, some Psalms, many Proverbs, Ecclesiastes written.*)	Gezer and Megiddo fortified (1 Kings 9:15-17). Temple and royal palace built in Jerusalem (1 Kings 9:1,15).

Canaanite altar at Megiddo, c. 2500–1800 B.C. It is approximately 26 feet in diameter. (L. Shaw)

Divided Kingdom: Israel

931–910	Jeroboam I (1 Kings 11–14).	
910–909	Nadab (1 Kings 15:25–31).	
909–886	Baasha (1 Kings 15–16).	
886–885	Elah (1 Kings 16:8–10).	
885	Zimri (1 Kings 16: 9–20).	
880–874	Omri (1 Kings 16:16–28).	Mentioned on Moabite Stone and in Assyrian annals. Samaria fortified (1 Kings 16:23–24).
874–853	Ahab (1 Kings 16–22).	Probably reinforced Samaria (1 Kings 16:29). Many ivory inlays from his period recovered. Mentioned in Monolith Inscription of Shalmaneser III, king of Assyria.
853–852	Ahaziah (1 Kings 22:51 to 2 Kings 1).	
852–841	Jehoram (2 Kings 3–9).	
841–814	Jehu (2 Kings 9–10).	Named on Black Obelisk of Shalmaneser III, c. 838.
814–798	Jehoahaz (2 Kings 10–13).	
798–782	Jehoash (2 Kings 13:10–12).	

782–753 (coregent from 793)	Jeroboam II (2 Kings 13–14). (*Hosea written probably during this period.*)	Jasper seal of Shema at Megiddo and the Samarian ostraca (records on bits of pottery) are contemporary 8th-century artifacts.
753–752	Zechariah (2 Kings 15:8–12).	
752	Shallum (2 Kings 15:13–15).	
752–742	Menahem (2 Kings 15:14–22).	Mentioned in Assyrian annals of Tiglathpileser III, *c.* 742, found at Nimrud.
742–740	Pekahiah (2 Kings 15:23–26).	
740–732	Pekah (2 Kings 15:25–31).	Mentioned in Assyrian annals of Tiglathpileser III, *c.* 742, found at Nimrud.
732–722	Hoshea (2 Kings 15–17).	Fall of Samaria in 722 mentioned in Khorsabad annals of Assyria.
Divided Kingdom: Judah		
931–913	Rehoboam (1 Kings 12–14).	The invasion of Palestine by his forces, *c.* 925, described in the Egyptian pharaoh Shishak's inscription at Karnak (photo on p. 73).
913–911	Abijam (1 Kings 15:1–8).	
911–870	Asa (1 Kings 15:9–24).	
870–848 (coregent from 873)	Jehoshaphat (1 Kings 15; 2 Kings 8; 2 Chron. 17–21).	
848–841 (coregent from 853)	Jehoram (2 Kings 8:16–24; 2 Chron. 21–22). (*Obadiah written?*)	

Bas relief on the Black Obelisk from Nimrud. King Jehu of Israel is shown bowing and bringing tribute to Shalmaneser III, king of Assyria. (ORINST)

841	Ahaziah (2 Kings 8–9).	
841–835	Athaliah (2 Kings 11; 2 Chron. 22–23).	
835–796	Jehoash (2 Kings 11–12).	
796–767	Amaziah (2 Kings 14:1–20).	
767–740 (coregent from 790)	Uzziah (2 Kings 14–15; 2 Chron. 26). (Some Proverbs, Amos, Micah written. Job? Joel? Jonah?)	
740–731 (coregent from 750)	Jotham (2 Kings 15; 2 Chron. 27).	
732–716 (coregent from 744)	Ahaz (2 Kings 16).	Appealed to Tiglathpileser III for Assyrian help against Syria and Israel (2 Kings 16:7). Judah made tributary.
716–686 (coregent from 729)	Hezekiah (2 Kings 18–20). (Some Proverbs, Song of Solomon written?)	Siloam tunnel (2 Kings 20:20) built in 701 when Sennacherib besieged Jerusalem.
687–642 (coregent from 696)	Manasseh (2 Kings 21:1–18; 2 Chron. 33). (Isaiah written.)	Commanded by Esarhaddon, king of Assyria, to visit Nineveh.
642–640	Amon (2 Kings 21:18–26).	
640–609	Josiah (2 Kings 21–23). (Nahum written.)	
609	Jehoahaz (2 Kings 23:31–34).	
609–597	Jehoiakim (2 Kings 23–24). (Habakkuk, Zephaniah written.)	
597	Jehoiachin (2 Kings 24:6–15).	Exiled by Babylonians.
597–586	Zedekiah (2 Kings 24–25).	Fall of Jerusalem in 597 and 587 confirmed by the Babylonian Chronicle. Lachish letters written just before Jerusalem fell in 587.
586–582	Gedaliah (2 Kings 25:22–25). (Jeremiah, Lamentations written. 1 & 2 Kings?)	

(Note: Ancient systems of reckoning have produced chronological problems for the divided monarchy period.)

597–538	Exile in Babylonia. (Some Psalms, Ezekiel, Daniel written.)	Ration tablets near Ishtar Gate in ancient Babylon unearthed, mentioning Jehoiachin as captive along with other royal princes. Seal impressions and a seal from Palestine show that Jehoiachin's property was probably under a steward.

On a wall of the temple of Amon at Karnak, Egyptian ruler Shishak is shown leading Palestinian towns captive during Rehoboam's reign. (H. Vos)

Ruins of Herod the Great's palace courtyard at the Herodium near Bethlehem.
(H. Vos)

538	Fall of Babylon and edict of Cyrus (Ezra 1:2–4).	Edict preserved on Cyrus Cylinder.
535–515	Return of exiles to Judea (Ezra 2).	
520	Haggai and Zechariah.	
516	Temple completed. (*Haggai, Zechariah written.*)	
486–465	Period of Xerxes and Esther (Esther 1–10).	
458–444	Work of Ezra and Nehemiah. (*Some Psalms, Joel written?*)	Geshem's name (Neh. 2:19; 6:1) attested on a silver 5th-century B.C. bowl. Tobiah (Neh. 2:10; 6:17) mentioned in Zeno Papyri. Family castle near Amman now in ruins.
440	Malachi. (*Esther, Ezra, Nehemiah, Malachi, 1 & 2 Chronicles written.*)	
Intertestamental and New Testament Periods		
331–65 B.C.	Greek period in Palestine.	Greek became common language of Near East. Greek culture widespread.
300–287 B.C.	Simon I High Priest in Jerusalem.	

190 B.C.	Dead Sea community probably founded.	Dead Sea scrolls.
175 B.C.	Antiochus IV Epiphanes (See 1 Maccabees in the Apocrypha of the Old Testament.)	
167 B.C.	Maccabean revolt (1 Maccabees).	
143–37 B.C.	Rule of Hasmoneans.	
65 B.C.	Roman period in Palestine.	
40–4 B.C.	Herod the Great.	Extended Temple, built magnificent structures, fortified Masada.
30 B.C. to A.D. 14	Augustus as Roman emperor (Luke 2:1).	Many inscriptions and public works.
C. 4 B.C.	Birth of Christ (Luke 2).	Quirinius (Luke 2:2) governor of Syria.
A.D. 14–30	Ministry of Christ (Matt., Mark, Luke, John).	Pilate (Matt. 27) procurator of Judea. (Josephus, *Antiquities*, 18,3,1; *Wars of the Jews*, 2,9,1).
A.D. 36	Conversion of Paul (Acts 9:1–30).	
A.D. 46–48	Paul's first missionary journey (Acts 13-14). (*Galatians, James written.*)	
A.D. 49–52	Paul's second missionary journey (Acts 15-18). (*1 & 2 Thessalonians written.*)	
A.D. 53–58	Paul's third missionary journey (Acts 18–21). (*Romans, 1 & 2 Corinthians written.*)	
A.D. 70	Fall of Jerusalem. (*New Testament documents completed by c. A.D. 95.*)	

Figure 5 Highlights of Old Testament History

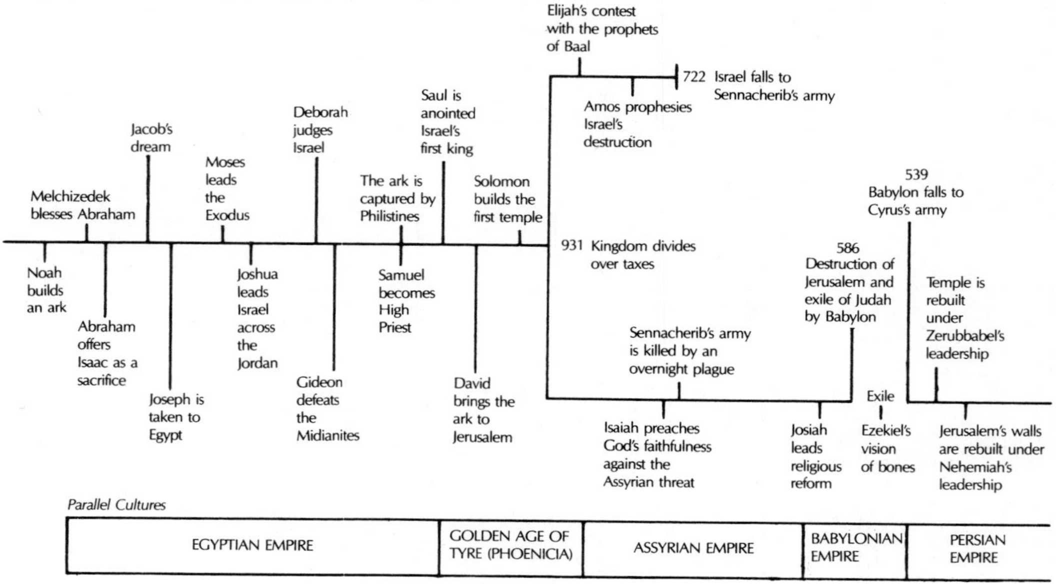

Parallel Cultures

EGYPTIAN EMPIRE	GOLDEN AGE OF TYRE (PHOENICIA)	ASSYRIAN EMPIRE	BABYLONIAN EMPIRE	PERSIAN EMPIRE

Timeline events:

Noah builds an ark

Melchizedek blesses Abraham

Abraham offers Isaac as a sacrifice

Jacob's dream

Joseph is taken to Egypt

Moses leads the Exodus

Joshua leads Israel across the Jordan

Deborah judges Israel

Gideon defeats the Midianites

The ark is captured by Philistines

Samuel becomes High Priest

Saul is anointed Israel's first king

Solomon builds the first temple

David brings the ark to Jerusalem

Elijah's contest with the prophets of Baal

Amos prophesies Israel's destruction

931 Kingdom divides over taxes

722 Israel falls to Sennacherib's army

Sennacherib's army is killed by an overnight plague

Isaiah preaches God's faithfulness against the Assyrian threat

Josiah leads religious reform

586 Destruction of Jerusalem and exile of Judah by Babylon

Exile

Ezekiel's vision of bones

539 Babylon falls to Cyrus's army

Temple is rebuilt under Zerubbabel's leadership

Jerusalem's walls are rebuilt under Nehemiah's leadership

Figure 6 Highlights of New Testament History

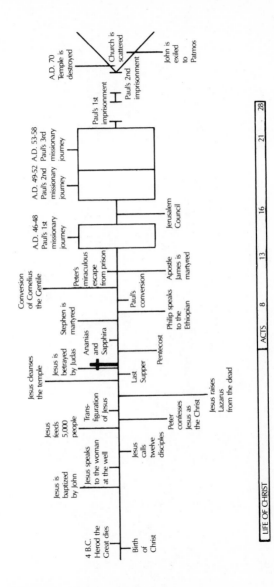

What the Bible
Teaches about Christ
& Christian Faith

2 / What the Bible Teaches about Christ & Christian Faith

The Life of Christ
by Walter A. Elwell

Jesus of Nazareth is the most important person who ever lived. He has influenced more lives and civilizations than anyone else. More people look to him for guidance and inspiration, even today, than anyone else who has ever lived. Why? The answer of the New Testament is that Jesus was not just another human being, but the incarnation of God. No apology, or even any defense, of that assertion is ever

An Arab boy on a donkey at Gaza. (R. Nowitz)

given. It is simply stated, with the offer to test it out in experience. That Jesus is who he said he was is proven in the reality of life day by day, not simply in thought processes.

The basic source of information about Jesus is the New Testament Gospels: Matthew, Mark, Luke, and John. From them it is possible to reconstruct an outline of what Jesus did and said. We are not told everything we would like to know, but enough is there so that we will not go astray.

Jesus' life may be conveniently divided into five periods: his birth and early years, his baptism and early ministry, his Galilean ministry, his ministry in Perea and Judea, and his death and resurrection.

Tiberias on the Sea of Galilee was founded about A.D. 20 and named for Tiberius, the Roman emperor referred to in the narrative of Jesus' ministry. (IIS)

Birth & Early Years of Jesus

The Gospels record several significant events that preceded the birth of Jesus because they provide information for a fuller understanding of who Jesus was and what he came to do. Those events center around Mary the mother of Jesus and Elizabeth the mother of John the Baptist.

There was an air of expectancy during the last few years of Herod's reign. He had been such a disagreeable leader that many people were looking to God to intervene in history and make things right. One such man was an older priest named Zechariah who was visited by an angel while exercising his priestly duties. He was told that his wife, who was beyond childbearing years, would have a son who was to be named John. Neither Zechariah nor his wife Elizabeth could believe it but it was true. During Elizabeth's sixth month of pregnancy, a young relative of hers named Mary also received an angelic visitation. Although she was a virgin, it was announced to her that she would be the earthly mother of God's Son. Her humble acceptance of God's will, in spite of the utter inexplicability of it all, stands as an example of how we should respond to God's will in our lives. Joseph, Mary's prospective husband, was also informed by God of what would happen. He, too, gladly accepted the will of God. Both of them realized that a life of puzzlement and pain awaited them. Mary made a visit to Elizabeth in Judea and stayed with her for three months. During that time it was confirmed that miraculous events were about to break in on the earth.

After Mary returned to Galilee a decree was passed by Caesar Augustus, ruler of the Roman empire, requiring that everyone return to their ancestral home for taxation enrollment. Mary and Joseph would have to travel to Bethlehem in Judea because they were descendants of David. There the birth of Jesus took place. The story is told simply in the Gospel of Luke. There was no room for the weary travelers in the inn so they were forced to spend the night in what seemed to be a barn. There, amid earthly poverty and indifference, but with divine acclamation, Jesus was born. Shepherds, told of the great event by God's messengers, came to marvel at the little family. How astonishing it all was. A more unlikely thing could not have been imagined, then or now—that the eternal God would choose to enter his world in such fashion. In his love, and for our good, God stooped down into the world in the form of a helpless baby, subjecting himself to the vicissitudes of human existence.

The Egyptian sphinx and pyramid shown were built long before Mary and Joseph fled with the infant Jesus to Egypt. (D. Birkey)

According to Jewish custom Jesus was circumcised on the eighth day and later was presented in the Temple 40 days after his birth. At the presentation, Simeon and Anna, inspired by the Holy Spirit, spoke of Jesus and what he would someday do. Jesus was to be for the salvation of the world, a sign for Israel, a discerner of hearts, and a sword through the heart of Mary. The ominous reference to a sword indicated that all were to pass through deep waters.

Visitors from the East later arrived, the Magi (or Wise Men), guided by a star, to offer their homage to the young king. That knowledge so enraged the unstable Herod that he ordered that all male children under two years of age in Bethlehem and its vicinity be killed, hoping to do away with the threat he perceived Jesus to be. The child was not there, however. Having been warned in a dream, Joseph took Mary and Jesus down to Egypt, where they stayed until Herod died.

After Herod's death, the family returned to Judea and evidently were going to settle there, but Archelaus, Herod's son, was ruling over the area. He was even more unstable than his father, so Joseph took the family to Nazareth in Galilee, where Jesus grew to manhood.

We are told almost nothing about Jesus from his birth to about age 30. One episode is recorded when Jesus was twelve years old. The annual trip to Jerusalem had been made and the boy was in the Temple discussing theology with the learned rabbis there. Other than that, we know nothing except that Jesus grew in mind and body, pleasing both God and man.

Jesus' Baptism & Early Ministry

John the Baptist appeared in the wilderness outside Jerusalem like one of the great prophets of the Old Testament. Word went around, in fact, that Elijah or Jeremiah had come back from the dead. John had a stern message of judgment for everyone who came to hear him preach. He said that neither privileges of birth nor being formally religious would do anyone any good. The times were too drastic for such things. The ax was already laid at the root of the tree and it was about to be cut down. Decisive spiritual reorientation was needed. Everyone, from high priest to lowest sinner to Gentile soldier, had to repent, confess their sins, be baptized, and live ethically, as proof of their sincerity. That would signify acceptance of a new life.

John said that One was coming who was God's anointed. He would baptize with the Holy Spirit, just as he, John, was baptizing with water.

Jesus went to the Jordan River to be baptized by John, much to John's puzzlement. Jesus had no sins to confess, so why should he be baptized? The answer lay in Jesus' words, "Let it be so now; it is proper for us to do this to fulfill all righteousness" (Matt. 3:15). Jesus was identifying with sin, not his own, but the sin of others, in order to do away with it forever. He was the Lamb of God, taking away the sin of the world (John 1:29). As Jesus was baptized, heaven was opened, and a voice was heard to say, "This is my Son, whom I love; with him I am well pleased" (Matt. 3:17).

Traditional site of Jesus' baptism in the Jordan River. (H. Vos)

Jesus' experience in the wilderness, which immediately followed his baptism, was of supreme importance for him. It helped to define what kind of Messiah he was to be. Three different models were offered: that of a humanitarian reformer (turn stones to bread); that of a miracle worker (leap down off the Temple); and that of one defying God's will (casting his lot with Satan). In each case Jesus ound strength by quoting Scripture, thus repelling Satan's attacks. He knew that to do God's work of salvation meant nothing less than paying the full price. Tempting as it was, he still rejected any compromise that would destroy what he came to do.

Jesus returned to Galilee, where the town of Capernaum became his base of operation. He was already gathering disciples, but no formal call had gone out to any of them to leave their occupations and follow him. They seemed to have gone back to their ordinary lives, waiting for the moment when Jesus would begin his public work. Jesus' disciples began baptizing, which created some strain with the disciples of John, but Jesus stayed in the background. His time had not yet come. Jesus made two trips to Jerusalem, one of them including an interview with a Jewish ruler named Nicodemus who was told he must be born from above (or "born again") if he wanted to enter the kingdom of God. Miracles were performed, as at the wedding in Cana, but for the most part this period was one of preparation for Jesus. He was getting ready for the time when he would be on the center stage of history. That moment came when John the Baptist was arrested. The time of preparation was over; the time for action had arrived.

Jesus' Galilean Ministry

When John the Baptist was thrown into prison by Herod Antipas, Jesus took it as a signal that he should step forward with a message of fulfillment. John was the last of the old order; he was in fact "Elijah" who was to come before the arrival of God's Messiah, but all that was now history. Jesus picked up the message of repentance, proclaiming that the kingdom of God was at the door. It had now broken into history in what he was doing and saying.

The ministry of Jesus in Galilee lasted for approximately a year and a half. A great deal took place that can be conveniently treated under three headings: what happened, what Jesus did, and what Jesus taught.

What happened. Four events stand out as of crucial importance during Jesus' Galilean ministry. First, Jesus chose twelve men as a nucleus of leadership (Mark 3:13–19). The importance of this is that Jesus recognized his need of help to get the job done, as well as the fact that his work would live on after him in the ministry of these individuals. The choice of twelve to be apostles was on the analogy of Israel with its twelve tribes; the church which would arise was to be a new people of God.

Second, John the Baptist sent a message from prison asking Jesus if for sure he was the One who was to come. Jesus' coded reply affirmed that he was (Matt. 11:2–19), but what is crucial here is the nature of Jesus' Messiahship. He was not going to be a conqueror like those of Rome, but One who healed the sick, gave sight to the blind, and brought hope to the lost. Jesus' message was spiritual, not political.

Third, Jesus fed a crowd of 5,000 men, along with their families (Matt. 14:13–21). After that, the crowd wanted to make him a king, but he refused. Again, it was important that he be the Messiah whom God intended, not what popular opinion wanted. The loneliness of his task was moving in on him as he realized that the people wanted the benefits of what he could do, but were not willing to pay the price of repentance and submission.

Fourth, Jesus withdrew to Caesarea Philippi, where he revealed that being the Messiah meant his going to Jerusalem to die (Mark 8:27–38). Peter resisted that possibility but received a stern rebuke from Jesus. The transfiguration that followed this momentous event (Mark 9:2–8) confirmed that the right decision had been made.

What Jesus did. Jesus' activity during this period was designed to show what it was like to have the kingdom of God present. He cast out demons, evil spiritual forces that opposed whatever was good for humankind. The kingdom of God meant the overthrow of the kingdom of evil. Where Jesus goes, evil retreats.

Map 4 **Palestine in the Time of Christ**

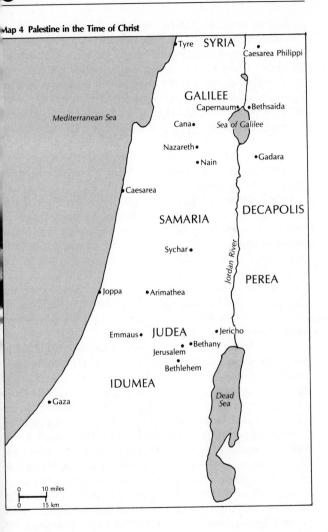

Second, Jesus healed the sick. The Gospels give representative examples of what he did, including his healing of fever, leprosy, deafness, inability to speak, blindness, paralysis, congenital illnesses, and others. God cares for his creation; Jesus was the concrete embodiment of that care. Where Jesus goes, disease retreats.

Third, Jesus ministered to every kind of human need. He encouraged the weak, fed the hungry, calmed raging storms, blessed normal human life with his presence (weddings, worship, travel, etc.), raised the dead, and brought peace where trouble existed. Where Jesus goes, human need retreats.

Fourth, Jesus graciously allowed for a spectrum of discipleship. Some people were disciples who stayed at home; some left everything in order to be with him; some followed him for awhile to learn and then returned to their usual occupation; some stayed at home for awhile and then joined him—it really did not matter. God wants us to be ourselves. He sanctifies our lives just as they are, as long as we give them to him. He fills our lives with meaning and purpose. Where Jesus goes, meaninglessness and despair retreat.

Finally, Jesus came into conflict with the comfortably religious of his day. It is ironic that ordinary people were more interested in Jesus than the prestigiously religious. But, as Jesus said, it is the sick who are in need of a physician. It is only when we realize that we need God that we can be helped. Where Jesus goes, hypocrisy retreats.

What Jesus taught. The teaching of Jesus during the Galilean period may be summarized briefly. To outsiders, it was "Repent and believe the gospel. The time is at hand and the kingdom of God is upon you." To those who came, it was "follow the precepts of God as found in the Sermon on the Mount" (Matt. 5–7). Most of all it is to love God with all our hearts, and love our neighbors as ourselves. Of himself, Jesus said, he came to fulfill the righteousness of God by going to Jerusalem to die and rise again. That was the nature of his Messiahship.

view of the Judean hills. (IIS)

Jesus' Perean & Judean Ministry

With full knowledge of what it meant to go to Jerusalem, Jesus left Galilee and headed south. His ministry in Perea and Judea would last about six months, culminating in his death and resurrection. During that time, he continued to preach, heal, work miracles, and cast out demons. Some changes, however, had taken place.

There was now more open conflict with the authorities as Jesus pressed for moral change in their lives. They, for their part, were more determined than ever to do away with this One who was such an embarrassment to them. Jesus also identified more closely with the lost and explained his coming death and resurrection in more detail. His parables now took on a new emphasis of salvation, as in the parables of the lost coin, lost sheep, and prodigal son (Luke 15:1–32). Finally, he strongly emphasized the cost of discipleship in the light of what was to take place.

This private tomb at Jerusalem is similar to the kind of tomb where Jesus was buried. (L. Shaw)

Jesus' Death & Resurrection

The climax of Jesus' ministry was reached during what we now call Passion Week. He had come to be the Lamb of God, and so it was. After entering the city of Jerusalem in triumph (on the day now celebrated as Palm Sunday), Jesus disputed with the authorities in such decisive fashion that they were determined to get rid of him, little knowing that their evil schemes would mysteriously accomplish the redemptive plan of God.

On Thursday night of that week, Jesus ate a Passover meal with his disciples. He explained that his blood was about to be shed as the blood of the "new covenant" foretold by Jeremiah the prophet (Jer. 31:31–34). Judas, for personal reasons unknown to this day, betrayed Jesus into the hands of his enemies, and Jesus was arrested after praying in the Garden of Gethsemane across the valley

from Jerusalem. Jesus was first tried by a Jewish court before the religious and civil leaders and was then handed
over to the Romans for official action, because they alone
were able to impose the death penalty. Both Herod and Pilate examined Jesus and were of a mind to let him go with

Map 5 Path of Jesus' Trial & Crucifixion (see Matt. 21–27; Mark 11–15; Luke 19:28–23:1; John 12–19)

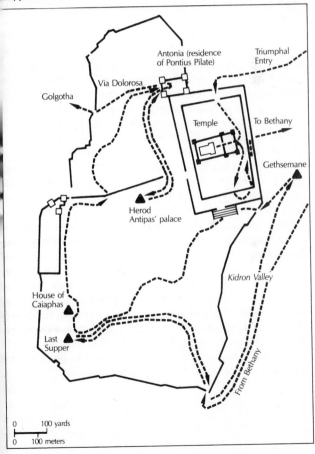

a stern warning, but were soon pressured by the Jewish authorities and the mob to put him to death. The shrewd but weak-willed Pilate consented and sent Jesus off to be executed. Jesus was scourged to a point of near death and then was publicly crucified. He suffered on the cross from about nine a.m. to three p.m. on Friday (our Good Friday), at which point he died saying, "It is finished," and "Father, into your hands I commend my spirit."

No one knows exactly what took place in those awesome moments. The New Testament tells us only that it was for us that Jesus died, thus freeing us from the penalty of sin, which is death. Jesus died, not as everyone dies, but *for* everyone, in the plan of God making atonement for our sins. It is the greatest mystery imaginable. It is enough for us to know that God's will was accomplished and all we must do is humbly acknowledge our need, bowing before the cross to receive pardon from God.

After being placed in a tomb outside Jerusalem, Jesus' body lay in peace for the equivalent of three days (according to Jewish reckoning, any part of a day may be counted as a whole day, so Friday through Sunday equaled three days). On Sunday morning the tomb was empty because Jesus had risen from the dead as he had said. He made numerous appearances to his friends, including Mary Magdalene, Peter, Thomas, Nathanael, James, John, the other apostles, and other unnamed disciples. Death was unable to hold Jesus down because he is the Lord of death—and of life as well. There is no rational explanation for the resurrection of Jesus. It was a display of the power and love of God, who controls all our experiences of life, including death. Forty days later Jesus returned to his heavenly Father, there to await his return in glory to end this age and bring to pass ultimate salvation.

he modern village of Bethany. In New Testament times Jesus' friends Lazarus, Mary, nd Martha lived here. (H. Vos)

The Teachings of Christ
by *Walter A. Elwell*

Jesus neither wrote books nor taught any systematic theology, but that fact does not mean he hadn't thought things through for himself. It is evident that he had. The task he set for himself, however, was a direct communication of the truth, and he went about it differently from what we might today.

Basically, his task was to speak the truth to those who already knew the answers, but in such a way that truth would become evident to them. They had heard it so many times that it had lost its urgency and power in their lives. In order to accomplish that, Jesus chose to use simple and direct language that cut to the heart of the matter. He used analogies, parables, and other imagery to bring truth to life. Jesus' teaching was never abstract; no one was ever in doubt about the point he was making. Some-

times he used paradoxical or highly graphic language t
wake up his hearers. He said such things as "The last sha
be first," or "Let the dead bury their dead," or "If on
would save his life he must lose it." Occasionally he use
hyperbole to shock his hearers into self-examination, a
when he said that to enter into life we must cut off ou
hand if it offends us. All of that was calculated to pres
home a personal choice on those who heard. It was impos
sible to remain neutral; either one pursued the truth t
the core and was saved, or set it aside as foolishness. Je
sus' words were designed to penetrate to people's heart
and force a decision for or against God.

Jesus' View of God

Central to Jesus' teaching is the existence of God. He no
where argued for the fact that God exists; it is too obvious
Everywhere one looks there is evidence of the reality o
God, whether in history, in the words of the prophets, i
nature, in our social lives, or in ourselves. God confront
us everywhere, at all times, and without ceasing.

But who is God? For Jesus, what was traditionally said
about God in the Scriptures was unquestionably true. He
is love, spirit, holy, good, all-powerful, glorious, righteous
all knowing, almighty, the wise ruler, the revealer of truth
and true. Supremely, God is our heavenly Father. He lov
ingly cares for us, knows and meets our needs, is mercifu
to us, is willing to forgive us our sins, gives good gifts to
his children, and delights in our prayers. Because God is
Father to us we need not live in anxiety but in confidence
of his attention and concern. There is no need to worry be
cause God knows what he is doing and is looking out for
our good. Granted there are times when this is not obvi
ous, but it is true, nonetheless.

Jesus' View of Himself

Jesus was a human being. Neither his virgin birth nor his
sinlessness detracted from that. He had the same physical

eeds as anyone else. He got tired, hungry, thirsty; possessed five senses like everyone else; experienced pain; suffered; and ultimately died. He had emotions. There were times when he was sorrowful, angry, zealous, distressed, upset, filled with yearning, loving, lonely, joyful, calm, patient, exasperated. He possessed a mind like ours. He was intelligent, witty, creative, imaginative; had common sense; was logical and consistent. Finally he had a moral and spiritual nature like other human beings. He was nonjudgmental, affirmative, courageous, determined, moral, trustworthy, truthful, committed to the truth, and conscious of God's presence.

But Jesus was more than just a human being. He possessed a consciousness that he was unique. He claimed equality with God, spoke with God's authority, accepted prayer and praise (due to God alone), and challenged anyone to find any fault in him. He claimed final authority over other human beings saying that their eternal destiny depended on how they related to him. He claimed power over all human life and promised peace to those who sought it in him. Using many metaphors, he said he was the bread of life, the light of the world, the good shepherd, the door to enter the sheepfold, the true vine, the way, the truth, the life and one from above.

Jesus never tried to explain how his human and divine natures were combined in himself; he simply lived out that reality. The church has not tried to explain it rationally either. It has been content to say that Jesus was "fully God and fully man."

Jesus' View of Humanity & Sin

Jesus presented no abstract teaching about human nature. He never discussed such questions as how our will relates to our mind or other such theoretical matters. Jesus' concern was practical. He viewed each human being as existing in relation to God, others, and himself. Looked at in this way, Jesus was able to define what human

The traditional Mount of Temptation near Jericho. (H. Vos)

life consisted of, not abstractly, but concretely. Negatively, human life does not consist of what we possess, our status, our pious acts, our human efforts, or our self-fulfillment. Positively, it does consist of loving God; loving our neighbor; possessing the spiritual qualities of meekness, purity, compassion, righteousness, and mercy; participating in the kingdom of God; and being committed to doing God's will. A powerful negative force works against all that, and that force is sin. Jesus never preached a sermon on sin as such, but he noted that its effects were everywhere to be seen. Sin is what keeps us from finding God and thus life. But, Jesus did not stress the destructive power of sin (that was evident enough); rather, his emphasis was that God was able to save us from the consequences of our sins. The solution to our problem lies in submitting to God's will as it is made known in the Scriptures.

Jesus' View of the Kingdom of God
The heart of what Jesus said about the relation of God to

the world is contained in the expression "kingdom of God (or heaven)," which occurs about 75 times in the Gospels. Essentially the kingdom of God is a spiritual reality or realm where the will of God is recognized as being supreme and where God exercises his sovereign right to rule. Because it is a spiritual reality and not a material place—like the land of Palestine or the Roman empire—it may exist anywhere and at all times. Because God is always God, his rule will never cease and we are invited to participate in it. In one sense of the word, everyone and everything is in the kingdom of God. God works in all things for the good of those who love him (Rom. 8:28). That truth is the foundation for statements like the apostle Paul's "Give thanks in all circumstances" (1 Thess. 5:18).

In another sense everyone is *not* in the kingdom, but only those who choose to enter. Jesus said that the kingdom of God had drawn near; to enter we must repent and believe the gospel (Mark 1:14). At another time Jesus said we must be born again (or from above) to enter the kingdom (John 3:3,5). A complete turnabout is required. We must set aside false confidence in ourselves and instead have complete trust in God. When we do that, we experience the benefits of living in the kingdom: fellowship with God, eternal life, freedom from anxiety, and possession of life's necessities. To enter the kingdom is the most important thing a person can do. We should be willing to lose all that we have to obtain it, even our lives if need be, because nothing can compare with knowing God now and eternally.

The Kingdom has a present and a future aspect. We may enter it now as a present reality, but its fullness will not exist until God is all in all. In the Lord's Prayer we are told to include a petition for that day to arrive: "Your kingdom come" (Matt. 6:10).

For Jesus, salvation meant life in the kingdom. When we are God's we are free from the destructive powers that dominate this world and are free to be ourselves in God's will. God as heavenly Father knows what we are and what we need, so we are never in ultimate want. For those who have eyes to see, the whole world is theirs. But just as the kingdom has a present and future aspect, so does salvation. In the future we may expect eternal life, resurrection, a new heaven and earth, and eternity with God in unending blessedness.

Jesus' View of the Christian Life

The foundation for what Jesus said about Christian living is threefold. First, he tied his ethical commands to our relationship to him. Not everyone who says to him "Lord, Lord," but those who do the will of God will enter the kingdom. Hearing Jesus' words and building on them is like building your house on rock. To neglect Jesus' words is to build on sand (Matt. 7:21–27).

Second, the Christian life is lived in the light of God's

A scene at the market in present-day Nazareth. (D. Birkey)

ove for sinners. We do not need to *be* righteous to enter
nto life; entrance into life opens the door for us to *become*
ighteous. God knows that we are sinful human beings yet
ne loves us anyway. We are not to shrink back from him,
out embrace him in the knowledge that God controls all
things. God made all things, has a purpose for all things,
ares for all his creatures, and works for the eternal good
of what he has made. Never once has he done anything
nurtful or mean. Human beings may do that, but not God.
The mystery of this is that God can weave his good pur-
ooses into the hurtful and mean things that humans do,
thus overcoming our evil intents.

Living the Christian life is not following a set of rules,
out living according to the principle of love. All the commands of God are covered in two statements. We are to
ove God with all our hearts. We are to love our neighbors
i.e. others) as ourselves.

When we love God and neighbor we recognize the value
of persons, ourselves, and all that God has created. We
can recognize that sin is not the essence of a person; sin is
what is chipping away or destroying that essence. We are
to call people back to what God intended: to be themselves in God's grace and favor. God values us as individuals so we must value individuals as well.

We must also recognize that to love God and neighbor
mplies that salvation has a social dimension. Government, rulers, laws, human welfare, care for the helpless—
all of these are included. Jesus went so far as to say that
what will separate those who are his from those who are
not ("the sheep from the goats") is how they have treated
their fellow human beings. Do we visit the sick, feed the
hungry, cloth the naked, give drink to the thirsty, and wel-
come strangers? (Matt. 25:31–46).

Finally, love of God and neighbor carries with it a stress
on the wholeness of salvation. Our whole life, both now
and forever, is included. Our talents, interests, desires,
needs, dreams, plans and values are included. Nothing is
eft out. When we lose our life for Jesus' sake and the gos-

pel's, we *find* it in a new and comprehensive way.

The teachings of Jesus are the most important words in human language. To hear and obey them is to find the "pearl of great price," he said. The testimony of countless people is that they have found God by simple trust in what Jesus taught.

uins of a magnificent 2nd century A.D. synagogue at Sardis in western Turkey. Chris-
an communal worship still shows the influence of Jewish synagogue services. (H. Vos)

What Christians Believe
by R.E.O. White

"If you confess with your mouth, 'Jesus is Lord,' and believe in your heart that God raised him from the dead, you
will be saved" (Rom. 10:9). With those words the apostle
Paul, like Jesus, emphasized the importance of confessing one's faith (Matt. 10:32). If belief is real, it is not opinion or head-knowledge, but something that stirs and
controls our heart.

Jesus asked for such a confession, and Peter gave it:
"You are the Christ," meaning that Jesus was the Messiah
the Jews were expecting (Mark 8:29). Non-Jews might say
"Jesus is Lord," or "Jesus is the Son of God." That simple
confession was required from converts seeking baptism
(Acts 2:38; 19:5; Rom. 10:9; Phil. 2:11).

The later church may have used a fuller form of confession at baptism, "the name of the Father and of the Son

and of the Holy Spirit" (Matt. 28:19). That was because, as Christianity moved out of Palestine to confront other gods and pagan saviors, it became necessary to define Christian faith more exactly. As Christians explored and defended their faith, still more titles and defining phrases were added to make clear who God was, who Jesus was, and what Christians believed.

By the year A.D. 350, in the Apostles' Creed, Christians were confessing their faith in words similar to those still used in worship all over the world. Quite possibly this creed came into being in Rome two centuries earlier. Although it was believed to state correctly the apostles' faith, the possibility that any apostle had any part in composing it is unlikely. We use it here as a summary of Christian doctrine, explaining it clause by clause, so that readers will be able to see what believers of every description have believed from the beginning of the church.

(As the church has grown, controversies about the faith have required more precise expressions of Christian beliefs. For this reason, at various times in history church leaders have gathered in council to reject heresy and set down orthodox doctrine in credal form. See page 113 for a brief explanation of some major church councils.)

The Apostles' Creed

In the words of this creed Christians confess: *I believe in God the Father almighty, maker of heaven and earth, and in Jesus Christ, his only Son, our Lord, who was conceived by the Holy Ghost, born of the virgin Mary, suffered under Pontius Pilate, was crucified, dead, and buried; he descended into hell. The third day he rose again from the dead. He ascended into heaven, and sitteth on the right hand of God the Father almighty. From thence he shall come to judge the quick and the dead. I believe in the Holy Ghost, the holy catholic church, the communion of saints, the forgiveness of sins, the resurrection of the body, and the life everlasting.*

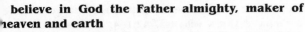

believe in God the Father almighty, maker of heaven and earth

That statement describes God as Christians know him. The word *Father* summarizes all that Christ had said about God's loving, providing, caring, forgiving, and answering of prayer. In his inmost nature, God is like a good father toward all people, though not all live as his children (Luke 15:11–32; John 1:12).

Almighty means that God is supreme over all, acting in total freedom within the limits he sets for himself—his own character—and the responsible freedom he has given to humankind. That means that God is supreme in history and will in the end outwit evil and get his own way. Because God is fatherly love, love is the ultimate power in the world.

The phrase *maker of heaven and earth* points to God as originator, fashioner, and sustainer of all that is. To him belong all things and all creatures. To believe in God is to worship, trust, pray, obey him, enjoy his world, and esteem everything in it with a sense of responsibility and care (Matt. 6:25–33; Rom. 11:33–36; 1 Tim. 1:17).

And in Jesus Christ, his only Son, our Lord

Here the foundations of Christian faith are laid in history—not in experiences or vision or emotion, but in Jesus of Nazareth, a first-century Jew, the Jesus of the Gospels. *Jesus* is the Greek form of *Joshua*, meaning "God saves," or "Savior" (Matt. 1:21).

The title *Christ*, meaning "anointed," signifies one sent on divine mission (John 17:18; 20:21; 1 John 4:14), but especially the expected king who was to restore the Davidic monarchy, rule in God's name, and establish God's kingdom. That hope was nourished by numerous prophecies (Deut. 18:15; 2 Sam. 7:16; Pss. 2;110; Isa. 9:2-7; Mic. 5:2; Zech. 9:9; Mal. 3:1–4) and was in part fulfilled by Jesus (Matt. 20:29–21:11; 22:41–45). But Jesus adopted from Ezekiel (2:1, etc.) and Daniel (7:13) the ambiguous title *Son of man* and reinterpreted Messiahship by other prophecies: those of the Servant of God who would suffer to achieve God's will (Isa. 42:1–4; 52:13–53:12; Matt. 12:17–21; Luke 4:16–21; Acts 8:30–35; 1 Pet. 2:21–25).

In calling Jesus God's *only Son* the church underlines Christ's uniqueness in history. Others are children of God by divine favor, through Christ, by rebirth (John 1:12, 13; 3:3, 5) and adoption (Gal. 4:4, 5). Jesus is Son of God, in likeness and in essential nature, originally, eternally, and by right (Matt. 21:37; John 3:16–18; Rom. 1:4; Heb. 1:1–3). He is, among all the religious heroes of humanity, the only divine Savior (Acts 4:12).

He is *our Lord,* Lord of mind (Phil. 2:5), of conscience (Rom. 13:14), of will (2 Cor. 10:5), of relationships (Rom. 14:3–4; 1 Cor. 7:39), of Scripture (Matt. 5:21–22), of the church (Col. 1:18), of life and death (Rom. 14:7–9). To believe in Jesus is to trust only and completely in him as Savior, to serve and follow him as Lord out of gratitude, admiration, and love.

Who was conceived by the Holy Ghost, born of the virgin Mary

In these words the creed asserts the central miracle of Christianity, the incarnation of God in Christ (Luke 1:35). Jesus was not produced by time and circumstances (though he was divinely prepared for). He came (John 13:3), intervening in human affairs by God's initiative, as one given (John 3:16) and sent (John 6:57). His origin and nature were divine (John 1:1). Yet he was born of a woman (Gal. 4:4), was truly human, grew, was tempted, asked questions, prayed, and was weary, hungry, sorrowful, suffering, rejected, and mortal (John 1:14; Phil. 2: 6–7; Heb. 2:5-18; 1 John 4:2).

In the words *born of the virgin,* Christ's divine origin is again stressed. He was born "not of the will of man" (see Matt. 1:18–25). (To many early Christians who were convinced that original sin was transmitted through human fathers, Christ's virgin birth also resolved the problem of how Christ could be truly human and sinless.) The name

f Mary in the creed reminds Christians of the true place
f this pious Jewess as mother of the Lord. To believe
hese things about Jesus is to wonder at his perfect hu-
nanity and strive to be conformed to his likeness.

uffered under Pontius Pilate, was crucified, dead, nd buried; he descended into hell

Here we have a five-fold insistence that Jesus really
lied. Here are listed the date, judicial circumstances,
ruel manner, obvious physical consequence, and ines-
apable spiritual consequence that he descended, not
nto the place of fire and torment popularly understood as
ell, but into hades, the abode of departed spirits (Luke
23:43; and the puzzling 1 Pet. 3:18–20; see Acts 2:27, 31).
5o the creed answered charges that Christ did not truly
lie, but swooned, was rescued, escaped—because, some
asserted, a son of God could never die.

It need not surprise us that nothing is said about why
Jesus died. The creed was recited at baptism, where the
convert accepted Christ's death on his or her behalf and
died with Christ to sin, self, and the world (Rom. 6:1–23;
Gal. 2:20; 6:14). It was also recited at the Lord's Supper,
where Christ's blood of the new covenant between God
and humankind was clearly and repeatedly set forth. Jesus died as the Lamb of God bearing away the sins of the
world, the righteous for the unrighteous to bring us to
God. He offered expiation for sin, redeeming humankind
(John 1:29; 1 Pet. 3:18; 1 John 4:10; Rom. 3:24–25; 2 Cor.
5:18–21). In so doing, he demonstrated God's love for sinful men and women (1 John 4:9–10). To believe that is to
live gratefully, pardoned, and at peace.

The third day he rose again from the dead

That assertion offers another dated historical fact. Jesus did not merely survive or pass through death; he rose
or, as Scripture often insists, God raised him "out from
among the dead" (Acts 2:32; 1 Cor. 15:15; 1 Pet. 1:21). The
central facts are that Christ conquered death and is alive

Frieze from an ancient Roman building. (J. Jennings)

forevermore, a living, present Savior. Here we have a second reason for Christ's uniqueness: he has risen from the dead. He returned from death as the same Christ, yet different, glorified. Far from the disciples' expecting the event, their hopes creating the conviction that it had happened, they were astonished, unbelieving, and afraid. At first they did not recognize him. Paul recited the evidence (1 Cor. 15). Later the Gospels record the remembered details with much of the wonder and confusion of the experience still in their stories.

The risen Christ is the focus of the Christian's daily faith. His resurrection confirms who he is (Rom. 1:4), that God accepted his sacrifice (Rom. 4:25), and that all who are in Christ will also someday rise (1 Cor. 15:20–23). Those holding such a faith live in Christ's company, sure of everlasting life, unafraid of death.

He ascended into heaven, and sitteth on the right hand of God the Father almighty

Here we have the church's declaration that Jesus was at last fully vindicated, crowned, in the sense of sharing God's throne, and victorious. The Jewish messianic prophecies of kingship were fulfilled beyond anything the prophets foresaw. The ascension of Christ is beautifully described in Luke 24:50–51, more fully in Acts 1:9–11, and dramatically (as the homecoming of a victorious Roman general) in Ephesians 4:7–10. Arguments about the meaning of *up* and *down* are somewhat childish. Christ passed into the eternal sphere of God's immediate presence in victory and glory. Remembering that these are human words for divine realities, how else can human language express such ideas except in three-dimensional terms?

To believe in Christ's ascension is to know that we have a friend at court interceding for us (Rom. 8:34). It is to be drawn upward in aspiration and hope to things above (Col. 3:1–3). It is to be reminded that the author and perfecter of our faith has himself gone all the way before us, through struggle and suffering to glory (Heb. 12:1–3).

From thence he shall come to judge the quick and the dead

Christian faith has a forward look, too. Christ's story is not ended. Just as Jesus promised to be with us always (Matt. 28:20), so he promised to return (Matt. 24:30; 25:31; John 14:3), thus consummating our spiritual fellowship with him in his manifestation in power and glory. The early church eagerly expected his return (Acts 1:10–11; Phil. 3:20–21; 1 Thess. 1:10; 2:19; 2 Tim 4:8). 1 Thessalonians 4:16 attempts to describe his coming. Usually that truth is expressed in metaphors, such as lightning (Matt. 24:27), the secret thief (Matt. 24:43; 1 Thess. 5:2), the arriving bridegroom (Matt. 25:6), the returning master (Matt. 24:46; 25:19). The time has been fixed by God but is unknown to us (Matt. 24:36, 42, 44; Acts 1:7), and even to Christ himself (Matt. 24:36). That point is emphatically made.

At Christ's coming, Christians will be changed into his likeness, bodily (1 Cor. 15:51–52; Phil. 3:20–21) and spiritually (1 John 3:2). To believe this is to be vigilant, faithful in service, lest he should come suddenly and find us asleep (Mark 13:35–37).

A second purpose of Christ's coming is for judgment of the living (*quick*) and the dead (John 5:22; Acts 17:31). Jesus himself said he will judge accordingly as people have served him in serving others (Matt. 25:31–46), that is, by the supreme law of love for God and neighbor. Such judgment will be universal (Rom. 2:5–11, 16; 14:10). But Christians need fear no condemnation, for they have passed from death to life (Rom. 8:1, 38–39; John 5:24). Yet we Christians must all appear before the judgment seat of Christ for assessment of our service (2 Cor. 5:10; Rom. 14:10–12).

Christian belief in divine judgment is therefore not self-

Chapel built on the Mount of Olives to commemorate the ascension of Jesus. (H. Vos)

ighteous nor vengeful, but is instead a deep confidence n the moral constitution of the world—that truth and ight are eternal and will triumph. In the end, God is king. To believe that fact is to live humbly and reverently, with enduring certainty that our struggle and sacrifice will prove worthwhile.

Completing its statement about Jesus, the creed seems to take a fresh breath before drawing very large conclusions from what God has done in Christ.

I believe in the Holy Ghost

Ghost is the old word for "disembodied spirit." In the Old Testament the invisible power of God at work in the world is called his *breath*. The same word also means spirit: God's personal activity, manifest only by its effects. Jesus was conceived by God's Spirit (Luke 1:35), anointed by the Spirit in baptism (Luke 3:22), and endowed by the Spirit for his ministry (Luke 4:18). At the end he promised the same spirit to the disciples (Luke 24:49; John 14:16–17, 26; 16: 7–15; Acts 1:8).

Pentecost is the record of the Spirit's coming on the church (Acts 2). At first, the spectacular effects—equipping and empowering Christians especially for communication and for healing—impressed onlookers (Acts 2:1–4; 3:1–10; 1 Cor. 12:4–11). Later, as the Spirit was recognized more clearly as the Spirit of Jesus (Acts 16:7; 2 Cor. 3:17), the deeper effects in Christian character were more highly valued. That especially meant love (Gal. 5:22–23; 1 Cor. 13; 2 Cor. 3:18). The Spirit teaches, leads into truth, convicts, shows things to come. One might say that the Spirit replaces Jesus.

The church experiences the Spirit as the Spirit of truth, purity (holiness), power, and progress. All Christians are born of the spirit (John 3:5) and possessed of the Spirit (Rom. 8:9; 1 Cor. 12:13). Regrettably, not all live in full enjoyment of his ministry and gifts. To believe in the Spirit is to open all the windows of one's soul in surrender and trust to his coming in.

The holy catholic church, the communion of saint

The Spirit of Jesus is not an abstract idea but is em bodied in the living church, the body of Christ (1 Cor 12:12–27), which Christ purchased (Acts 20:28), loves and cherishes (Eph. 5:22–30), and indwells (1 Cor. 3:16; Eph 3:16–17). Despite its faults the church is rightly called holy, a people set apart for Christ. Because there is only one body of Christ through the whole world and all time i is rightly called *catholic,* although several sections of the church have adopted that title as meaning orthodox or true. Christianity is corporate as well as individual. It cre ates a kingdom, a family of God, a band of disciple: bound together by a law of love.

Differences of tradition, government, and culture do not destroy our essential oneness in Christ. The communion of saints extends from the church militant on earth to in clude the church triumphant in heaven. When we believe in Christ, we identify with some convenient local outcrop ping of the church. We love it, are loyal to it, serve it, yet we cherish fellowship with all who acknowledge Christ as Lord. We emphasize things that unite us; we are honest and tolerant about things that divide us.

The forgiveness of sins

Fatalists, some psychologists, and remorseful, guilt-ridden souls find it hard to believe that forgiveness is pos-sible. What's done is done, they say. Physical and social consequences of wrongdoing are indeed sometimes per-manent. Restitution for wrongdoing is part of penitence; the Christian convert should never expect to be let off from doing what can be made right, or from receiving what is deserved from wrongdoing. At times it happens that we do escape the consequences of our sin. Other times we must receive help from God to bear whatever the undesirable results.

Forgiveness is essentially a changed relationship with God. It is being accepted, reconciled (2 Cor. 5:18–21), loved, trusted—with all concealment ended, sin confessed

Figure 7 Major Creeds & Councils in Church History

Early Church

Apostles' Creed c. 150?	A summary of the faith held by the early Christian church, the Apostles' Creed was not codified in a precise form until many centuries later, but the doctrinal content remained consistent in all versions.
Council of Nicaea (325)	The Council of Nicaea responded to the rise of heresies questioning the deity of Jesus. The creed affirms the divinity of Jesus, stating that he was not a created being but was in existence with the Father before all creation.
Definition of Chalcedon (451)	The Chalcedonian Council responded to questions regarding the humanity of Jesus. While in total agreement with the Nicene Creed, this creed states that Jesus was a man like us in all respects (except sin), affirming the true humanity of Jesus along with his true divinity.

Middle Ages

Fourth Lateran Council (1215)	The greatest of the Medieval councils, the 4th Lateran Council was called for the purpose of reforming the church. As a statement of Medieval Christianity, this creed outlines the roles of both clergy and laymen within the church.
Council of Florence (1438-45)	The Council of Florence dealt with the division between the Greek and Latin churches. The creed specifically addresses the role of the sacraments in the church, and in the life of the Christian.

Reformation

Augsburg Confession (1530)	The Augsburg confession is a Protestant statement of Christian faith, pepared by theologian Philipp Melanchthon, and reflecting the teachings of Luther. It emphasizes justification by faith and the experience of salvation, and calls for correction of moral abuses within the Catholic Church.
Council of Trent (1545-1564)	This Roman Catholic response to the Protestant Reformation addresses crucial issues of doctrine and practice raised by the Reformers and expresses a desire for moral and spiritual renewal of the church.
Westminster Confession (1647)	Written by a theologically diverse assembly that met in Westminster Abbey (London), the Westminster Confession presents a comprehensive and fully developed Reformed theology.

Modern

Barmen Declaration (1934)	A response by Reformed & Lutheran theologians to the Third Reich and "German" Christianity of the period, the Barmen declaration proclaims that Jesus Christ is the only one the Christian is to follow.
Council of Vatican II (1964)	This council, called by Pope John XXIII, was the first major theological reform of the Catholic Church since the Council of Trent. The theological and ecclesiastical depth of the creed marks the beginning of a progressive and ecumenical Catholicism.

Remains of an early Christian church which was built into a corner of the columned Temple of Artemis at Sardis. (H. Vos)

and put away. God forgives, initially, for Jesus' sake (Eph. 4:32), then cleanses (1 John 1:7) and strengthens (Eph. 3:16), enabling us to overcome temptation (Rom. 6:6–7, 12–14). The catalyst of forgiveness is penitence, confession, and faith (Acts 2:37–38; 1 John 1:9). The fruit of forgiveness is a healing peace (Rom. 5:1) and a spirit of forgiving toward others (Matt. 6:12, 14–15; 18:23–35).

he resurrection of the body, and life everlasting

Christian belief in eternal life rests in part on human-
ind's almost universal intuition of the indestructible na-
ire of the human spirit. It rests on the promises and res-
rrection of Christ. It rests on our present experience of
ellowship with the eternal God, who will not allow the soul
e made, loves, and has redeemed, to be extinguished.
'ss. 16:10–11 and 73:23–26 lay a foundation for Matt.
2:31–32; Rom. 8:38–39; Phil. 1:21, 23; John 10:27–29).

As an unborn child cannot imagine the world that
waits it after birth, so our imagination now fails to pic-
ure the life to come. Our personality will endure. "Be-
ause I live," Jesus said, "you also will live." "I will raise
iim (the one who believes in Christ) at the last day" (John
4:19; 6:39–40, 44, 54).

Hebrew thought resisted the widespread dividing-up of
he human being into body and spirit. Each person is an
mbodied spirit. Disembodied we are naked (2 Cor. 5:1–4),
ess than human. Immortality, therefore, involves a
esurrection-body. But the Gospel resurrection-stories and
he writings of the apostle Paul insist on our continuing
dentity amid that change (1 Cor. 15:36–53; Phil. 3:20–
!1). The immortal soul inherits a body transformed to be
appropriate for its new life, imperishable, glorious, power-
ul, spiritual (1 Cor. 15:42–44). To believe this adds realism
o our thoughts of eternal life and profound sacredness to
our present body (1 Cor. 6:13–14; Rom. 8:10–11, 23).

The Apostles' Creed is thus a beautiful and concise
statement of faith that has been adopted or used over the
centuries by virtually every branch of Christendom.

The Bible:
A Book
for People Today

3 / The Bible: A Book for People Today

How the Bible Came to Us
by H.D. McDonald

The Bible is a general name given to the literature accepted by the Christian church as revealing God's purposes for the world. The term *Bible* comes from the Greek word *biblion* (book). The New Testament uses the phrase "the scriptures" to specify the Old Testament either in part or as a whole. In one New Testament reference, the writings of the apostle Paul are included in that designation (2 Pet. 3:16). Paul added the prefix *holy* (KJV) or *sacred* (RSV) when he said that from childhood Timothy knew the "holy scriptures" which make wise unto salvation through faith in Jesus Christ (2 Tim. 3:15; compare Rom. 1:2).

The designations *Old Testament* and *New Testament* to

For more than 3000 years, God's people have found his Word a limitless source of wisdom, strength, and light. (D. Singer)

characterize the Bible's two divisions came into use in th
late second century (see 2 Cor. 3:14 KJV). The word *testa*
ment means "covenant." The Christian addition to the ea
lier Hebrew volume contrasts the "new covenant
prophesied by Jeremiah (Jer. 31:31f.) with the former on
(Heb. 8:13). Christ is the mediator of the new covenan
(Heb. 8:6f; 10:9).

Compilation

The Bible is a composite of 66 books, 39 in the Old Testa
ment and 27 in the New. The various writings of the Ol
Testament appeared at first as separate scrolls in the He
brew language. It is not known just how and when the
were gathered into one volume. By Jesus' time, howeve
the Old Testament was clearly a completed collection. It
threefold division into the Law (of Moses), the Prophets
and the Writings (the Psalms and other books of "wisdom
literature") was generally accepted, as is reflected in th
words of Luke 24:27 (cf. 16:29; Matt. 5:17, etc.). The ulti
mate bringing together of the scattered writings tha
make up the Old Testament took place under the superin
tendency of God. Christ authenticated it as "the word o
God" and as divine scripture which cannot be broker
(John 10:35).

The authenticity of the Old Testament text as we now
have it can be confirmed from a number of externa
sources. Beyond that, the Jews were exceedingly meticu
lous on this score. If a single error was discovered in a
manuscript, or some kind of blemish after use in public
worship, the manuscript was promptly destroyed and the
whole retranscribed. There is reasonable certainty, there
fore, that the text of the Old Testament manuscripts that
we now have preserves with substantial accuracy the bib
lical word from Israel's earliest times.

The New Testament stands to the Old Testament in a re
lationship of *promise* to *fulfillment*. The first Christians
saw in the former Testament a disclosure of God's deal-

ngs with his chosen people, Israel. The Old Testament
prophecies and word pictures of the Christ to come were
et in the context of God's choice and preservation of Is-
ael until the time should fully come (Gal. 4:4). The Old

eginning of Ephesians from a Beatty-Michigan papyrus c. A.D. 200. The Chester Beatty
apyri are some of the earliest-known Greek N. T. documents. (U. of M. Library)

Testament records what God spoke in times past by the prophets concerning the Messiah (Heb. 1:1; cf. 1 Pet. 1:11). The New Testament records God's final word in his Son (Heb. 1:2), the Word become flesh (John 1:14).

The initial destinations of the various writings that make up our present New Testament were widely scattered. Some, like the Gospel of Luke and the book of Acts, were written to single individuals. Most of Paul's letters were addressed to specific Christian communities; some of them, written before the four Gospels, are among the earliest New Testament writings. Of the Gospels—Matthew, Mark, Luke, and John—Mark is thought to be earliest. According to an ancient source, it reflects the preaching of the apostle Peter. Mark's first readers were mainly Greek, so he found it necessary to translate specific Hebrew words, e.g., Boanerges (3:17), Talitha koum (5:40), and Abba (14:36), and to explain Jewish customs (7:3; 14:12). Matthew's audience was mainly Christians of Jewish background. He therefore appealed to the history of Israel and Old Testament prophecy as fulfilled in Christ (e.g., Matt. 4:4, cf. Deut. 8:3; Matt. 4:6, cf. Ps. 91:11; Matt. 4:7–12, cf. Deut. 6:16, etc.). Matthew traced the genealogy of Jesus to Abraham and David, and left specific Jewish ideas unexplained (e.g., "Son of David," "end of the age"). The third Gospel was written by Luke to give a man named Theophilus an accurate account of the ministry of Jesus "until the day he was taken up" (Luke 1:1–4; Acts 1:1).

Mark, Matthew, and Luke are called the *Synoptic Gospels* because, in spite of their differences, when "seen together" (*sunopsis*) they follow the same general pattern. The fourth Gospel has a more theological and spiritual perspective.

Although all of the New Testament writings had a precise destination they soon became the common property of the scattered Christian communities. Paul's letter to a specific church was passed on for reading in others (cf. Col. 4:16). Copies began to multiply. In the course of time the original writing was either worn out or lost so that no actual *autograph* now exists. By comparing existing manuscripts—and there are very many—scholars can bring to light with almost a hundred percent certainty what was on the first parchments. One famous manuscript, the Codex Sinaiticus (Alpha), discovered by Tischendorf in 1844, contains the full New Testament in Greek. The Codex Alexandrinus (A), now in the British Museum, has both Testaments in Greek. The Codex Vaticanus (B), in the Vatican Library, contains the Old Testament in Greek and the New Testament as far as Hebrews 9:14. Exactly when the writings were brought together to form the New Testament as we have it today cannot be determined, but it was early. The process was well under way by the end of the first century.

Canon

The Christian church from the first accepted without question the sacred volume of Judaism as its scriptures. It was enough that Christ had stamped it with his divine approval. His view of the Old Testament as the living voice of God, his use of it, conditioned the attitude to it of the believing communities. In all these Scriptures of the Old Testament, Jesus saw the holy task it was his to accomplish. In Christ, Christians saw "the word of the prophets made more certain" (2 Pet. 1:19). Moses and all the prophets truly wrote of him (Luke 24:27). The principle running through the varied literature of the Old Testament, that God had a redemptive purpose for the world through Israel, was almost sufficient to bring its writings together into one composite volume. By the testimony of the Holy Spirit in their hearts, New Testament believers responded to its evidence and outline of God's unfolding revelation and its focus on the Savior whom they had come to know. Thus the church came to honor the Old Testament as Christ honored it, and found in it divine truth.

It was, however, left to the Christian church to discover for itself, in addition to the Old Testament, a like body of accepted writings. The various New Testament authors wrote to meet the needs of their own times, but in the purpose of God these writings have become his word for all times. This collection of writings forms what is called the canon of the New Testament.

Roman catacombs, underground burial chambers. Because of persecution, early Christians met here in secret. (D. Singer)

The word *canon* is derived from the Greek *kanōn* (related to *kanē*, "cane"). In classical Greek it refers to a straight rod or carpenter's rule and is used in a variety of metaphorical senses. It appears in Galatians 6:16—"all who follow this rule" (cf. Phil. 3:16). Applied to Scripture the *canon* is the rule of faith and truth. The canon of the New Testament refers to that collection of books to which a prescribed rule has been applied and which have "passed the test." These books, then, constitute the "rule of faith" by which all doctrine and behavior must be tested.

Why the formation of a canon, you may ask. Jesus was the redeemer to whom the Old Testament gave witness. His words, it was felt, could not be less authoritative than

hose of the Law and the Prophets. Convinced of that,
hristians repeated them often and put them into written
orms that became the nucleus of the canon.

Time was passing. As long as the traditional rule of "ap-
stolic doctrine based on Christ's teaching and interpreta-
on of his work" was generally held in the churches there
as no need of a written rule. But as the apostles one by
ne died, an oral tradition was insufficient. Dissensions
ithin churches also made appeal to the written Word
oth natural and necessary.

Yet the fiat of a church council did not make a specific
riting canonical. No book could be declared scripture
at did not hold within itself those forces which made it
o. An amazing unanimity prevailed among the churches
s to which writings spoke compellingly of God. That fact
as uppermost in determining canonicity. The New Testa-
ent canon grew under the guidance of a spiritual in-
inct rather than by the imposition of an external
uthority.

The writings accepted were authored by those held in
onor in the church—Matthew, John, Paul, Peter—as well
s by less known figures behind whom was an apostolic
uthority—Peter behind Mark, Paul behind Luke. Some
ooks, like the epistle to the Hebrews, took longer to at-
in the status of canonicity. Others, like Clement of
ome's epistle to the Corinthians and the Shepherd of
ermas, were candidates for canonicity for some time,
ut did not finally succeed.

nspiration

od's revelation in Scripture declares itself to be God's
ord. The Old Testament's 4,000 usages of "Thus says the
ord" specifically relates its origin to God. That recurring
ffirmation, "God spoke," or "God has spoken," calls hu-
ankind to hear his voice from the eternities. The prophet
eremiah was assured by God, "Now, I have put my words
 your mouth" (Jer. 1:9). To Ezekiel, God said, "You must
peak my words to them" (Ezek. 2:7). David declared, "The

Spirit of the Lord spoke through me; his word was on my tongue" (2 Sam. 23:2).

The New Testament writers at times use the phrase "the word of God" for the revelation preserved in the Old Testament. Beyond that, they identify the message of the gospel as the true meaning of that former Testament. What they had to declare was, then, no less authentically the word of God. When the first Christian believers accepted certain newer writings as Scripture (2 Pet. 3:16), it was with the sureness that here too God was speaking.

The word *scripture* in its derivation means something that is written. Scripture is God's word written. The Bible is eloquent with the speech of God in written form.

Inspiration is the term used for God's direct action on the biblical writers. While the individuality of each was preserved, they were at the same time moved, guided, and guarded by the Holy Spirit so that what they wrote constitutes for humankind the one all-sufficient Word of God.

As that statement makes clear, the Bible is both a human and a divine product. We see something of its human author—his outlook, style, temperament, and the like. But it everywhere carries the stamp of the divine impulse to indicate that behind and within the work of the human author is God himself. Thus God, by the process of inspiration, is the direct author of Scripture.

Two passages are specific about that. "For prophecy never had its origin in the will of man, but men spoke from God as they were carried along by the Holy Spirit" (2 Pet. 1:21). These writers were "borne along" by a special influence of the Holy Spirit that caused what they wrote to be "inspired," the product of God's breath. Although the above passage from 1 Peter is referring to spoken prophecy, Peter certainly had in mind the divine origin of Scripture as a whole (cf. 1 Pet. 1:23-25). "All Scripture is God-breathed" (2 Tim. 3:16). As "by the word of the Lord were the heavens made, their starry host by the breath of his mouth" (Ps. 33:6), so by God's "out-breathing" the Scriptures were produced. As God breathed out life into

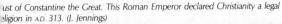
ust of Constantine the Great. This Roman Emperor declared Christianity a legal
religion in A.D. 313. (J. Jennings)

man, and man became a living soul bearing God's image
(Gen. 2:7; 1:27), so God breathed out, through human
writers, words that are able to lead us to salvation and instruct us in righteousness.

Inspiration is plenary; it is full, entire, complete. Scripture in all its parts is God-breathed. Inspiration is *verbal.*
The Bible does not simply convey ideas about God. Rather,
the biblical writers put God's revelation into words that
are to be received as God's words. The Bible therefore can
be trusted.

This title page is from the first complete Bible printed in English, translated by Miles Coverdale and dated 1535. (British Museum)

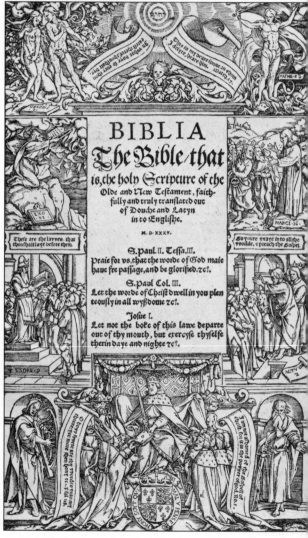

Translations

The Bible first began to be translated into other languages in Egypt in the third century B.C. At that time the Hebrew Old Testament was rendered into Greek. According to tradition, 70 (some say 72) Jewish scholars worked at that task, thus giving the version its title, the *Septuagint* (Latin, *Septuaginta*, for "seventy" = LXX, the symbol by which that version is now known).

At the time of Jesus, Greek was the universal language, to be superseded by Latin (with the extension of Roman rule). By the mid third century A.D., parts of the New Testament appeared in that language as well as in Coptic and Syriac. A collation of the various Latin portions was made early. Later Jerome (c. 345–419), bishop of Milan, at the instigation of Pope Damascus made a revision known as the *Vulgate* (c. 382). The Vulgate was the Bible of the church during the Middle Ages, and was accepted among Roman Catholics up to and long after the Reformation.

In Britain, Latin fell into disuse among the common people. Yet it continued to be the medium of communication in the church and among the intelligentsia. That situation inspired the Venerable Bede (c. 673–735) to translate sections of the Old and New Testaments into the vernacular Anglo-Saxon, the language of ordinary people.

After the Norman invasion of Britain in 1066, no further translations were made for some time. The Word of the Lord was scarce in those days. Meanwhile the Anglo-Saxon language changed and was supplemented by what is now known as Middle English. Under the guidance of John Wycliffe (1330–1384), two complete translations of the whole Bible were then brought out. Another two hundred years passed before further translations appeared. In 1516, Erasmus produced the New Testament in the original Greek, which in turn became available to biblical scholars through the printing press (invented in 1450). William Tyndale (1494–1536) in Britain and Martin Luther (1483–1546) in Germany produced translations in the language of the common people.

In Britain other translations quickly followed Tyndale
Matthew's Bible in 1537; the Great Bible in 1540; the Bis
ops' Bible in 1568. In 1611, at the suggestion of Kir
James I (1566–1625), there was produced the Bible th
remained for centuries the Authorized Version in th
English-speaking world. In 1881 a Revised Version a
peared but had little impact.

From the beginning of the present century new transl
tions have multiplied remarkably (see chart on p. 132
Many of these are the work of single individuals: R.T. We
mouth's New Testament in The Modern Speech (190:
James Moffatt's A New Translation of the Bible (1924); Ch
rles B. Williams' New Testament, "A translation in the la
guage of the People" (1937); Ronald Knox's Cathol
Version, The Holy Bible, (1944–50); J.B. Phillips's The Ne
Testament in Modern English (1958). Unquestionably th
best-known single-author translation is Kenneth N. Ta
lor's The Living Bible (TLB). It began its life in 1962 as Li
ing Letters and by 1971 the entire Bible was released.
has sold in massive quantity and continues to be the mos
controversial of all the modern Bible translations, praise
by many, condemned by some. Detractors of The Livin
Bible point out that it is a paraphrase and not a transl
tion, that it is sometimes a very loose rendering of th
text's meaning, and that it is inconsistent in its treatmen
of theological ideas and very uneven as a whole. Sup
porters of the work argue that it communicates as n
other modern translation does, that it is wholly conserva
tive in its theological orientation, and that it is quite clea
to anyone who picks it up to read. The Living Bible is, n
doubt, what both groups say it is: a valuable, widely use
Bible for today that possesses some peculiarities of i
own, so that readers would be wise to keep a more litera
translation handy to clear up any confusion about th
text's meaning.

Many other translations have been produced by variou
committees of scholars. The Revised Standard Versio
(RSV) was intended to be a revision of the American Sta
dard Version (ASV) of 1901 in the light of the results of mo

ern scholarship and using the simple, classic English style of the *King James Version* (KJV). The RSV New Testament appeared in 1946 and the Old Testament in 1952. It has been very popular in liberal denominational circles, but less so among the conservatives, who have been disturbed about a certain liberal bias displayed by the translators. On the whole, the RSV is an excellent translation that is readable and reasonably accurate. While it does contain some questionable material, the problems are not serious enough to warrant a wholesale rejection of one of the most widely used translations of this century.

The *New American Standard Bible* (NASB) was prepared under the guidance of 55 evangelical scholars, and was a new translation based on the principles used to translate the ASV of 1901. The New Testament appeared in 1960 and the Old Testament in 1971. This version, like the RSV, tried to make use of the best of modern scholarship, including a revised (or critical) Greek text and the Qumran findings. As a translation it is easy enough to read but lacks literary flair. It is wholly conservative in its choice of theological vocabulary and hence is acceptable to orthodox Christians. The NASB is perhaps overly literal in places but still represents an advance over the KJV or the ASV.

The *New English Bible* (NEB) was published in 1970 and was the work of a group of scholars, mainly from Britain. The group's goal was to put the Bible into the current English of our day without falling into the trap of becoming faddish. The NEB was received with mixed emotions by the English-speaking world. Some felt that it was too "British" (i.e., stuffy), hence was not really a Bible for the average person. North Americans especially felt this way. Others praised its flowing, elegant style. The truth probably lies somewhere between the two extremes, with the translation being sometimes glorious and inspiring, and other times verbose and snobbish.

The *Good News Bible* (GNB) was released first as a New Testament called *Good News for Modern Man* in 1966, followed by the whole Bible in 1976. Illustrated with over 500 line drawings, it is worded in common language, intended

Figure 8 A Bible Spectrum—Scripture translations arranged according to translator's purpose

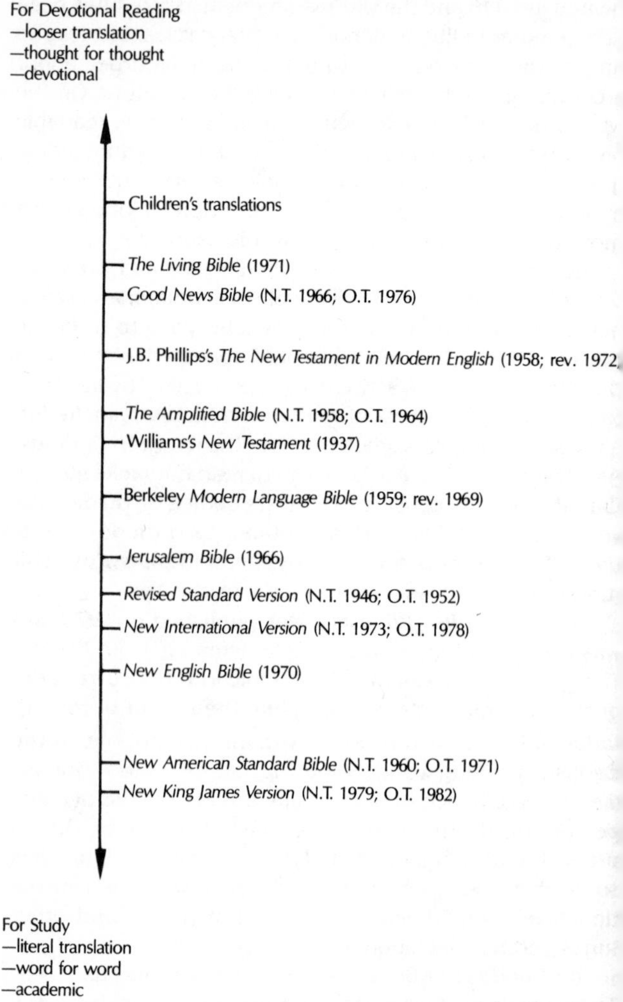

For Devotional Reading
—looser translation
—thought for thought
—devotional

— Children's translations

— *The Living Bible* (1971)
— *Good News Bible* (N.T. 1966; O.T. 1976)

— J.B. Phillips's *The New Testament in Modern English* (1958; rev. 1972)

— *The Amplified Bible* (N.T. 1958; O.T. 1964)
— Williams's *New Testament* (1937)

— Berkeley *Modern Language Bible* (1959; rev. 1969)

— *Jerusalem Bible* (1966)

— *Revised Standard Version* (N.T. 1946; O.T. 1952)
— *New International Version* (N.T. 1973; O.T. 1978)

— *New English Bible* (1970)

— *New American Standard Bible* (N.T. 1960; O.T. 1971)
— *New King James Version* (N.T. 1979; O.T. 1982)

For Study
—literal translation
—word for word
—academic

o be read like a newspaper, and put together following a translational theory called "dynamic equivalence." This theory says the translator must aim to express what the original author *meant*, not simply what he *said*. Therefore he must look for dynamically equivalent statements, not statically exact equivalents. This enormously popular Bible has been praised as the first of a new breed of Bible translations and hence the best available, and condemned as a version off on the wrong track. In actual fact, it is neither. The GNB has many good points, but it is far from perfect. It is wise to read a less expanded translation along side this version for reference.

The *Jerusalem Bible* (JB) began as a collection of commentaries on the books of the Bible that was finished in 1956. This led to a one-volume French edition of the Bible with commentary notes, published in 1961. The English version begun in 1959, was virtually a new translation from the original languages, but retained the notes from the French edition. It was produced by essentially 27 scholars and released in 1966. The JB was designed for student reference, not for reading in the church, and aimed to help believers keep abreast of the times and deepen their theological thought. Hence, new cadences, words, and expressions were used; simplicity and directness were sought to facilitate understanding.

The *New International Version* (NIV) was the work of more than 110 evangelical scholars drawn from around the world, hence the name "International." The New Testament was published in 1973 followed by the Old Testament in 1978. This version was based upon critical texts for both the Old and New Testaments and the translators attempted to strike a middle course between being overly literal and paraphrasing excessively. The translation is accurate, impressive, and conservative in theological tone. Some have found its conservatism to be a fault, and some have complained of a dullness in certain passages.

The *New King James Version* (NKJV) is the product of over 130 evangelical scholars and it is intended to be a replacement for the KJV of 1611. The New Testament appeared in 1979 and the Old Testament in 1982. The strengths of this translation are its fidelity to the KJV tradition, its modernization of obsolete terminology, its accuracy, and its flowing cadences. Its weakness is basically that it is based on an outmoded theory of textual criticism, thus making the project out of date and perhaps even unnecessary.

While it is interesting to examine the strengths and weaknesses of Bible versions, we must realize that the important thing is not which translation a person reads, but that he reads something. No translation is perfect, but no translation is so poor that it obscures the message that God intends us to have. The Word of God speaks clearly to us as we read. Of the many versions it may be said, as Paul said of the many preachers of his day, "Some indeed preach Christ from envy and rivalry, but others from good will," but "whether in pretense or in truth, Christ is proclaimed; and in that I rejoice" (Phil. 1:15, 18 RSV).

How to Read the Bible More Effectively
by Walter A. Elwell

An appalling amount of biblical illiteracy exists in our churches these days. Recent polls by Gallup and others have shown that many people do not know even the simplest of facts, such as the city of Jesus' birth (Bethlehem) or the names of the four Gospels (Matthew, Mark, Luke, John). There is no way to justify such ignorance. Because God gave us his Word, we ought to make every effort to find out what it says. The Bible is, in fact, the most important book in existence. In it we find the words of eternal life, and of life here on earth as well. If we do not know what God says, is it any wonder that we go off in wrong directions?

By studying the Bible we get to know who God is and what he is like. The Scriptures include over 15,000 references to God and a thorough study of those passages alone could change our lives. We should also study the Bible in order to test out what we believe. The world is filled with false ideas about God and his purposes for us. So when we hear someone stating what God's will is, we ought to check it out for ourselves in his Word, and then reject what is false and keep what is true. Finally, we need to study the Bible in order to grow spiritually as it encourages us to love and serve God and others, calls our attention to our own sin, and helps us live like Christ.

But how do we read the Bible more effectively? These few pages don't provide a comprehensive answer to that question, but they do offer guidelines and point us in the right direction.

The Basic Quest

What we are trying to do when we read the Bible is to see what is there. Exegesis (the term used to describe biblical interpretation) is the art of seeing the obvious. Too many

Both Jews and Christians continue the ancient tradition of studying God's Word. Here two generations of Jews study Scripture and commentaries in Jerusalem. (R. Nowitz)

people try to think profound or deep thoughts when they read the Scriptures. But the Scriptures are deep enough; all we need to do is find out what is there. Another way of defining exegesis is to say it is the art of asking the right questions. If we ask the right questions of the Bible when we read it, we will get the right answers. Some suggested questions are given below for approaching the text with a keen eye, an inquiring mind, and an open heart.

The Living Book

So now we open the pages of the Bible. What do we have? In one sense, we have a book like any other book. It has words, ideas, grammar, figures of speech, history, poetry, etc. The rules that make possible our understanding and interpretation of these data will be little different from those we refer to when reading other literature of a similar type. In another sense, however, the Bible is completely different from any other book. The Bible is God's inspired Word and when we read it, we are not examining it, rather, it is examining us. We do not interpret it; it interprets us. As God's Word it has a life of its own and we must *listen* to what God says to us through it.

Bible Translations

Many excellent translations of the Bible are available, so finding one that is readable should not be a problem. (See pp. 130–134 for a discussion of several.) We need to recognize, however, that all are translations of the original Hebrew, Aramaic, and Greek. Therefore we should be careful not to push our own opinions too hard on the basis of our English versions; they are not the originals, but translations. These translations do in fact express the original quite accurately, but the wise person will always speak with a certain amount of humility. Not even the greatest experts in the world know all that there is to know about the Bible. So we must pick a translation that is appealing, read it with care, and leave room for adjustments in our understanding when attempting to comprehend it.

Questions to Ask

As we have seen, reading the Bible with understanding (exegeting) essentially means asking the right questions to see what is there. What are the right questions? Following are some we need to ask.

Who wrote the book? When we know this we can compare what is said here with what the writer said elsewhere.

What language did the writer use? Of course, we may not know Greek or Hebrew, but we can appreciate the fact that what was said in Greek or Hebrew might not be exactly what is conveyed by the translation. This forces us to seek for information, perhaps even investigating different meanings of the original, rather than assume we already know every answer. As an example, there are three Greek

A restored street in the Jewish quarter of old Jerusalem. (L. Shaw)

words translated "love" in English, and each of these words has a distinct meaning. We might miss shades of meaning like this if we close our mind to everything but the English words printed in our versions.

What do these words mean? We must proceed through the text asking over and over again "What does this mean?" We cannot zip through and gather only vague impressions. We must formulate in a language understandable to us what the writer is saying. Usually the meaning is close enough to the surface that it does not take a great deal of digging to figure out what is being said. This is not always the case, of course, and at times we should seek help from a good commentary.

What sort of literature am I reading? The Bible's contents are not limited to a single style. This holy book contains history, poetry, songs, exhortations, prayers, commands, theology, personal defenses, allegories, parables, sermons, letters, typology, quotations from other books, speeches, and other forms of literature. Each of these forms must be interpreted according to appropriate guidelines. For instance, we interpret history in a much different way than we interpret a poem or a love song. By recognizing the diversity that exists and being careful to adjust the way we look at the text we can get a clearer idea of the meaning of biblical passages.

Why did the writer say this? We need to know what the writer had in mind, his reasons for writing what we are reading. This question often takes some research and can be answered only after we have answered the questions already mentioned.

To whom is the book written? The books of the Bible were written to people of various nations over a time span of approximately 1500 years. We need to know whether the book's content was for Christians in Roman times, or for Hebrews during the exile in Babylon, etc. If we don't know this information, we cannot adequately understand what is being said.

Archaeological discoveries continue to add to our understanding of the Bible.
(D. Birkey)

Finding Answers to Difficult Questions

Answered together, all of the above questions help us to understand the Bible. But what if we do not know the answers? Where do we go then? A list of helpful books has been provided on pages 390–391, but following are four basic suggestions. First, many answers can be found by using a concordance. Simply looking up a word in its various places in the Bible may help the meaning fall into place. Second, we can consult a good Bible dictionary; J.D. Douglas's *New Bible Dictionary*, revised (Tyndale) is excellent. Third, we can refer to a readable commentary, such as *The New Layman's Bible: Commentary in One Volume* (Zondervan), edited by G.C.D. Howley, F.F. Bruce, and H.L. Ellison. Finally, we can refer to *How to Read the Bible for All It's Worth* (Zondervan) by Gordon Fee and Douglas Stuart, for more information on the methods used to understand the Bible.

One Final Question

The Bible is God's eternal Word. In order to understand it properly we need more than just good tools and the text. We need to be spiritually in a position to know what is there. God does not dispense his truth to the sinful or the merely curious. He will reveal himself and his will to us only if we sincerely want to know what he reveals. This means we must be prepared spiritually as well as intellectually to read the Bible. Since in the final analysis it is the Holy Spirit who reveals the truth to us, we should be reading prayerfully and open to his voice. He will give us understanding and help us answer the question, "How does God want me to apply this truth in my life?" For, in the end, it is not the one who hears, or knows, or even understands, the will of God who is blessed, but the one who *does* it.

Concise Summaries of the Books of the Bible

4/Concise Summaries of the Books of the Bible by Walter A. Elwell

Old Testament

The Old Testament consists of 39 books that were written over a period of about a thousand years. The material was drawn from every walk of life and was written by numerous individuals, from uneducated herdsmen to highly skilled priests and kings. It consists of four sections: the Pentateuch (Genesis–Deuteronomy); History (Joshua–Esther); Poetry (Job–Song of Solomon); and the Prophets (Isaiah–Malachi). (See chart on p. 146 for a chronology of these writings.)

Pentateuch

The first section of the Old Testament consists of five books (Genesis–Deuteronomy). These writings contain the story of the beginning of the world up to the entrance of Israel into the promised land of Canaan. This collection of books is referred to as "the five books of Moses," "the Law," "the Pentateuch," or "the Torah." They were considered especially sacred by the Jews, since they contained the Ten Commandments and the history of the founding of their nation.

Moonrise over Jerusalem, a city of great theological and historical significance in both Old and New Testaments. (R. Nowitz)

Figure 9 Chronology of Old Testament Books

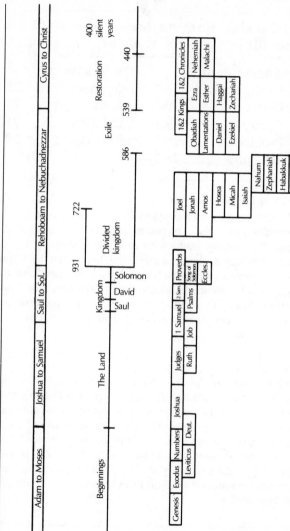

is fine metalwork from a Sumerian temple gateway (c. 2600 B.C.) is made of copper, e of the first metals used by man. (H. Vos)

Genesis
Author: Moses
Date: c. 1400 B.C. or c. 1200 B.C.

Content
The book of Genesis is a theological explanation of the beginnings of our universe. It tells about the lower orders of creation, like plants and animals; the human race; the nations of humankind; the selection of Abraham and one nation, Israel, to be the historical vehicle of God's redemption; the narrowing of God's purposes within that nation; and God's providential protection of one branch of that nation, the line of Joseph. There are other realities of our existence whose first appearance is noted in Genesis: evil, sin, rebellion, redemption, election, providence, and covenant. Other obvious realities that underlie the stories in Genesis, such as the creation of Satan or angels, are not described.

After a careful look at all this, it becomes clear that Genesis is a selective description of the origin of things. Moses, under the guidance of God, did not intend to discuss how *everything* came to be, but only things that contributed to a religious or theological understanding of

history. This is not to say that Genesis is only "theolog
cal," whatever that may mean, or is untrue in any factua
sense. When Genesis speaks factually it may be assume
to be true. But the facts primarily convey theological sig
nificance, rather than scientific or historical explanations
So, from a modern point of view, much is left out tha
would be of great interest to scientists, sociologists, psy
chologists, linguists, and others, but that would be of less
value to theologians.

Map 6 Modern Nations on the Fertile Crescent (center of Old Testament culture, agriculture, & trade)

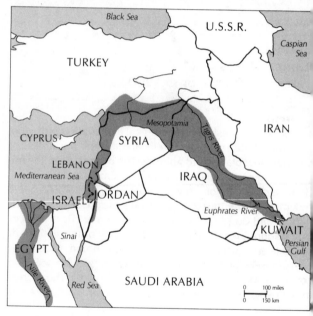

Theological Themes

Several underlying ideas in Genesis help us understand the diverse elements that otherwise might seem only distantly related. The first fundamental fact is that God exists. The world exists only because God *is* and because he chose to make it. The world does not *have to be*. If nothing else had ever been created, God would still *have been*, throughout all of eternity.

Second, everything depends on God and is his. Nothing can rightly claim to exist by its own power or purpose. God is in control and knows what he is doing.

Third, it is possible to reject God, but that is a very foolish and destructive thing to do. When God is effectively in control, all is well; when we choose to take charge ourselves, the result is evil, chaos, destruction, and pain. Sin is a tragic fact of human existence.

Fourth, in spite of our rejection of God, he has not rejected us. Even now, God is redeeming people on earth. Genesis shows that the essence of God is love and compassion for his lost creation.

Finally, God acts in history. His involvement does not begin when we die and go to heaven; it is happening now. In the midst of human history, with all its problems, struggles, and uncertainties, God's presence is certain. It was known by the patriarchs of our faith and, as Genesis teaches us, it can be known by us too.

Outline

1. The initial creation   *1:1–2:25*
2. The fall of humankind and its tragic results   *3:1–5:32*
3. Crime and punishment: the flood and after   *6:1–10:32*
4. The diffusion of people throughout the earth   *11:1–32*
5. The story of Abraham   *12:1–25:11*
6. The story of Isaac and Ishmael   *25:12–27:46*
7. The story of Esau and Jacob   *28:1–36:43*
8. The story of Joseph and the last days of Jacob   *37:1–50:26*

Figure 10 Genealogy of Adam to Abraham

Name	Age at Death	Genesis Reference
Adam	930	5:5
Seth	912	5:8
Enosh	905	5:11
Kenan	910	5:14
Mahalalel	895	5:17
Jared	962	5:20
Enoch	365	5:23
Methuselah	969	5:27
Lamech	777	5:31
Noah	950	9:29
Shem	600	11:10–11
Arphaxad	438	11:12–13
Shelah	433	11:14–15
Eber	464	11:16–17
Peleg	239	11:18–19
Reu	239	11:20–21
Serug	230	11:22–23
Nahor	148	11:24–25
Terah	205	11:32
Abraham	175	25:7

Figure 11 Genealogy of Abraham to David

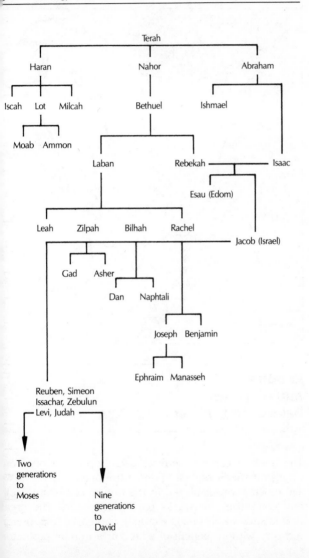

Map 7 The Exodus Wanderings

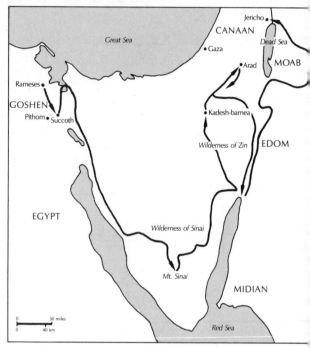

Exodus

Author: Moses
Date: *c.* 1400 B.C. or *c.* 1200 B.C.

Content

The book of Exodus, with its backdrop of history, con
tinues the theme of redemption introduced in Genesis. We
see redemption displayed in the nature of history itself
and epitomized in Israel's particular history. The great
drama shows God's people cruelly oppressed in a foreign
territory, without benefit of a land or a human protector

iod hears the cries of his people and sends a deliverer, Moses, to be the agent of his divine redemptive power. It was necessary for God to work a series of miracles in order to dislodge the Pharaoh from his tyranny over Israel, which results in Israel's release and equally miraculous passage through the sea made dry.

The redemption pictured in the book of Exodus is not just escape from oppression. We also see its positive side, as God leads his people through a wilderness, providing for all of their needs. Then at Mt. Sinai he renews the covenant he had made with Abraham in Genesis, binding himself to all the people of Israel. Here laws are given, summarized in the Ten Commandments, which are a further evidence of God's love and concern for his people. Rules are given for all of life, and a religious structure (tabernacle, priesthood, regulations) is established.

The book of Exodus therefore describes a "going on" as well as a "going out." After the Israelites went *out* of Egypt, they went *on* as his people in the wilderness, trusting the promises God gave at Sinai.

Theological Themes

The first significant theme in Exodus is the power of God. Nothing can withstand his awesome might. Nations, people, the sea, the natural elements, the wilderness—all are subject to his control.

Second is the benevolence of God. He *cares* for his people, hears their cries, and rescues them.

Third is the mystery of evil. It is present, both in Egypt and in Israel, but God's will is still being accomplished.

There is also a mystery in the relation between human and divine action. Pharaoh hardened his heart against God, but it is equally true to say that God hardened Pharaoh's heart. Who can understand the mystery of these two seemingly irreconcilable ideas?

Finally, there is the importance of our human existence as part of God's plan. He makes provision for all our needs by providing divine guidance for us in the form of guide-

Ancient Egypt's agriculture depended totally on the Nile's annual flooding. Nilometers or river level gauges, such as this permitted close observation of the river's rising. (H. Vos)

ines (or laws). These laws relate to every aspect of our existence, showing us that God is concerned about all we do and are.

Outline

1. Bondage in Egypt and a deliverer sent *1:1–11:10*
2. The passover and exodus from Egypt *2:1–14:31*
3. Conflict and guidance in the wilderness *15:1–18:27*
4. The laws of God given and accepted *19:1–34:35*
5. The presence of God in Tabernacle and priesthood *35:1–40:38*

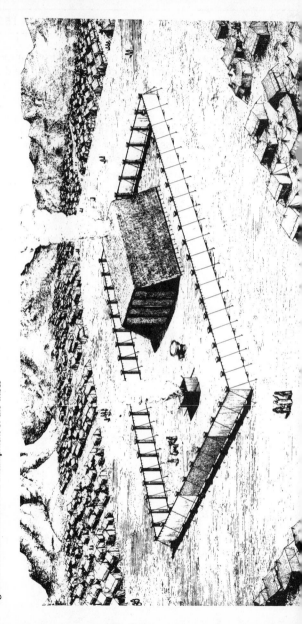

Figure 12 The Tabernacle & the Encampment of the Tribes

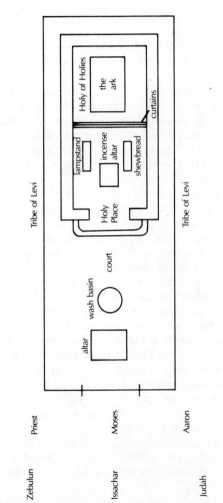

Ephraim

Manasseh

Benjamin

S
E —|— W
N

Gad

Dan

Holy of Holies

the ark

curtains

lampstand

incense altar

shewbread

Holy Place

Tribe of Levi

Tribe of Levi

Simeon

Asher

court

wash basin

altar

Reuben

Naphtali

Priest

Moses

Aaron

Zebulun

Issachar

Judah

Leviticus
Author: Moses
Date: *c.* 1400 B.C. or *c.* 1200 B.C.

Content
The book of Leviticus served as a handbook for the an
cient priests of Israel. Much of it is devoted to specific reg
ulations concerning offerings, sacrifices, ritual purity
ordination, feasts, and festivals. (See charts on pp. 16
and 256 for more information on offerings and feasts
There are also regulations that go beyond the religious in
stitutions and that deal with the events of life. The impl
cation of those regulations is that all of life is, in fact
religious. All that we do, whether in direct worship or not
is part of our relationship to God.

For example, we should not separate life into categorie
of sacred and secular, imagining that only the so-called
sacred areas belong to God. God sees us as totalities, an
all of our life—work, worship, relationships, creativity
family—is important to him. That awareness is a source o
great comfort in the book of Leviticus. It says that w
should not worry that the writing is of no interest or valu
simply because these rules were formulated for a basicall
rural, agricultural, and ancient people, whereas we are, fo
the most part, urbanized, industrialized, and modern
Some may wonder about the rules themselves, which
seem to have no bearing on contemporary life. A sligh
shifting of our mental gears should help us to overcom
these problems. Looking at the basic idea rather than a
the specific rule, we can see how each rule embodies
principle that is just as valid today as it was in Moses' day
In fact, it is amazing how current the ideas are. For exam
ple, the rules about sexual purity (15:1-33) may be seer
as emphasizing the sanctity of sex and warning against
its casual treatment. The need for such advice today is ob
vious.

Theological Themes

The theological themes that run throughout the book of Leviticus are of great value for us to consider. The first important theological theme in Leviticus is that God is holy, and that he expects his people to be holy. This practical holiness is to govern our whole life.

Second, all of life should be viewed as God's. We must never imagine that we can cut God out of what we are doing. He is vitally concerned with all that we do.

Third, sin needs to be atoned for. The system of sacrifices established by God showed atonement in a graphic way and pointed to the great sacrifice eventually to be made in Christ. The blood of bulls and goats can never remove sin ultimately; the death of Jesus can and does do that.

Finally, our lives are to be lived horizontally as well as vertically. Our relationship to other human beings is just as important as our relationship to God. We are to love our neighbor as ourself (19:18). Jesus said that this was of equal importance to loving God with all our hearts and, in fact, formed a commandment with it (Matt. 22:37–40; Mark 12:30–31; Luke 10:27).

Our devotion to God is part of a total understanding of life; all of life is God's. The book of Leviticus was written to show the ancient Israelites, and us too, how to live in a consecrated way before God.

Outline

1. Regulations about sacrifices and offerings   *1:1–7:38*
2. The priesthood and the Tabernacle   *8:1–10:20*
3. Regulations about human life   *11:1–15:33*
4. The great day of atonement   *16:1–34*
5. Holiness before God as ethical living   *17:1–22:33*
6. Festivals, feasts, and various other regulations   *23:1–27:34*

Figure 13 Old Testament Offerings

	Burnt	Cereal (Grain) and Drink	Peace	Sin	Trespass (Guilt)
General Character	Acknowledgement of a gracious Lord			Recognition of our sinfulness	
Purpose	to demonstrate total dedication	to offer tribute or a gift	to demonstrate unity and faithfulness	to atone for our sinful nature	to atone for a specific sin
How Purpose Is Symbolized	The animal is completely burnt before God.	This offering from agriculture is often combined with an animal sacrifice, demonstrating that the whole of life belongs to the Lord.	The priest waves his portion of meat before the Lord as a wave offering before eating it and the offerer shares his portion with his friends.	The animal must be without blemish.	The offerer repays offended parties (God & man) with an animal sacrifice plus compensation.
Offerer's Intent	to be accepted by God	to show thanks	to depict harmony with God and man	to pay for his sin	to offer compensation
Received by God as	a soothing aroma	a soothing aroma	a soothing aroma	an atoning action	an atoning action

Numbers

Author: Moses

Date: *c.* 1400 B.C. or *c.* 1200 B.C.

Content

The book of Numbers narrates Israel's wide-ranging experiences in the wilderness. Jewish scholars from ancient times until today have referred to it by the title "In the Wilderness," which is the first word in the Hebrew text. Others refer to it as "Numbers" because the numbering of the people plays a prominent part in the book.

Numbers is a difficult book to outline because it consists of a collection of material that covers numerous events in Israel's wilderness life. There are problems, travels, judgments, rules, admonitions, complaints, battles, and conflicts. All of these are designed to show that human life is a series of difficulties that need to be dealt with by the grace of God. With such an approach, they can be turned into blessing.

The most significant events that stand out in the history of Israel in the wilderness are: the departure from Sinai; the sending of the spies into Canaan, the Promised Land; the rebellion of the people in refusing to enter the land; the judgment of God, condemning the people to 40 years of wandering; the failure of Moses; and the final victories of the people at the end of 40 years.

Theological Themes

Certain things stand out theologically in the book of Numbers. First is the fact that the Tabernacle is central. It points to the centrality of God in their lives. Tragically, Israel's worship later degenerated into outward formality—a lesson to all of us.

Second, God is in control of the whole situation. At no time is there any doubt as to who is running things. This is a comfort and a warning: a comfort, in that we can rest in

The lifestyle of these present-day nomads is remarkably similar to the lifestyle of nomads living during the early days of Israel's history. (J. Jennings)

God's power and sovereignty; a warning, in that rebellion is futile.

Third, it is clear that God demands obedience. We cannot simply ask God to do everything. He expects, and demands, that we fight battles, face enemies, and overcome obstacles—all with his help.

Fourth, life is seen as a pilgrimage. This theme is found in the New Testament's use of the book of Numbers. Paul, in 1 Corinthians 10:10–11, says that all of these things were written for our admonition and learning.

Finally, it is clear that sin is a problem that needs to be faced among the people of God. It is sad to read that even Moses was not without fault before God, but the way he handled his problem is a lesson for us all. Earth is not heaven. That is certainly no news, but all too often we expect our lives to be without difficulty or temptation. Numbers shows us that such an expectation is wrong. We must always be on guard, lest we too "fall in the wilderness." The book of Hebrews in the New Testament makes a big point of this, pointing to the "rest remaining" for the people of God and the struggles we must face here below (Heb. 4:1–16).

Outline

1. Organization of the people of Israel *1:1–8:26*
2. The memorial passover ceremony *9:1–10:10*
3. Wandering in the wilderness; various judgments and regulations *10:11–21:35*
4. Further wandering (in Transjordan); more judgments and regulations *22:1–36:13*

Jebel Musa, traditionally thought to be Mount Sinai. Deuteronomy reviews the event at this mountain, where God gave Israel his covenant and laws. (J. Jennings)

Deuteronomy
Author: Moses
Date: c. 1400 B.C. or c. 1200 B.C.

Content
Deuteronomy is the fifth book of the Pentateuch. It is something of a bridge between the earlier events of Israel's (and the whole world's) existence, and what follows after Israel's entrance into the Promised Land of Canaan. As such, it looks in two directions. It looks back to the events that brought Israel to the point of going in to the land to claim their inheritance and it looks forward to what life will be like when they are there. It also shows us how Moses, the great leader of Israel, finished his years of leadership and then passed from the scene, handing over the reins to Joshua.

For the most part, Deuteronomy is a rehearsing of the laws and regulations given to the people while they were in the wilderness. Most of what is said can be found in the earlier books of the Pentateuch. Any differences in the formulation of the laws is slight and consists of constructing them a little more in the light of what life will be like when they are in the land.

Theological Themes

Theologically, three things stand out in Deuteronomy. First, the importance of our remembering our past is emphasized. We need to look back to see where we have come from in order to know where we are going. If we have made mistakes, we should not make them again; if we have done the right things, we need to keep on doing them.

Second, the importance of God's laws stands out. These rules were not given to be a burden to us, but to help us. God is an orderly Person and has planned things so that our lives run best when they are ordered too. It makes sense to obey God. He knows what is best for us and has shown us how to live.

Third, the importance of knowing God and worshiping him is stressed. There is only one God over all the heaven and the earth. He is to be worshiped. The wonder is that God not only allows this, but desires it. The highest act a person can perform is to find himself or herself in worship of God. Following directly upon our worship is service to those around us. Worship and service are two sides of the same coin according to Deuteronomy.

Outline

1. Review of Israel's wilderness wandering   *1:1–4:43*
2. Review of Israel's laws   *4:44–26:19*
3. Final acceptance of God and his covenant   *27:1–30:20*
4. The last days of Moses   *31:1–34:12*

History

The second major section of the Old Testament contain basic historical material concerning the nation of Israel. consists of twelve books, from Joshua to Esther. The na ration goes sequentially through the capture of the lan (Joshua); the history of the early nation (Judges, Ruth the period of the united and divided monarchie (1 Kings–2 Chronicles); and the exile and return (Ezra Esther).

Joshua

Author: probably Joshua
Date: c. 1350 B.C. or c. 1150 B.C.

Content

The book of Joshua picks up where Deuteronomy leave off. Moses is gone and the role of leadership is Joshua's Joshua had been one of the two spies (Caleb was th other) who had brought back a favorable report and urge the Israelites to enter the land. They would now enter afte 40 years of wandering.

There are essentially three battle campaigns describe in this book. The central campaign goes through Jerichc and Ai, and concludes with the treaty made at Gibeor The occurrences in each of the three cities give us some thing to ponder: Jericho shows us the power of God; A shows us the wages of sin; and Gibeon shows us the foo ishness of human beings. To leave the Canaanites in th land turned out to be a disaster a century or two later.

The southern campaign involves a coalition of kings le by Adoni-Zedek, king of Jerusalem. Joshua's army is abl to defeat them by the direct help of the Lord.

The northern campaign brings Jabin, king of Hazor, int battle against Israel and sees his eventual defeat.

The land thus has rest from war (11:23) and the peopl

is defense tower of ancient Jericho (c. 7000 B.C.) was part of the site's earliest town, ablished more than 5000 years before Joshua's time. (J. Jennings)

of Israel now settle in to live in this new territory, which [is]
apportioned to the twelve tribes. (See Map 8.)

Theological Themes

Numerous important theological ideas may be seen in the
book of Joshua. The focus on the centrality of God continues from the earlier books. God is God and his will is being done. His power to act is also evident, as well as his
control over the forces of nature and history. The holiness
of God is evident in the judgment meted out to the Canaanites whose iniquity was now "full," but also in that Israel, too, was judged when it sinned. God is an absolutely
impartial judge who will not regard one person above another. The mercy of God is also to be seen in the sparing of
many from the horrors of war.

The importance of human involvement and response is
a central theme of the book of Joshua. God could have defeated his enemies directly had he chosen to do so, but he
didn't. He used Joshua and the people of Israel. They
made the decisions, marched through the land, fought
the battles, set up the cities, and lived their lives. Through
those actions God accomplished his will. It is important to
keep both facts firmly together in our minds: God works;
we work.

One other thing stands out: the necessity to make the
right choices. The choice was thrust upon the new dwell-
ers in the land: Choose whom you will serve, either God or
the gods who were worshiped by the Canaanites. Joshua
made the right choice for his people as an example for us.
The temptation to follow false gods is just as strong today
as it was back then.

Outline

1. The time of preparation   *1:1–2:24*
2. The entrance into the land   *3:1–5:15*
3. The conquest of Canaan   *6:1–12:24*
4. The division of the land   *13:1–21:45*
5. Settling under Joshua's leadership   *22:1–24:33*

Map 8 Inheritances of the Twelve Tribes

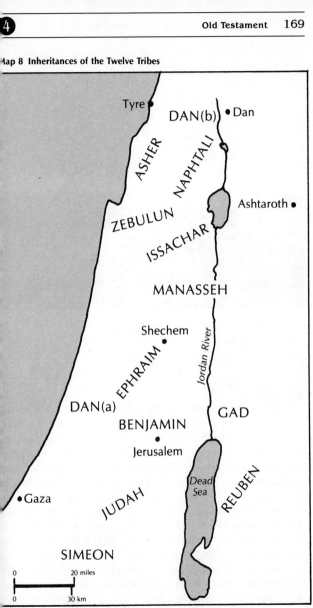

Mount Tabor. When Deborah & Barak judged Israel, Barak led his troops down this mountain to attack the armies of the Canaanite leader Sisera. (J. Jennings)

Judges
Author: unknown
Date: *c.* eleventh century B.C.

Content
After the conquest of Canaan, the Israelites divided up the land into large sections and settled there tribe by tribe. They faced numerous problems: building houses, plowing the land, planting vineyards and trees, digging wells, and generally getting established as a nation. It was not easy, for the new settlers were attacked by invaders. In order to protect his people, God sent judges to lead them. These judges were not legal experts, as the name seems to imply, but military leaders. They were specially empowered by God to gather an army together, defeat the enemy, and rule over their district until things quieted down.

There are about fourteen episodes mentioned in the book of Judges. One man, Abimelech, may not have been a judge, but his story is given anyway, probably to show

Figure 14 Judges of Israel

Judge	Accomplishment	Years the judge led Israel	Reference in Judges
Othniel	Led Israel to freedom from Mesopotamian oppressors	40	3:7–11
Ehud	Led Israel to freedom from Moabite oppressors	80	3:12–30
Shamgar	Led Israel to freedom from Philistine oppressors	10	3:31
Deborah Barak	Led Israel to freedom from Canaanite oppressors	40	4-5
Gideon	Led Israel to freedom from Midianite oppressors	40	6–8
Abimelech	Terrorized the Jews as self-proclaimed king of Israel	3	9
Tola		23	10:1–2
Jair		22	10:3–5
Jephthah	Led Israel to freedom from Ammonite oppressors	6	10:6–12:7
Ibzan		7	12:8–10
Elon		10	12:11–12
Abdon		8	12:13–15
Samson	Led Israel to freedom from Philistine oppressors	20	13–16
Eli	Exercised the office of judge as High Priest	40	1 Sam. 4:18
Samuel	Exercised the office of judge as High Priest	21	1 Sam. 7:15

what a disgrace he was. Several judges became popula
heroes whose names are remembered even today, such a
Deborah, Gideon, and Samson.

The book closes with two particularly grisly stories, on
involving religious deceit and the other murder. The
show what happens when people forget the Lord and rel
on their own strength.

Theological Themes

The book of Judges has a carefully followed pattern that i
used to show how God works in history. It goes like this: Is
rael serves the Lord, then turns from God and falls awa
from his favor. In order to bring his people back, God al
lows them to suffer the consequences of their sin by pun
ishing them through a foreign invader. Israel cries out t
God, who sends them a judge or deliverer. Israel is the
serving the Lord again. This starts a new cycle, following
similar pattern.

A great deal can be learned from looking thoughtfully
at this cycle of events. There is the fact of God's involve
ment in our lives as well as the fact of our own actions. I
isn't an either-or situation. When we are doing God's will
all is well; when we sin, we bring disaster on ourselves. No
tice, as well, the mercy of God. No matter how long it was
when the people cried out to him, he answered them. It is
comforting to know that God is always there to hear ou
prayers.

Finally, notice the awful results of sin. When we choose
to reject God's ways, terrible things result. The stories told
are object lessons for us to learn from. It does not make
any sense to rebel against God. In the end, no one benefits
from wrongdoing. This holds true even for God's people.
After all, Samson was not a pagan, but an Israelite, and
sin destroyed his life, too.

Outline

This man is winnowing grain the same way it was done in Ruth's time—by tossing the threshed grain into the air so the wind blows away the chaff. (J. Jennings)

Ruth
Author: unknown
Date: c. eleventh century B.C.

Content

The times of the Judges were extremely difficult years. That book concluded with the observation that anarchy reigned. No one was answerable to anyone else. The book of Ruth shows a different side to this period, no doubt included to provide some relief to the otherwise almost completely bad situation.

It tells of a famine that drove Elimelech, his wife Naomi and their family from Bethlehem to Moab to settle there. A young Moabite woman named Ruth married into the family and, after being widowed herself, refused to stay in her native land when her mother-in-law Naomi, also widowed by then, returned home. Her beautiful words, "Your people shall be my people, and your God shall be my God" (1:16), have inspired generations of struggling people. An act of kindness from a kinsman, Boaz, is recorded, providing an heir for the family of Elimelech. Boaz was to be an ancestor of David the king, and ultimately of Jesus himself. It is significant that Ruth, though born a pagan, was part of the ancestry of Christ.

Theological Themes
The religious truths found in this book relate more to practical life than to abstract theology. Loyalty, love, kindness, the value of persons, and the need to understand one another stand out. In the midst of the chaos then in the land, meaning could be found by returning to the first principles of simple truth. The book of Ruth tells us that no matter how bad things may be, goodness can exist, if we are willing to make the effort.

Outline
1. In a foreign land   *1:1–22*
2. Ruth and Boaz   *2:1–23*
3. The redemption of Ruth   *3:1–4:15*
4. The ancestors of David and Christ   *4:16–22*

1 & 2 Samuel

Author: unknown

Date: probably tenth century B.C.

Content

These two books carry us into the period of time following the judges. Samuel, as the last of the judges, was the leader just before a king was appointed for the nation. Things were still chaotic, with new problems arising with regrettable regularity. The religious affairs of the nation were getting worse. The economic situation was bad. But most difficult of all was the presence of the Philistine army, which threatened to destroy the nation of Israel. In an epic battle, Israel was defeated and the Ark of the Covenant captured.

In the midst of this national confusion, Saul was appointed to be the first king. (See the map of his kingdom on p. 177.) He was a strange figure, who alternated between doing the reasonable thing and insane acts of violence. Because of Saul's fear of others, David in particular, he spent excessive amounts of time fighting the wrong people. Rather than concentrating on ridding the nation of its enemies, he was in effect chasing out its friends. Things could not last long that way, and in the end Saul died an inglorious death in battle with the Philistines. It was a sad chapter in the history of Israel.

David was a different sort of king. (See the map of his kingdom on p. 178.) He showed his military ability early, but he had remarkable administrative skills as well. When the time came, he was ready to structure the people along national lines and establish a government that would work. His biggest job was to defeat the Philistines in battle, and he did this. We are not told how, but it must have been a resounding victory because the Philistines never again presented any serious threat to Israel.

David was not perfect, however. At one point during a

crucial battle he allowed his passions to overcome his rea
son and seduced the wife of one of his soldiers. He late
deeply regretted that act, composing a psalm of repen
tance that even today is moving to read (Psalm 51).

Theological Themes

Several theological principles shine through the pages of
these two books. Foremost is the continued fact that God
is active in history to work out his purposes. He could im
pose his will on us, but he chooses not to do so. Rather, he
weaves his purposes through our acts in such a way that
our good is affirmed and our evil is judged. It is a great
mystery how God can keep it all straight, but we are en
couraged to believe that all will turn out well because God
is in control.

Another important point is that God cannot be manipu
lated. When the Israelites were losing the war, they
thought that bringing the Ark into battle would bring
them the victory. But God will not be forced like that. If our
lives are not right, no amount of superficial piety will save
the day.

God's love and forgiveness also stand out. On numer
ous occasions, God was forbearing toward those who of
fended him. The marvel of it all is that God does not deal
with us according to our sins, but in mercy.

Outlines

1 Samuel
1. The life of Samuel   *1:1–8:22*
2. The life of Saul until his split with David   *9:1–20:42*
3. David in exile until the death of Saul   *21:1–31:13*

2 Samuel
1. The rise of David as ruler   *1:1–4:12*
2. The life of David as king of Israel and Judah   *5:1–14:33*
3. Rebellion within the nation   *15:1–20:26*
4. David's latter years   *21:1–24:25*

Map 9 Saul's Kingdom

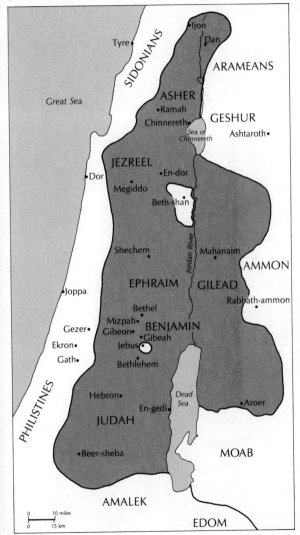

Map 10 David's Kingdom

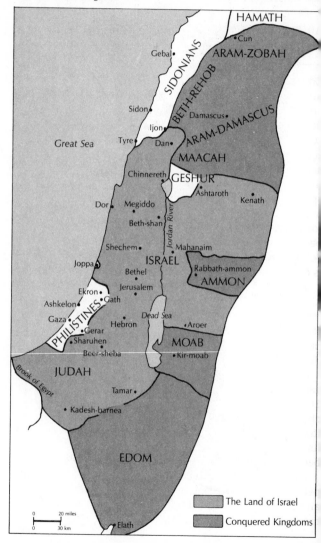

& 2 Kings
Author: unknown
Date: sixth century B.C.

Content

After the death of David, his son Solomon ruled the still united kingdom. His was a marvelous reign and the nation prospered as never before or since. He built a magnificent Temple for worshiping God, established a sound economy, expanded foreign trade, modernized the army, and built a series of fortifications for defense. Great as all this was, however, there were also problems. Solomon spent more than he took in, angered the various regions of his country, increased taxes to the breaking point, and took himself too seriously as a leader. So the good and the bad more or less balanced each other out, and as long as Solomon was around things went well. With his death, as is often the case with strong personalities, it all fell apart.

Solomon's son, Rehoboam, was not able to keep the kingdom together. Following some bad advice, he took a hard line with his critics and the nation split in two, along regional lines. The North became Israel, led by a man named Jeroboam and the South was called Judah, led by Rehoboam. (See map of the divided kingdom on p. 181.)

Here we read of the various fortunes of the rulers of each kingdom down to the end of each. (The chart on p. 185 shows all of these rulers.) The northern kingdom was characterized by instability and bloodshed, but was visited by prophets from God, like Elijah and Elisha. Few of its rulers were very spiritual people and the best remembered are its worst representatives, Jezebel and Ahab.

The southern kingdom had good and bad rulers, with periodic revivals taking place, notably under Hezekiah and Josiah. Prophets of great stature were sent to Judah, too, men like Isaiah and Micah.

Theological Themes

The theological principles found in these books are similar to those found in the books of Samuel. The control of God is emphasized. In the midst of the chaos of human history, God reigns supreme. God's rule is based on moral absolutes. When the Ten Commandments were given, they were not to be seen simply as good advice, but rather as rules to live by. Any person or nation that disregards them does so at their peril. To stand idly by when abuse of the poor, the innocent, or the helpless is taking place is to invite the judgment of God. The nations of Israel and Judah are testimony to this dread but solemn fact.

Another emphasis here is God's care for his people. Time after time, God sent prophets to plead with them to return to his ways. A refrain often heard was God's cry, "Why will you die, O Israel?" (Ezek. 18:31; 33:11). The tragedy was that it did not have to happen. Sin had come between God's people and God, but that did not cancel out God's love. To choose sin, however, was to choose death instead of life.

Another fact that stands out is the value of ordinary life. Throughout the centuries of Israel's and Judah's rise and fall, life went on with God at work in it. The people's biggest task, and ours, was just to live each day as it came, making the most of things, whether good or bad.

Outlines

1 Kings
1. The death of David   *1:1–2:11*
2. The reign of Solomon   *2:12–11:43*
3. The early history of the divided kingdom, to Jehoshaphat and Ahaziah   *12:1–22:53*

2 Kings
1. The divided kingdom to the fall of Israel   *1:1–17:41*
2. The history of Judah until its fall   *18:1–25:21*
3. Judah under Gedaliah   *25:22–30*

Map 11 The Divided Kingdom

Interior view of the Most Holy Place, the Holy Place, and the porch of Solomon's Temple, Howland–Garber model. (E.G. Howland)

1 & 2 Chronicles
Author: unknown
Date: fifth century B.C.

Content

The books of Chronicles seem boring to some people because of all the genealogies and because they cover the same material as Kings. Isn't that unnecessary? When properly understood, however, these Chronicles are important books. The key to understanding them is to remember that the Bible was written with a religious purpose in mind, not a political or historical one. This is not to say that history isn't there, or is false, but that whatever is said is recorded primarily for religious reasons.

The genealogies are important because the Messiah would someday be a human being. These records show the family histories of God's people as a whole, from which the Messiah came, as well as of his family in particular. They are also important because they show God's faithfulness through the passing centuries. His promises can be checked by looking at the records.

These books also lay heavy stress on Judah's history, rather than Israel's. This is because Judah represents the family of David and it was from David's line that the Messiah would come. The northern kingdom of Israel lived in a state of virtual anarchy, with assassinations and governmental turmoil almost a way of life. There was a measure of stability in Judah, with the rulers all coming from one family. Chronicles attributes this to religious faithfulness on the part of the South and apostasy on the part of the North. Not that God didn't love the people of Israel. He continually sent prophets to them to plead for their return. They would not come, however, and their destruction in 722 B.C. was the result of their hardheartedness.

The religious aspects of Judah's history are also prominent. A lot of space is given to the Temple, its worship, the priests, and the Levites. Stress is also laid on the revivals that took place under Hezekiah.

Theological Themes

Certain theological principles stand out in the Chronicles. First, there is the centrality of worship. So much time is devoted to the Temple because it was to be central in the life of God's people. The same is true today. Where worship is routine or missing, whether in a nation or a person's life, spiritual death is just around the corner.

Second, the faithfulness of God is clearly seen. Throughout the many years when the nations' behavior merited only judgment, God remained true to his agreements (called covenants in Old Testament times) with his people. He remains true to them today.

Third, the justice of God is painfully clear. As much as he disliked doing it—and the Old Testament says this clearly—God had no other choice but to punish his people. This should be a warning to us all. God does not play favorites. All will be blessed and judged alike.

Finally, the need for daily watchfulness is evident. Too often our concern is for what *might* be, or for tomorrow. What we ought to do is watch out for today. Israel and Judah never seemed to learn that, and the result was their destruction. This need not happen to us, if we learn from their tragic examples.

Outlines

1 Chronicles
1. Genealogies from Adam to Saul   *1:1–9:34*
2. The life of Saul   *9:35–10:14*
3. The life and reign of David   *11:1–21:30*
4. The organization of David's government   *22:1–27:34*
5. The death of David and the inauguration of Solomon   *28:1–29:30*

2 Chronicles
1. The life and reign of Solomon   *1:1–9:31*
2. The history of Judah   *10:1–36:21*
3. Footnote on Persia   *36:22–23*

Figure 15   Kings of the Divided Kingdom

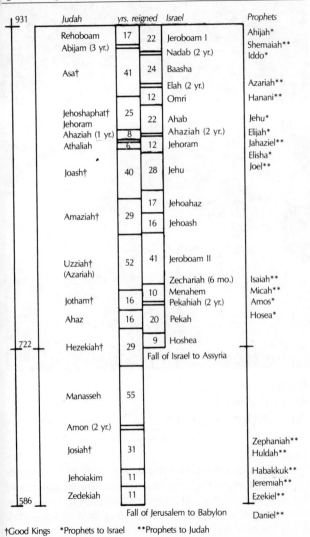

Judah	yrs. reigned		Israel	Prophets
931				
Rehoboam	17	22	Jeroboam I	Ahijah*
Abijam (3 yr.)			Nadab (2 yr.)	Shemaiah**
				Iddo*
Asa†	41	24	Baasha	
			Elah (2 yr.)	Azariah**
		12	Omri	Hanani**
Jehoshaphat†	25	22	Ahab	Jehu*
Jehoram			Ahaziah (2 yr.)	Elijah*
Ahaziah (1 yr.)	8			Jahaziel**
Athaliah	6	12	Jehoram	Elisha*
				Joel**
Joash†	40	28	Jehu	
		17	Jehoahaz	
Amaziah†	29	16	Jehoash	
Uzziah† (Azariah)	52	41	Jeroboam II	
			Zechariah (6 mo.)	Isaiah**
		10	Menahem	Micah**
Jotham†	16		Pekahiah (2 yr.)	Amos*
Ahaz	16	20	Pekah	Hosea*
722		9	Hoshea	
Hezekiah†	29		Fall of Israel to Assyria	
Manasseh	55			
Amon (2 yr.)				
Josiah†	31			Zephaniah**
				Huldah**
Jehoiakim	11			Habakkuk**
				Jeremiah**
Zedekiah	11			Ezekiel**
586			Fall of Jerusalem to Babylon	Daniel**

†Good Kings   *Prophets to Israel   **Prophets to Judah

Children on a kibbutz in Israel participate in a Seder, the Passover meal. Ezra 6:19–22 describes a Passover celebrated by the returned exiles. (R. Nowitz)

Ezra
Author: Ezra
Date: fifth century B.C.

Content
When the northern kingdom was destroyed in 722 B.C., its inhabitants were scattered throughout the ancient world and were lost track of. The land was filled by the Assyrians with foreigners, who became the Samaritans of Jesus' day. When the southern kingdom fell in 587 B.C., its prisoners

vere almost all taken and settled in one place by the Babylonians. As a result they did not lose their national consciousness. Although life in exile was hard for them, thoughts of Jerusalem sustained them over the many years that passed until they were allowed to return home by Cyrus, king of Persia. Psalm 137 is a beautiful but melancholy reflection on those days.

The book of Ezra picks up with the decree of Cyrus to let the people of Judah return home. Ezra was to be one of those who led a group of refugees back to establish the Jews in the land once more.

The first wave of settlers, who arrived in Palestine during the 530s B.C., did not find things easy going. Cities had to be rebuilt, farms plowed, walls constructed for protection, homes built, lives reestablished, and a new life begun. All of it was done in the face of opposition by enemy forces. The Temple was also rebuilt and dedicated in 516 B.C. Ezra then led a new wave of refugees and was appalled to find the people so demoralized. A revival took place, and life was more tolerable for a while.

Theological Themes

The religious value of this book is to show us that although life is never easy, it can be lived with God's help. The struggles of God's people seemed overwhelming but day by day they made it through. Their strength came from the Lord. If we could learn this lesson, we could make it through as well. No one ever knows what difficulties a day may bring, but reflection on Ezra and his times can bring renewed confidence. God has not changed, even if the way he accomplishes his purposes is different today.

Outline

1. The decree of Cyrus   *1:1–11*
2. The census of the people   *2:1–70*
3. The rebuilding of the Temple   *3:1–6:22*
4. Ezra's return   *7:1–10:44*

A section of the current eastern wall of Jerusalem, viewed from inside the city with the Mt. of Olives in the background. (H. Vos)

Nehemiah
Author: Nehemiah
Date: fifth century B.C.

Content

This book is in some ways a parallel account to the one given by Ezra. Nehemiah was a trusted servant in the court of the Persian king, but was committed to his nation and his own people. When he heard of the problems they faced, he requested permission to go to Palestine to help them. His specific concern was the rebuilding of the walls. Without walls, Jerusalem was helpless. Nehemiah must have been a man of immense energy and personal charisma because within 52 days the task was accomplished.

However, Nehemiah found more than just broken walls. He found broken lives. Discouragement had set in, God's commandments were being transgressed, and religious laxity, even among the priests, was common. The situation was not much better than it was before the nation had gone into exile. Realizing that something had to be done, Nehemiah took concrete steps to remedy the situation. The result was a reformation that brought the peo

le, the aliens who lived in the land, and the priests back
n line religiously and morally.

As a person, Nehemiah was in marked contrast to Ezra,
vho worked along with him. Ezra was a rather quiet,
scholarly type who wanted to reason things out. Nehe-
niah was a man of action who literally threw people out
nto the street if the occasion demanded it. Together they
got the job done.

Theological Themes

Two things are significant in this book. First, there is the
ever-present danger of backsliding. We must always be on
the alert. If spiritual attrition could happen in Israel, it can
happen in anybody.

Second, God uses people, and they don't all have to be
alike. Ezra and Nehemiah were different personality types,
but God used them both. He will use us, too, if we let him.

Outline

1. Jerusalem's walls rebuilt   1:1–7:53
2. The people's repentance   8:1–10:39
3. The nation reformed   11:1–13:31

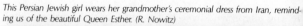

This Persian Jewish girl wears her grandmother's ceremonial dress from Iran, reminding us of the beautiful Queen Esther. (R. Nowitz)

Esther

Author: unknown

Date: fifth century B.C.

Content

The book of Esther tells a straightforward story. It takes place in Persia, where Jews were to be found after the return to Palestine had taken place. Not everyone went home. For over a thousand years the largest concentration of Jews outside Palestine was to be found in the region where they had formerly been exiled.

The king of Persia married a Jewess named Esther, who uncovered a plot against her people led by Haman, the prime minister. Genocidal actions were common in antiquity and have carried down to our own day, as was the case in Nazi Germany. When Esther and her cousin Mordecai brought the plot to the attention of King Ahasuerus, Haman was deposed and replaced by Mordecai. Those who had taken part in the aborted plan were all executed, and the Jews narrowly escaped a frightful slaughter. To commemorate the event, a feast called Purim was established.

Theological Themes

Some persons have objected to the presence of this book in the Bible because it does not seem to have any specifically theological themes, nor is the name of God mentioned in it. Religious content, however, is there; it is below the surface, rather than obviously presented. The main point is that ordinary life is not ordinary but filled with eternal significance. Events fit into a normal pattern of cause and effect, but woven through it all are the hidden purposes of God. Human choices are of great importance and have profound consequences, whether for good or evil. The book of Esther says, in effect—watch what goes on and do not be deceived by appearances. More is happening than you think.

Outline
1. Esther becomes queen   *1:1–2:23*
2. The plot of Haman   *3:1–15*
3. Haman's plot uncovered   *4:1–7:10*
4. The consequences of Esther's bravery   *8:1–10:3*

Poetry

The third major section of the Old Testament contains books written mainly in poetic style. There is an epic poem (Job), a collection of hymns (Psalms), a collection of traditional wisdom (Proverbs), an ornate meditation on life and its vanity (Ecclesiastes), and a love poem (Song of Solomon). Hebrew poetry is different from English poetry in that it stresses a balance of ideas, rather than sounds, rhythm, and images.

A flock of sheep in Israel. Throughout the Bible, and especially in the books of Poetry, sheep have metaphorical significance. (H. Shaw)

Job
Author: unknown
Date: perhaps as early as tenth century B.C.

Content

Job, one of the most complex and interesting books in the Old Testament, deals with a profound human theme. Why do people suffer, if God is in control? That problem has exercised the best minds of virtually every society from the beginnings of civilization until today. The book itself, a very long and highly structured poem, is about a man named Job who lost all that he had within a short period of time. He found himself an outcast, waiting for death near the city dump, when some of his former friends came to comfort him. The hidden backdrop to the story is the will of God and the sneering challenge of the Devil.

The first set of speeches made by Job's friends has the general theme that Job is sinful. The all-wise, all-powerful God, they say, is only giving him what he deserves. All three friends speak—Eliphaz, who is a kindly mystic; Bildad, a rather unsympathetic traditionalist; and Zophar, a narrow dogmatist. These three men represent different approaches to the problem of suffering, as does Job himself. Job replies to them all, ending with a touching appeal to God ("Though he slay me, yet will I hope in him"—13:15), and longs wistfully for an afterlife of peace and tranquillity.

The second set of speeches hammers on the theme that divine judgment is coming for the wicked. It never seems to occur to these three speakers that there might be a *mystery* to human life and that simple answers might not work. Job agonizingly replies, reaching a high point (some would even say the watershed of the book) in 19:23–29 where he affirms his deep personal faith in God and the future. "In my flesh I will see God."

The third set of speeches extols God's wisdom and con

trol of life, implying that Job is an ignorant fool who has no right to reply to God. Job reaffirms his position that he does not deserve what is happening to him.

A new person enters the scene, Elihu, who approaches the subject from a different angle. In essence he says that pride has entered Job's heart and a mysterious correlation exists between that and the suffering that Job is having to endure.

Before anyone can speak, God replies to them all. Job's friends, Elihu, and even Job are all wrong. None of them has all the facts, and consequently none of them is in a position to make a final judgment. Attempts to justify God fall short for lack of knowledge; attempts to justify oneself fall short for lack of honesty. Only God is in a position to put everything together correctly, and Job is invited to learn this lesson. When we have nothing left but God, only then do we realize that God is enough.

After Job learned that lesson, his fortunes were restored and he was comforted and consoled. "The Lord blessed the latter part of Job's life more than the first" (42:12).

Theological Themes

Many theological points are made in this book, but two stand out: the majesty of God and human finitude and need. If we could simply keep these two realities in their rightful place, we would need little else when crises arise in life. The solution to our problems comes when we see God for who he is.

Outline

1. Prologue: scene in heaven   *1:1–2:13*
2. First set of speeches   *3:1–14:22*
3. Second set of speeches   *15:1–21:34*
4. Third set of speeches   *22:1–31:40*
5. The speech of Elihu   *32:1–37:24*
6. The reply of God   *38:1–42:6*
7. Epilogue   *42:7–17*

King David's instrument was the harp or lyre. This third century A.D. mosaic from Tarsus shows a later development of that instrument. (H. Vos)

Psalms
Author: principally David, but also others
Date: tenth century B.C. and later

Content
Psalms is probably the best-known and best-loved book of the Bible. It is the sole book from the Old Testament that is regularly bound with the New Testament when only the New Testament is wanted—as though no Bible would be complete without it. It has provided more personal comfort, imagery, hymns, and poems than any other book that has ever been printed. In some ways it is the Bible in miniature.

The Psalms were written over a long period of time, perhaps 600 years. A large number of them were written and collected by King David (hence the name "Psalms of David"), but many were added to the collection after his day. The book was used by the Israelite community and by single individuals, much as it is used today. The community used it in their public worship. They read from it or sang from it, depending on the circumstances. Some of the psalms were written for special services, such as the coronation of the king. Thus, many of the psalms were hymns, anthems, and special music, sung by the congregation, choir, or both. The Israelites were fond of antiphonal music.

The Psalms were used privately for personal devotion. Almost every possible emotion or situation is covered in them. There are psalms of thanksgiving, lament, devotion, prayer, grief, praise, confession, penitence, and meditation. The psalter (book of Psalms) is therefore a book for all seasons, able to meet all our needs.

Theological Themes

The Psalms contain some of the richest theology in the whole Bible. This in part accounts for the book's continued popularity. Underlying the psalmist's outlook is the concept of the power of God. God is in control of this universe. Although it may appear at times that things have gotten out of hand, this is not so. God is beyond our knowing, but we are not beyond his power. He acts at the right moment, in the right way. Our job is to learn how to trust him.

God's providence, or effective working, is also prominent in the book. He works like a master craftsman, weaving his will in and out of our free choices, so that in the end we have a blend of divine and human activity. Indeed, he works *in* our free choices as well, accomplishing his own good purposes. This should give the believer great comfort and courage; beyond all disappointments and problems we can know that God is there, caring, and able to work out his loving purposes.

The tenderness of God is constantly emphasized. Like a

father who pities his children, or a hen who gathers he
chicks under her wings, so God deals with us. He remem
bers how he made us, he knows that we are but dust. Con
sequently he does not expect what we cannot give. He is
compassionate and merciful, fully aware of every possible
angle to every situation. He knows how to make allowance
for human frailty.

God is also depicted as just. No wrongs will go un
righted. No evil done to God's people is unseen. In due
time, all will be made right. The temptation either to give
up on the one hand or to join the evildoers on the other
must be resisted with the strength that God provides. Evi
will not win because the justice of God will not let it.

The proper response of God's people is also evident. We
are to live lives of prayer, praise, humility, thanksgiving
and faith. Each one of these ideas, explored in depth in
the Psalms, should be the fabric of our existence. In them
we find the secret of living.

The beauty of the world, the value of life, the goodness
of the natural order, and the sheer joy of living are also de
scribed. From the grass that grows beneath our feet to the
loftiest thoughts in our heads or the highest stars in the
sky, the majesty that God wrote into the world is undeni
able. It is there for all to see. However, there is also mys
tery. Ambiguities exist that are unresolvable apart from
God. Glory, mystery, ambiguity—these are the essence of
human life, and God is their source and answer.

Outline
1. Book 1   *1–41*
2. Book 2   *42–72*
3. Book 3   *73–89*
4. Book 4   *90–106*
5. Book 5   *107–150*

The Dome of the Rock, a Muslim mosque, now occupies the area where King Solomon built the magnificent temple in Jerusalem. (L. Shaw)

Proverbs

Author: principally Solomon, but also others

Date: tenth century B.C. and later

Content

The book of Proverbs embodies the collective wisdom of Israel. Usually attributed to Solomon, it is a collection of sayings that reflects Israel's views about how one was to live life in the presence of God. To live this way was wise; those who taught these epigrams were "sages" or wisemen.

The idea of wisdom is common in the Old Testament. In its fullest and highest sense, wisdom belongs to God alone. He is the originator of all life. He knows everything that occurs or could occur. To him belong the earth, humanity, all other living things, the stars, heavens, and angelic hosts. All are evidence of the wisdom of God. In one place it is even said that wisdom was a mastercraftsman along with God (8:22–31). God's wisdom guides the affairs of nature and of humankind, and his ways are past knowing. His ways are not our ways. Consequently we should never second-guess God in order to attempt an explanation of things.

God has revealed some of his wisdom to us. When speaking of wisdom in this way, the Bible uses the term in three ways. Sometimes a skill is described as wisdom. A person who has the technical ability to do something, like build a ship or a building, is called wise. Sometimes the art of making the right decisions is called wisdom, whether moral or nonmoral. Preachers need wisdom to succeed but so do architects; both are called wise when they make the right choices. Finally, wisdom among human beings is the art of right living. It includes all aspects of our lives and begins with the "fear" (respect) of the Lord. It is a religious and practical knowledge that unifies our lives in the presence of God.

The book of Proverbs sums up this idea of wisdom with a collection of aphorisms that cover every aspect of life— relation to parents, growing up, serving God, resisting temptation, practical advice, seeking the truth, the folly of riches, situations to avoid, the knowledge of God, the perfect wife, to name just a few.

Theological Themes

The central theological idea of the Proverbs is that God is creator and ruler. He made the world to function a certain way, and if we have any sense at all we will look to him as supreme. Life is filled with mysteries, but God understands them all and invites us to turn to him for guidance. A second theme, related to the first, is that all of life can be redeemed. Since God made all of life, all of it may be offered to God. Not a single phase of legitimate human existence is outside God's concern. A third theme is that serving God makes sense and leads to a full and satisfying life. This stands to reason. If God made life to function best by living a certain way, to live that way produces meaning and fullness in our lives. Finally, only fools choose death. Two roads are open before us: the way of life and the way of death. The wise person chooses life, the fool chooses death. The way we go depends eventually on us.

Outline

In Old Testament times camels were used for long-distance transport and were an important part of a person's wealth. (J. Jennings)

Ecclesiastes
Author: probably Solomon
Date: tenth century B.C.

Content

The author of Ecclesiastes calls himself Koheleth (the preacher). His exact identity is not known, but traditionally he is identified with Solomon, king of Israel. Ecclesiastes is a difficult book to understand, partly because it is structurally disjointed, but mainly because it seems to have two different sets of ideas in it. It reads a bit like a collection of sermon notes rather randomly put together, leaving it to the reader to decide what to make of it all.

Basically there are two interpretations to the book. One sees the book as a pessimistic statement of life that represents the true view of the preacher. He has tried everything and all is vanity. His conclusion is to live life to the fullest, die, and pass into a state of eternal nonexistence where there is no feeling or consciousness and from which there is no return. Interpreters who adopt this view explain the optimistic passages, those that imply a belief in God or in justice, as later additions. Such an interpretation has a certain appeal to it, especially in our skeptical age, but it runs so counter to everything else the Old Testament says that it ought not to be taken too seriously.

The other interpretation sees the book as a sermon, or a series of sermons on the vanity of life. The preacher adopts a secularized point of view in order to show that if one lives according to those rules, all he or she can expect is disappointment. In this view, the statements that speak of the meaninglessness of life represent the secularism of the preacher's day, and not his own view. His outlook is expressed in the passages that speak of belief in God and trust in him. In order to make his point, the preacher shows that life lived apart from God, no matter how desirable it might seem, is in the end frustrating and unsatisfying. He shows that wisdom, material possessions, sensual pleasure, wild parties, power, and prestige cannot satisfy. The best a secular philosophy can come up with is something like this: Life is short, full of uncertainty, meaningless, and void of any real peace of soul. Because death ends everything, we should simply live now and when we die be done with it. Having said all this, the preacher has proved his point; life lived apart from God is a hopeless affair.

But that is not the whole story. Throughout the book, running alongside the secular philosophy of despair, is the assertion that God sees through our pretensions and sorrows, and will meet us in love if we want him (3:17; 8:12; 11:9; 12:14). Koheleth's conclusion to the whole matter is this: "Fear God and keep his commandments" (12:13). That is not a bad evangelistic message.

Theological Themes

Two theological points stand out in the book of Ecclesiastes. First, the power and redemption of God are the ever-present background for all that is said. God is there, always available, waiting for the moment when wayward seekers after pleasure realize that this world cannot really satisfy. Second, there is the fact that life is not able to meet our needs if we go at it in the wrong way. Not being ultimate, it cannot provide for our ultimate longings and needs. If, however, we see life as under God's control, it may be used by us in the proper way. The world makes a very good servant, but a very hard taskmaster.

Outline

1. Preface   *1:1–11*
2. The futility and oppression of life   *1:12–4:12*
3. The vanity of life in all its forms   *4:13–7:14*
4. Secular philosophy and its failure   *7:15–10:3*
5. Summary of the vain life and how to overcome it   *10:4–12:14*

Fig tree, olive tree, and grape vine (l. to r.). The fruits of these plants are mainstays of life in the eastern Mediterranean region. (H. Vos)

Song of Solomon
Author: probably Solomon
Date: tenth century B.C.

Content
This book represents one of those grand surprises that pop up from time to time in the Bible. Because most people understand the Bible to be a book about religion and spirituality, it cannot be imagined that a book dealing with a theme like human love could be found there. The Song of Solomon tells about a Shulammite woman and her beloved. There is the mutual admiration expressed by each one for the other, as well as descriptions of their physical love. It is a beautiful and touching picture, going to the heart of human emotion and life.

Over the centuries, there have been numerous interpretations of this book. Some commentators have seen in it a vivid picture of the love of God for Israel or the love of Christ for the church. By looking at it in this way, these writers reinterpret the sensual imagery on a more spiritual plane. This book, however, gives no evidence that it is discussing the subject of God's love. Other interpretations say that it deals with ancient ritual, dramatic presentations, or liturgical rites. Those views also seem a bit overdone.

Probably the best way to take the Song of Solomon is at face value. It deals with human love and the beauty of it. When God made humankind he made us "male and female" (Gen. 1:27). That is a simple and fundamental fact of existence. That two people should love each other, and that their love should express itself physically ought to embarrass no one. The Song of Solomon celebrates that love in what could be called a collection of love poems or reflections.

Theological Themes
The basic truth taught in this book is that the structures of our humanity (psychological, physical, emotional, etc.) were created and blessed by God. The proper human response is to accept ourselves as we are in glad thankfulness for the way God made us.

Outline
1. The dream of the bride for her beloved   *1:1–3:5*
2. The arrival of the bridegroom   *3:6–11*
3. In praise of the bride   *4:1–5:1*
4. Night thoughts of the bride   *5:2–6:3*
5. The beauty of the bride   *6:4–7:9*
6. The beauty of love   *7:10–8:14*

Prophets

The fourth major section of the Old Testament contains the writings of the prophets of Israel. It is divided into two groups, the major prophets (Isaiah–Daniel) and the minor prophets (Hosea–Malachi). The words *major* and *minor* do not imply any value judgment but refer to the length of the books. Major prophets are long, and minor prophets are short. (See the chart on p. 236 for more information about the individual prophets.) This section of the Old Testament contains prophecies concerning the coming of Jesus Christ.

Because of its similarity to a skull, "Gordon's Calvary" was pointed out in 1849 as a possible setting of the Messiah's death. (H. Shaw)

Isaiah
Author: Isaiah
Date: eighth century B.C.

Content

The book of Isaiah is one of the best-known books of the Old Testament. It is the book most frequently quoted in the New Testament and the one used most frequently by Jesus. Throughout the history of the church it has been used in worship, in hymns, and by theologians. The reason for its popularity is twofold. First, it contains the clearest Old Testament presentation of the gospel. The depiction of sin, the helplessness of the sinner, the marvelous love of God, his provision of a savior, and the call to repentance and faith are all to be found there. For that reason, Isaiah has been called "the world's first evangelist." Second, the book abounds with memorable phrases including the following from the King James Version, all of which are found in our general church vocabulary or hymnody: "Though your sins be as scarlet, they shall be as white as snow"; "Behold, a virgin shall conceive"; "For unto us a child is born, unto us a son is given . . . and his name shall be called Wonderful, Counselor"; "The desert shall . . . blossom as the rose"; "Comfort ye my people"; "All we like sheep have gone astray"; "Come ye to the waters"; "They that wait upon the LORD shall renew their strength; they shall mount up with wings as eagles".

Isaiah wrote during a period of impending doom in Judah, in his time the southern half of what had been the nation of Israel. The mighty Assyrian army was devastating the northern regions and Isaiah's nation appeared to be next. Isaiah urged Hezekiah the king, against all logic, to cast himself on the Lord for protection, promising that God would be true to his word by sparing Judah. When Hezekiah dared to trust God, a plague broke out in the Assyrian camp, killing most of the army and forcing the Assyrians to withdraw. Thus the tiny nation of believers was pared. Isaiah's book covers those difficult times with messages, sermons, historical accounts, exhortations, and prophecies.

Theological Themes

The theological content of the book of Isaiah is one of the high points of the Old Testament. Paramount in the book is Isaiah's stress on the holiness of God: God is called "The Holy One of Israel." God's holiness is the foundation of all his dealings with the world. Because of this, Judah could rest secure; God would never do anything that was not just and fair. Isaiah tried to draw Judah's attention to the covenant (binding agreement) that God had made with his people. They were his. He might find it necessary to judge them for their sins, but he would never abandon them. If they got carried away into captivity, a remnant would return to pick up where their ancestors left off. In wrath, God would remember his mercy.

Perhaps the most prominent theme in Isaiah's message has to do with the coming Messiah, God's Servant. Four extended psalms, or poems, deal with the Suffering Servant of God. In them the ministry of Jesus is foretold; at another level they are descriptive of Judah, too, which as a nation was also God's servant: 42:1–7; 49:1–7; 50:4–11; 52:13–53:12. The Servant is to suffer for the world, establish justice, provide salvation for the nations, be a light to the Gentiles, teach the truth to all who will listen, give sight to the blind, offer release to the prisoners, be a covenant to the world, treat the weak with compassion and care, dispense God's Spirit, bear the sins of the world, make intercession for sinners, provide the knowledge of God to those who seek it, and secure peace for all people. All of these dimensions have been figuratively (and were sometimes literally) fulfilled by Jesus Christ.

Finally, the book of Isaiah offers a promise of salvation in some of the most beautiful imagery in all of the world's literature (see 1:18; 11:1–9; 35:1–10; 40:1–31; 52:7–10; 55:1–7; 61:1–11). The message concerns God's forgiveness and mercy, freely offered to all who respond in faith.

Outline

1. Judgment pronounced on Judah   *1:1–5:30*
2. The call of Isaiah as a prophet   *6:1–13*
3. Judgment and blessing pronounced on Judah   *7:1–12:6*
4. Judgment pronounced mainly on other nations   *13:1–23:18*
5. The apocalypse of Isaiah   *24:1–27:13*
6. Judgment and blessing on Judah, Israel, and Assyria   *28:1–39:8*
7. Future blessing and comfort for Judah   *40:1–66:24*

Modern Jerusalem. Jeremiah warned Judah of the coming destruction of Jerusalem by Babylon and he lived to see the city fall in 587 B.C. (H. Vos)

Jeremiah

Author: Jeremiah
Date: sixth century B.C.

Content

The prophet Jeremiah is one of the best-known figures in the Old Testament because of the biographical detail to be

found in his book. In most other instances the man is sub-
ordinated to the message, so that little is known about the
preachers as individuals. In Jeremiah's case, his life was
so woven into what he said that it is hard to separate the
two.

Jeremiah lived during the darkest days of Judah's history, spanning the reigns of five kings, and ending with
the destruction of Jerusalem in 587 B.C. He called for a national renewal of faith during the days of Josiah (640–609
B.C.) and was partly successful. When Josiah was killed in
battle, he was succeeded by a king who submitted to international blackmail. Jeremiah continued his stern message of repentance, urging the people to accept the heavy
hand of God as punishment for their sins. For this he
spent many of his remaining years in jail. He was heart-
broken over the evil that surrounded him, often weeping
over the impossible situation in which he found himself.
When the nation finally fell to the Babylonians, Jeremiah
was spared and allowed to live in the rubble that was Jerusalem, where he continued to preach. Ultimately carried
off to Egypt as a hostage, he died in exile.

Theological Themes

Jeremiah the prophet is a triumph of faith and courage. In
the midst of terrible difficulty, he was able to speak with
conviction and strength. He was virtually the only one
who saw clearly what was going on. His dedication to the
call of God was such that he never wavered, no matter
what the cost. Because of this, he is a monument for all
times of how to live when darkness surrounds us.

The foundation of Jeremiah's message was his concep-
tion of God as sole creator and ruler of all that is. God acts
according to his own will, he knows human hearts, he
helps those who trust him, he loves his own. He demands
that his people respond with obedience and faith. Because
God knows what he is doing, the desperate situation in
which Judah found itself was not outside God's knowledge or plan. If Judah would only accept God as Lord, ac-

cept his judgment on them, God would show himself as their deliverer in due course.

A second point stressed by Jeremiah was human responsibility to God. The people had no one to blame but themselves. They were trying to put the blame on their parents, the surrounding nations, the prophets who pointed out their faults, or even on God—but never on themselves. Jeremiah wanted them to see that restoration can come only when we are able to accept the fact that we are accountable for our own lives. Granted that all those things might be factors that influence us, they can never be used as excuses for our wrongdoings. "Not my sister, not my brother, but it's me, O Lord, standin' in the need of prayer."

Jeremiah also urged Judah to trust in God alone. For too long the people had been trusting in their military abilities, their money, or even their own religiosity. They thought that mere attendance at religious services was enough to make them pleasing to God. It was a rude shock to be told that God was not impressed with how much money they had or whether they "went to church" or not. God would allow no rivals, Jeremiah said.

Finally, Jeremiah opposed the false religion and preachers of his own day. Truth must exist within our hearts. Someday God would make a new covenant with his people (31:31), which would write the law inside their lives, not on tablets of stone. Jesus came to introduce that new covenant and establish true religion forever.

Outline

1. The call of Jeremiah   *1:1–19*
2. The sins of Judah outlined   *2:1–13:27*
3. Jeremiah's ministry to Judah   *14:1–33:26*
4. Jeremiah and the last days of Judah   *34:1–39:18*
5. Jeremiah after the fall of Jerusalem   *40:1–41:18*
6. Jeremiah in exile in Egypt   *42:1–52:34*

Prayers at the wailing wall in Jerusalem. For centuries Jews have read Lamentations
here every Sabbath eve to commemorate the city's fall. (J. Jennings)

Lamentations

Author: Jeremiah
Date: sixth century B.C.

Content

Although the book of Lamentations is anonymous as it
now stands, there has never been any real doubt that Jer-

emiah was its author. It was written by someone who wa
an eyewitness of the destruction of Jerusalem, lamenting
that fact—hence its name, Lamentations. It is a funeral
song, written in the rhythm and style of ancient Jewish
dirges, or funeral chants. The first line of the two-line
couplets has three parts to it and the second line only two
(A, B, C; A¹, B¹). The repetition of this rhythm, known since
ancient times as Kinah rhythm, with the third element
systematically missing, is a stylistic reminder of the ab
sence of the loved one, in this case, the city of Jerusalem

What Jerusalem's fall meant to the Jews of the Old Tes
tament is hard for us to imagine because most of us have
never experienced so severe a loss. To them it was the loss
of everything—their Temple, priesthood, sacrificial sys
tem, capital city, nation, and, in most cases, large num
bers of their loved ones. For the survivors of the
destruction, it meant a forced march of about 2,000 miles
to Babylon, where they then had to live in exile, servitude
and misery. Lamentations was written to bewail those aw
ful facts.

Theological Themes

The spirit of the book of Lamentations goes beyond
merely weeping over the past. Here we have an implicit
warning that to transgress is to invite disaster. The
prophets had predicted that God would judge the sins of
his people if they did not repent. Now, the ashes of the city
were testimony to the fact that God had spoken and was
true to his word. History was thus a vindication of God and
his righteousness. It was also a declaration of the wrath of
God, never a popular concept. Most people choose to em
phasize the softer side of God, and properly so, but that
understanding must never obscure the fact that God is
not to be trifled with. When we ignore the needs of those
around us, trampling on justice, God will step in to right
those wrongs. Beginning in the Middle Ages, the Jews
read this book every Sabbath eve at the wailing wall in Je
rusalem, commemorating the city's fall. It is a grim re-

inder that it does not pay to rebel against God.

Lamentations has another side, however. Although the ation of Judah is cast down, it is not without hope. The eople may yet trust God and find pardon. God is one hose mercies are renewed every morning, whose faith- lness is great (3:19–39). We see the value of patience, ayer, and confession of sin. God does not hold grudges nd is willing to start over anytime we are willing to ac- nowledge our errors and resubmit ourselves to him.

utline

The Mt. of Olives viewed from Jerusalem's temple area. God's presence hovered here (Ezek. 11:23) before leaving the city to Babylonian destruction. (H. Vos)

Ezekiel

Author: Ezekiel

Date: sixth century B.C.

Content

Ezekiel was born sometime near the end of Judah's existence, perhaps as early as 620 B.C. He was from a priestl
family, but was called by God to be a prophet. He was de
ported to Babylon in 597 along with Jehoiachin the king
and was settled in the village of Tel-Abib on the river Che
bar. Five years later, he received a formal call to become
prophet to the exiles and the remaining Jews in Jerusa
lem, although he never actually went there. We do no
know how long he lived but it was at least another 2:
years (29:17). Ezekiel's message was at first rejected, bu
later, when a messenger from Jerusalem arrived announc
ing that the city had fallen, the people began to listen
Ezekiel's prophecies had come true (33:21). He now gave
himself to preaching about the coming restoration, jus
as earlier he had given himself to preaching about the
coming judgment.

Ezekiel was an extraordinary person in at least three respects. First, he had remarkable powers of imagination, seen in his descriptions of the heavenly beings and the coming age. Second, he was possessed of supernatural gifts that allowed him to see events in Jerusalem in detail, even though he was over 1,000 miles away. Third, he was a man of great courage and determination. He was not discouraged by the rejection of his message, but kept preaching the truth. When he was finally vindicated, he did not gloat—but kept to the task God had given him.

Ezekiel set an interesting task for himself as a prophet to his nation. He saw himself as a shepherd, watchman, and defender of God. As a shepherd, his task was to look out for his people, tending them from within. He saw himself as a symbol of the Greater Shepherd who was to come, the Messiah, Jesus Christ. As a watchman, he was to warn of the coming judgment. Just as a military guard peers into the dark of night to see the approaching enemy, so Ezekiel peered into the darkness of time and cried out that judgment was coming. As a defender of God, he explained that the nation fell, not because God was weak, but because the people were sinful.

Theological Themes

At the heart of Ezekiel's message is the transcendence of God. The prophet's opening vision, with all of its strange imagery and figures, emphasizes this. God is so far above his creation that words cannot fully describe him. As a result, strange figures of speech are needed to convey the message that God is exalted above creation. Ezekiel exhausted his powers of description trying to explain who God is. At the end of this magnificent vision in chapter one, it is important to note that Ezekiel fell on his face before the Lord to worship. Ezekiel also emphasized the Spirit of God. The other prophets had used the phrase "the word of the Lord," to emphasize the presence and activity of the Lord. Ezekiel said that the Spirit of God was leading him. The purpose of the Spirit's leading Ezekiel was to give the people a message that would lead them to God. The problem was that they had lost touch with God; they no longer knew God. Not that they didn't know *about* him, but they did not know him personally. To know God in that sense is to acknowledge God as sovereign over history and over ourselves. God must be acknowledged as our God.

Ezekiel also brought a message of judgment. Because Judah had sinned against God, God's judgment must come. Judah had disobeyed God's laws, profaned his Temple, desecrated his Sabbath, listened to false prophets, indulged in uncleanness and defilement, and entered into foreign alliances.

Finally, Ezekiel had a message of restoration. The nation would rise from the ashes of its death like a dead body from the grave. That hope is vividly portrayed in the vision of the dry bones (ch. 37). A new age is coming, in which God will reign supreme.

Outline

1. Prophecies of doom for Judah and Jerusalem   *1:1–24:27*
2. Messages to the pagan nations   *25:1–32:32*
3. The renewal of life and the ideal age   *33:1–39:29*
4. The new Temple and the new age   *40:1–48:35*

his reconstruction of Babylon, where Daniel was taken captive by Nebuchadnezzar,
ows the Ishtar Gate (c.), and the ziggurat and Hanging Gardens (r.). (ORINST)

Daniel
Author: Daniel
Date: sixth century B.C.

Content
Daniel's name means "God is my judge." He was either of
royal descent or from a distinguished family of Jerusalem.

He was taken into captivity by Nebuchadnezzar during th reign of Jehoiakim, which would make it before the fall o Jerusalem in 587 B.C. Because his potential was recog nized, he was allowed to study in Babylon along with othe Babylonian youths. His course of study consisted of lar guage and science, probably in preparation for royal se vice. During that time of training, he was allowed by hi advisor to live on vegetables and water, rather than eatin rich food and wine. Daniel's dedication made him a bette student than his Babylonian counterparts.

In the second year of his reign, Nebuchadnezzar had dream that only Daniel was able to interpret. As a resul Daniel was given a position of authority over the Babylc nian scientists (magicians). After Nebuchadnezzar's deatl (562 B.C.), Daniel apparently lost his job because of th change of government. During Belshazzar's reign, how ever, Daniel was restored to government as Third Chie Governor after interpreting some mysterious handwritin on the wall during a banquet. Daniel held that post durin the subsequent reigns of Darius and Cyrus the Persian Daniel was obviously an intelligent, righteous person trusted even by pagans in high places. He was protectec by God in miraculous ways and was in a position to write a book such as this. About his later years and death we know nothing.

The book of Daniel consists primarily of a series of pro phetic dreams and visions. Some historical material is also there, but as background for the prophetic material Daniel interpreted Nebuchadnezzar's first dream (2:1–49 to mean that four great kingdoms would fall. Nebuchad nezzar's second vision (4:1–37) pointed out his vanity and pride.

Daniel's dream (7:1–28) in many ways parallels Nebu chadnezzar's first dream, only fantastic beasts represent the kingdoms of the world, rather than different metals in a gigantic statue. In this dream a figure called the "son of man" appears (v. 13). (In the New Testament, Jesus used this term with reference to himself.)

Daniel had another vision (9:24–27), perhaps the most important in the book. It speaks of a time when God's work would be completed. Many Christians see this prophecy as fulfilled in Christ, the one who atoned for iniquity and will bring in everlasting righteousness. Daniel had other visions (8:1–27; 11:2–20; 11:21–12:3), also prophetic, dealing with the events of world history.

Theological Themes

We can see four elements in the message of Daniel. First, God is all-knowing. He can predict future events, and he revealed some of those secrets to the prophets. Second, God rules over human affairs. This does not mean that we are not free to act, but it does mean that God works in and through our choices. This gives us confidence to live because ultimately no one can defy God and get away with it. God is still on the throne. Third, evil will ultimately be overcome. Although God's enemies may get the upper hand at times in history, the final chapter has not yet been written. When it is, God will come out the victor, along with those who have chosen to live for him. Finally, God's Messiah, Jesus, is vital in his plan for the world; Daniel had an intimation of that redemptive mystery.

Outline

Cedars of Lebanon. Hosea said that when Israel repented God would forgive them and make them strong, flourishing, and fragrant like a cedar of Lebanon. (H. Vos)

Hosea
Author: Hosea
Date: eighth century B.C.

Content

Hosea was a prophet to the northern kingdom of Israel fo about 50 years. His ministry began during the reign of Jer oboam II, making him a contemporary of Amos, who als preached to the North, and of Isaiah and Micah, wh preached to the southern kingdom of Judah. Hosea live to see the fall of his nation to the Assyrians in 722 B.C.

Hosea's unhappy family life became a tragic model fo his prophetic message. He married a woman (Gomer) wit the highest ideals of marriage. Hosea 1:2 says "a wife o harlotry," but this is in retrospect, considering what sh had become by that time, not what she was at marriage. I she had been impure at marriage the analogy to Israe would not fit—Israel was pure and became impure, as Go mer had done. His first child, a son, was symbolicall amed Jezreel, pointing to the coming judgment. The second child, a daughter named Lo-Ruhamah ("she-who-never-knew-a-father's-love"), was not Hosea's, and the father would never be known. The third child, a son named Lo-ammi ("not-my-kin") was not Hosea's child either. When Hosea reflected on the pain of his marital situation, he was reminded of the pain his faithless nation had inflicted on God. Just as Hosea loved Gomer in spite of her infidelity, so God loved Israel.

After six years Gomer left home to become a prostitute. Even then Hosea did not cease caring for her. After a time she slipped to the point of actually being sold into slavery. Rather than let that happen, Hosea bought her himself, bringing her back home.

The book consists of two unequal sections. The first, chapters 1–3, is mostly biographical, detailing the events of Hosea's turbulent life. The thought is difficult to follow because the narration is a mixture of Hosea addressing his wife, God addressing his nation, and combinations of both. The second section, chapters 4–14, consists of addresses, reflections, prophecies, sermon notes, comments, and pronouncements of doom. Because they are undated, it is difficult to know whether they came before or after the fall of Samaria in 722. Probably some are before and some are after.

Theological Themes

The message of Hosea stresses the steadfast love of God, who continues to care for his people despite every provocation imaginable. There was simply no reason why God should continue to love his people, but because his love was steadfast he did. A touching illustration of this can be found in 11:1–4. A second theme is that God takes the lead in his dealings with his people. Grace is mercy extended to those who do not deserve it. Like Gomer, Israel qualified on that count. Third, Hosea emphasized the reality and enormity of Israel's sin. He was not blind to the fact that what Gomer and Israel were doing was wrong and he could not ignore this in the name of sentimentali‹ mistaken for love. True love sees what is really at stak‹ and calls things by their right name. What Israel and G‹ mer were doing was sin and would ultimately be their u‹ doing. Fourth, Israel's basic problem lay in their havin‹ "rejected knowledge" (4:6). Knowledge in this instanc‹ means understanding, not so much recollection of fact‹ Israel did not understand God at all. Neither did Gom‹ understand Hosea. Fifth, repentance must precede r‹ newal. God asked Israel to acknowledge its sin and retur‹ to him.

Outline
1. Hosea's life as prophecy   *1:1–3:5*
2. Hosea's message of judgment to Israel   *4:1–13:16*
3. Promise of blessing if Israel repents   *14:1–9*

Ruins of a Crusader castle at Sidon. The prophet Joel prophesied that God would punish Sidon for its crimes against his chosen people Israel. (H. Vos)

Joel

Author: Joel

Date: probably eighth century B.C.

Content

Little is known about the prophet Joel except that his father's name was Pethuel, he probably lived in Jerusalem, and he prophesied to the southern kingdom of Judah. His book has been considered the earliest prophetic book written, the latest prophetic book written, or just about anywhere in between. Joel made an effort to round out his rhythm and balance his sentences. His book is one of the most elegant literary pieces in the Old Testament.

An atmosphere of impending doom pervades this prophecy. The major nations of the world, Babylon and Assyria, are not mentioned, so we are left to guess whom Joel had in mind as he thought about the coming judgment. A plague of locusts had just swept through the land, providing a background for Joel's visions of doom.

As the book opens, we hear the sound of a mighty army of insects stripping the vegetation bare.

Theological Themes

Using the plagues of locusts as an example, Joel meditates on the coming wrath of God. His words concern the present existence of Judah, but then shade off into discussing a future judgment, usually associated with the end of the age. This twofold approach provides the student of the Bible with an excellent example of what is known as prophetic "foreshortening." Two future events, although separated by many years, are spoken of as though they were one event: the events are telescoped together, giving the appearance of being one. Joel called the plague of locusts "the Day of the Lord" (1:15–2:1, 2, 31). A second theme in Joel is that, after judgment, a time of blessed prosperity may be expected (3:17–18). Like the other prophets of Israel and Judah, Joel emphasized that God stands ready to forgive, if people repent. God is gracious and slow to anger, abounding in steadfast love. If Joel's contemporaries would genuinely change their lives and attitudes ("Rend your heart and not your garments"), God would withhold judgment from them (2:13). Finally, Joel foresaw a future outpouring of the Holy Spirit (2:28–31). The apostle Peter later quoted these verses from Joel's prophecy as foretelling the day of Pentecost (Acts 2:16–21).

Outline

1. The plague of locusts and the judgment of God   *1:1–2:27*
2. The day of the Lord: blessing and judgment   *2:28–4:21*

The prophet Amos was a shepherd and tree farmer from Tekoa, a small town in Judah. (D. Birkey)

Amos

Author: Amos
Date: eighth century B.C.

Content

Amos prophesied during the reign of Uzziah in Judah (767–739 B.C.) and Jeroboam II in Israel (782–753). Israel was about to fall to the Assyrians (722), just 30 years after Amos preached.

The 50 years preceding Amos were a time of relative calm and prosperity for both Israel and Judah. Trade routes had been reestablished through the land, commerce flourished, wealth was piling up, and peace prevailed. In the midst of that apparent prosperity, however, an inner sickness was developing. The poor were being oppressed, the weak were intimidated, justice was ignored. Religion was a pretense, corruption a way of life.

Into that situation Amos came. He was not technically a prophet, nor a member of any prophetic community. Rather, God called him to leave his occupation as a shepherd and tree farmer in order to make God's will known to

Israel. The fact that he was from the South (Judah), a small town (Tekoa), and was not formally educated, made his mission to the North (Israel) all the more difficult. He was run out of the country when he pointed out that God was not impressed with outward pietistic show, devoid of moral content. Because of his courage, Amos is remembered as a model of sticking to one's calling in the midst of adversity.

Theological Themes

Amos depicted God as the ruler of history—past, present, and future. God, he said, is righteous, patient and long-suffering, impartial. God seeks fellowship with his people and demands a righteous life on their part. Amos took pains throughout his book (which is basically sermons) to point out the grace that God had shown to Israel and how that had been ignored by Israel. He selected Israel for special blessing; he gave them the law; he established a place of worship in the Temple and gave them the sacrificial system; he fought their battles; he worked miracles; he led them through the wilderness; he prepared a place for them in Canaan; he sent them prophets and special leaders (Nazarites); he gave them wealth, food, clothes, and homes; he caused business and commerce to flourish. And he gave them his word.

Amos cataloged the sins of Israel, describing them as guilty of cruelty, genocide, dishonesty, anger, greed, lawlessness, sexual excess, desecration of the dead, rejection of the prophets, violence, robbery, selfishness, injustice, deceit, and pride. Amos pointed out that such behavior is self-destructive. Sin is contradictory to God's will and will not be taken lightly by God.

Amos drew attention to the judgment to come: the Lord will roar from Zion and the people will writhe. Along with that, in the midst of a series of pronouncements about the coming wrath, Amos pointed out that God weeps over people's sins, takes no delight in judgment, and offers repentance if they want it. But he is clearly not optimistic about the prospects of Israel's actually repenting.

Finally, Amos tells the nation of Israel what God requires. They are not to bring more sacrifices or offerings to the Temple, but are to seek justice, good, honesty, and the well-being of all their people. Justice should roll on like a river, and righteousness like a never-failing stream (5:24).

Outline

1. Judgment on the nations   *1:1–2:16*
2. Three prophetic sermons   *3:1–6:14*
3. The visions of Amos   *7:1–8:8*
4. Epilogue   *8:9–9:15*

A tomb at the rock fortress now known as Petra. Obadiah prophesied the downfall of the Edomites, whose capital occupied this stronghold. (J. Jennings)

Obadiah

Author: Obadiah

Date: sixth century B.C.

Content

The shortest book in the Old Testament, Obadiah deals with the relationship between Judah and its southern neighbor, Edom. Obadiah is prophesying the fall of Edom because of its inhumane treatment of Judah. The fact that the two peoples were distantly related is important in understanding the book. Esau, to whom the Edomites traced their ancestry, was the brother of Jacob, to whom the Judahites traced their ancestry. Esau rightfully was to inherit the blessing of his father, Isaac, but sold it for a bowl of porridge. Jacob, though deceptive, received the blessing instead. Because of Esau's act, he became a symbol in Judah of a profane person, insensitive to spiritual values.

Judah's descendants settled just north of where Esau's

descendants settled, and relations between the two groups were never very cordial. There were frequent border clashes between the two countries, usually with Judah winning. The two major cities of Edom were Sela and Bozrah. Teman, mentioned by Obadiah, was in the southern part of Edom. Sometimes the whole country is called Mt. Esau, in contrast to Mt. Zion, which stood for Jerusalem or Judah.

When the Babylonians arrived, Edom saw its chance. The Edomites followed the Babylonians in, letting them do most of the fighting and then took whatever they wanted for themselves. That behavior earned them the scorn of the prophet and the punishing hand of God. Edom was destined to fall, said Obadiah, and fall it did, in 312 B.C. So two nations fell for their sins. Judah, however, would learn its lesson and be allowed to return to start over. Edom would remain a heap of ruins forever.

Theological Themes

The message of Obadiah is simple. Edom will be destroyed for its indifference, cowardice, and pride, as will all who choose to live in defiance of God.

Outline

1. Prophecy against Edom   *1:1–14*
2. The day of the Lord and Judah's blessing   *1:15–21*

This human-headed winged bull is from the entrance to the throneroom of Assyrian ki... Sargon II, who ruled from 722–705 B.C. (ORINST)

Jonah

Author: Jonah
Date: eighth century B.C.

Content

The prophet Jonah is known primarily for his extraordinary encounter with the "big fish." Born in a small town in Israel during the reign of Jeroboam II (782–753 B.C.), Jonah's mission was to preach repentance to one of Israel's dreaded enemies, Assyria, in its capital city, Nineveh.

Founded many centuries earlier, Nineveh was named after a female goddess, Ishtar, or Nina. In Genesis 10:11,

Nimrod is said to be the one who laid its foundations. Archaeological discoveries have confirmed that the site has been occupied from prehistoric times on. It was important as early as 1800 B.C. Both Ashurnasirpal II (883–859 B.C.) and Sargon II (722–705 B.C.) had palaces there. Sennacherib (705–681 B.C.) rebuilt the city, its walls, and its water supply. Inside the city there were administrative buildings, parks, private homes, temples, statues to Assyrian victories, and palaces. Accounts of Assyrian history and foreign policy were drawn up and stored in public libraries. At the height of its power, Nineveh had a wall over seven miles long surrounding its 175,000 people.

When God commanded Jonah to leave his native city in Israel to go to Nineveh and preach, Jonah was furious. Why should God care about those pagans? So Jonah deliberately took a ship headed in the opposite direction. A great storm arose and Jonah accepted responsibility for the danger, requesting that he be thrown overboard. A great fish (perhaps a whale, although we cannot be sure) swallowed him and after three days he was disgorged onto the land. Chastened, Jonah then went to Nineveh to preach. When the people of Nineveh repented, Jonah, rather than being glad, was resentful. He sulked outside the city in a field. God then taught him a lesson, using a plant. The point was, if Jonah could have pity on a bit of vegetation, couldn't God have pity on an entire city full of people?

Most of the discussion that surrounds the book of Jonah concerns whether or not these events could have actually happened. Some argue that it reads like an extended parable, and hence was not meant to be taken literally. The rabbis frequently used teaching devices, like parables, as did Jesus. Others believe that it is better to let the account speak for itself. The book looks like history, with the prophet being named and the events of his life being rather carefully described. That it took a miracle for Jonah to survive his long stay inside the fish is not denied. If God could create a world, fish, and Jonah, he certainly could handle a matter like that (1:17). Interestingly, there are actual cases on record of fishermen being swallowed by fish and surviving, even in our day. Other arguments used against the book, such as the size of the city or the unlikelihood of the city repenting, are more apparent than real. Archaeology has shown that the city was quite large, and who is to say whether they repented or not? All in all, it is best to take the book as a startling but true account of God's offer of repentance to the Assyrian nation at Nineveh.

Theological Themes
The purpose of the book of Jonah is plainly stated: "Should I not be concerned about Nineveh, that great city?" (4:11). The compassion of God for all people, even Israel's enemies, is at the heart of the book.

Outline
1. Jonah's refusal to follow God's command   *1:1–17*
2. Jonah's repentance   *2:1–3:10*
3. Jonah's remorse at the city's acceptance of God   *4:1–10*
4. The pity of God for Nineveh   *4:11*

Micah
Author: Micah
Date: eighth century B.C.

Content
Micah was born in the small town of Moresheth, about 25 miles southwest of Jerusalem in Judah. Nearby lay the great coastal road running north and south from Egypt to Mesopotamia, along which the armies of antiquity passed.

Micah's ministry was during the reigns of Jotham, Ahaz,

and Hezekiah, roughly parallel to Isaiah. He lived to see the arrival of the Assyrian army, the fall of Damascus in Syria, the war between Israel and Judah, the conquering of Galilee, the destruction of Samaria and the northern kingdom of Israel, and Sargon's defeat of Egypt. It was a violent, unsettled period of time.

The book of Micah is a collection of sermons and prophecies, largely arranged by topic rather than by when they were preached. The style varies, depending on the time and circumstance. Sometimes Micah is harsh and vigorous, at other times tender and compassionate. His language is always straightforward and forceful.

Micah's message was directed primarily to Judah, the southern kingdom, although he mentioned Israel and the surrounding nations. He was particularly concerned to defend the oppressed. He saw a society in which wealthy landowners took advantage of the poor, oppressing them unmercifully. Farmers, peasants, and small landowners were harassed by those who had connections in high places. Such abuse of power was singled out for scathing rebuke by Micah. Although Micah came from a rural area, he was well aware of the corruptions of city life and denounced Jerusalem in particular. He saw the city as a symbol of national corruption: corrupt law courts, government officials, religious leaders.

The basis for Micah's message was the righteousness of God, much like the emphasis of the prophet Amos, who was preaching to the northern kingdom of Israel. Micah stressed that God demands righteous actions from us, not outward show. In one of the best-known verses of the Old Testament, Micah summed up what God requires of us— to do justice, love kindness, and walk humbly before God (6:8).

Theological Themes

Micah presented a message of judgment. God will bring judgment on the land to destroy it if it does not mend its ways (3:12). A century later, Jeremiah remembered those words and referred to them in his prophecy (26:18).

Micah also gave one of the most detailed Old Testament accounts of the coming Messiah (5:2–15). The redeemer will come from Bethlehem and be a human being (i.e., not an angel). He will have been pre-existent from eternity, will bring together a righteous group of believers, will introduce a kingdom of righteousness on earth, and will care for those in need. The New Testament sees this as fulfilled in Jesus Christ.

Micah proclaimed a universal reign of peace that will be for all people. Swords will be beaten into plowshares and spears into pruning hooks. It will be a time of peace, prosperity, and plenty (4:1–5). God will rule over all, and war will cease to exist.

Outline
1. The wrath to come   *1:1–16*
2. Judgment on evildoers   *2:1–3:12*
3. Future blessedness   *4:1–5*
4. Prophecies of blessing and judgment   *4:6–5:1*
5. The Messiah to come   *5:2–15*
6. God confronts the nation   *6:1–7:20*

Figure 16   Books of the Prophets

Prophet	Spoke to	Message
Pre-Exile Prophets (931-586)		
Joel *	Judah	Joel calls out for national and personal humility and repentance warning that destruction awaits the wicked on the Day of the Lord but the Spirit's outpouring awaits the faithful.
Jonah	Nineveh	Jonah prophesies against the wicked Gentile nation of Nineveh and God accepts their repentance, demonstrating the extent of his love and mercy.
Amos	Israel	Amos pronounces judgment against Israel because of their social injustice, moral decadence, apostasy, and lack of concern for the needy.
Isaiah	Judah	Isaiah warns of judgment because Judah's careful attention to religious ritual is not combined with love for others and holiness before God. He offers hope through God's Suffering Servant to come.

Prophet	Spoke to	Message
Micah	Judah	Micah warns that the nation's corruption will bring imminent judgment but consoles the people with the promise of the future messianic kingdom.
Hosea	Israel	The unfaithfulness of Hosea's wife depicts Israel's infidelity to God. Hosea calls the nation to return to their first love.
Nahum	Nineveh	A century after Nineveh's repentance, Nahum proclaims their doom because of unprecedented pride, oppression, and idolatry.
Zephaniah	Judah	Zephaniah speaks of a universal judgment to begin with Judah, yet concludes his message with a promise of restoration.
Habakkuk	Judah	Habakkuk learns that God will judge Judah by using the ruthless Chaldeans, and that no matter what the circumstances the just always live in God's faithfulness.
Jeremiah	Judah	Jeremiah tells the people of Judah that judgment awaits them because they have left their first love by forsaking their covenant with God.

Exile Prophets (586-539)

Obadiah*	Edom	Obadiah predicts Edom's destruction as punishment for this people's sins against Israel. Not even their supposedly-impregnable mountain fortress will protect them.
Daniel	Babylon	Daniel foretells the judgment and overthrow of the Gentile world powers as well as the future deliverance of God's people.
Ezekiel	Exiles	Ezekiel has a message of destruction for Jerusalem. Then, after Babylon's conquest of Judah, Ezekiel tells the exiles of hope in the future messianic kingdom.

Post-Exile Prophets (539-400)

Haggai	Judah	Haggai rebukes the returned exiles for concentrating their efforts on their own prosperity rather than first rebuilding the temple and reestablishing the priestly offerings.
Zechariah	Judah	Zechariah moves the people beyond rebuilding the temple toward individual spiritual reconstruction while warning that the messianic kingdom lies in the distant future.
Malachi	Judah	Malachi warns a lethargic and spiritually-indifferent Judah that they must repent and humbly obey God in view of the coming Day of the Lord when the wicked will be judged.

*Date Unknown

Ruins of colossal statues at Thebes, once Egypt's magnificent capital. Nahum compared Nineveh's fate to the devastation of this city. (J. Jennings)

Nahum
Author: Nahum
Date: seventh century B.C.

Content

Nahum, born in Elkosh, in Judah, was a prophet whose primary ministry was to the city of Nineveh. Jonah had been sent by God about 100 years earlier to preach repentance to the Ninevites and a large portion of them had responded favorably. The intervening years, however, brought a change of heart as well as a change of government, and Nineveh went back to its old ways. God therefore gave Nahum the task of preaching judgment to the Assyrian capital sometime between 664 B.C. and the city's fall in 612 B.C. Although his message was directed to Nineveh, there is no evidence that Nahum ever went there in person.

Theological Themes

Nahum's message is one of coming judgment for the Ninevites. Their sins will be punished, specifically their idolatry (1:14), arrogance (1:11), murder, lies, treachery, superstition, and social sins (3:1-19). For all of this the city will be destroyed. Nineveh was, he said, a city filled with blood (3:1), a graphic description of the awful depths to which the nation of Assyria had sunk.

The foundation of Nahum's message is that God rules over all the earth, even over those who do not acknowledge him as God. Nineveh's gods and goddesses were nothing according to Nahum. The only God who exists holds us all accountable, whether we know it or not, whether we accept it or not. God alone is God. The Ninevites would soon see that to trust in idols is to trust in wood and stone.

Nonetheless, Nahum pointed out, God was willing to save the city if they repented. God is always seeking the lost, is slow to anger (1:3), is good (1:7), and is a strong-

hold to those who trust him (1:7). God sends good news to
those who will listen (1:15), a theme later taken up by the
New Testament writers when describing the work of Jesus
and the preaching of the *gospel* (a word that means good
news).

Outline

1. A prophecy of judgment   *1:1–15*
2. The fall of Nineveh   *2:1–13*
3. The reason for Nineveh's fall   *3:1–19*

Habakkuk

Author: Habakkuk
Date: seventh century B.C.

Content

Habakkuk prophesied during the last days of Judah, just
before its destruction by the Babylonians in 587 B.C. In the
year 605, at the great battle of Carchemish, the Babylonians defeated what was left of the old Assyrian army and
the Egyptians. That opened the way for Babylon as the
new world power to exert its influence along the major
trade route that ran from the Fertile Crescent down to
Egypt, running right through Judah. It was only a matter
of time before Judah would feel the heavy hand of Babylon, and Habakkuk, with prophetic insight, knew that.

Habakkuk did not cry out against the sins of Judah as
such, but came at the problem in a different way. Because
he was convinced that God is good and all-powerful, he

An arched street in Jerusalem today. Habakkuk prophesied in the final days of the southern kingdom, not long before the fall of Jerusalem. (L. Shaw).

wondered out loud why God allowed these things to happen. Granted Judah was sinful, but God was strong enough to do something about it, so why didn't he? That kind of approach to the problem is almost unheard of in the Old Testament. The book of Job looks at evil in some what this fashion, but Habakkuk is alone among the prophets in doing so.

Theological Themes

Habakkuk got his point across by using the question and answer method; he asked a question and God supplied the answer. Question #1 is found in 1:2–4. It asks, in essence, why God allows evil. Justice has failed, the poor are oppressed, violence is to be seen on every hand, and God seems to let it happen. Answer #1 is in 1:5–11. God responds that he is about to enter in and punish the sin he sees in Judah. He will accomplish this by using the Chaldeans (Babylonians) as the rod of his anger. They are terrible in warfare, proud, worshipers of their own strength, merciless to captives, and destined to win.

That raised an even more serious question in Habakkuk's mind. How could God use an even more evil nation to punish Judah (1:12–2:1)? God is so pure that he cannot look on evil, yet he is about to make use of the Babylonians. How could that be? God gave a two-part answer. In 2:6–19 the practical, historical aspect of the question is answered. Babylon, too, will be judged. In 2:2–4 the theological aspect of Habakkuk's question is answered in some of the most important words to be found in the Bible—the just shall live by faith. God told Habakkuk that human logic might fail, but God's wisdom will not. Even though we cannot understand the way things are going, that doesn't mean there is no answer. God has the answer and the one who would be just (righteous) before God must learn to trust him and live by faith. In one sense this is not so much an answer to the question as an invitation to realize who God is. That made Habakkuk understand he had been talking too much. The proper attitude to have in the presence of God is silence: the silence of quiet acceptance, not the sullen silence of resignation to our fate (2:20). Next comes one of the most beautiful prayers in the Old Testament, ending with Habakkuk's affirmation of faith (3:17–19). We can rejoice in the Lord even if everything is taken away from us. Because that actually happened in Habakkuk's case, he is an example of how to face the worst that life has to offer us.

Another point is significant in this book. Habakkuk shows how God was able to use the Babylonians, even though they did not acknowledge him as God. God is Lord of all the earth, even over those who refuse to accept him as such. It doesn't really matter to God, because he is the only God who exists. That realization should provide us with a great deal of comfort when we are tempted to imagine that God is not able to act, just because people we care about don't acknowledge that he is there.

Outline

1. Introduction   *1:1*
2. The problem of Judah's sin   *1:2–4*
3. The judgment of Judah's sin   *1:5–11*
4. Habakkuk's second question   *1:12–2:1*
5. God's answer and call to faith   *2:2–19*
6. Habakkuk's triumph of faith   *2:20–3:19*

Zephaniah
Author: Zephaniah
Date: shortly before 621 B.C.

Content

Zephaniah was the first of a series of prophets sent by God to the southern kingdom of Judah before its fall in 587 B.C. and after the fall of the northern kingdom of Israel in 722. Isaiah and Micah had lived to see the fall of Samaria, the capital of the northern kingdom, but had died before Zephaniah's time. Zephaniah was followed by Jeremiah, Habakkuk, and Ezekiel, all of whom had a special message to Judah in the south. Regrettably, that nation, too, paid no attention to the warnings sent from God.

The historical situation went something like this. After the death of Hezekiah, a righteous king in Judah, his son Manasseh ascended the throne. He was a thoroughly evil man who rejected his father's ways and allowed wholesale corruption back into the land. He was also instrumental in reintroducing pagan religious practices like Baal worship, astrology, spirit worship, and child sacrifice. Manasseh persecuted the prophets and suppressed the true worship of God. Jewish legend has it that he was party to executing the prophet Isaiah, although this cannot be proven one way or another. His son Ammon was just as bad, but his grandson Josiah (639–609 B.C.) tried to reverse the trend toward disaster. In 621 Josiah made sweeping reforms, partly because of Zephaniah's warnings.

Theological Themes

Zephaniah concentrated on denouncing the evil that abounded in the land, with the dire warning that if Judah did not repent, all would be lost. He also brought further insight to the concept of the "day of the Lord." Popular opinion assumed that the day of the Lord meant vindication for them in the face of their enemies. Zephaniah told them it meant judgment first for them and then for their

oes. The prophet ended with a promise of restoration
(3:9-20), looking beyond a mere return to the land to a
time of universal blessing for the whole earth.

Outline

1. General prophecy of God's judgment   *1:1–2:3*
2. Judgment on specific nations   *2:4–3:8*
3. Future blessings promised   *3:9–20*

Impression of a cylinder seal, (c. 2200 B.C., Iraq) used as a mark of authority and authenticity. Haggai 2:23 speaks of Zerubbabel as God's seal or signet. (ORINST)

Haggai
Author: Haggai
Date: 520 B.C.

Content

After the fall of Jerusalem in 587 B.C., the survivors were
carried off into captivity in Babylon. An international up-
heaval, resulting in a change of world leadership, then put
Cyrus the Persian in charge of what was left of Babylon
(539). One of the first things Cyrus did was to allow former

captives to return home if they wanted to go. A sizable number of Jews returned, although by no means all of them, and work was begun in the restored community. It was a difficult time. There were walls to be built, houses to construct, a Temple to dedicate, farms and fields to plant, forests to clear, roads to build, and an army to raise for protection. What to do first? After a zealous start on the Temple in Jerusalem, interest waned and work ceased in 536. After sixteen years of inactivity and divided interests, the prophet Haggai preached his message, demanding that work be resumed on the Temple so that God would have a fit dwelling place. His book consists of four messages all preached in 520 B.C. The first was directed to Joshua, the religious leader, and Zerubbabel, the civil leader. It denounced the people for spending time on their own amusement while the Temple lay in ruins. The second encouraged those who wanted to build, but were afraid the results would be insignificant. The third and fourth messages denounced the present state of corruption and promised God's protection, if the people responded to God.

Theological Themes
The basic message of the book of Haggai is simple: our spiritual state is more important than our material state. We must make a home for God, whether on a hill (then) or in our hearts (now), if we expect God to bless us.

Outline
1. Message to Joshua and Zerubbabel *1:1–15*
2. Word of encouragement *2:1–9*
3. Things will change for the better *2:10–19*
4. God will preserve the leaders *2:20–23*

Zechariah

Author: Zechariah

Date: between 520 B.C. & 500 B.C.

Content

Zechariah preached to the restored community at exactly the same time that Haggai did. The people had returned home from exile only to find an enormous task confronting them. There were homes to build, walls to erect, fields to plow, forests to clear, roads to build, and a Temple to construct, all in the face of strong opposition from the people who had moved into the land after the Jews had been carried away into captivity. Haggai concentrated on encouraging the people to rebuild the Temple, while Zechariah preached on more general issues. His book consists of a short introduction, eight visions, and a collection of miscellaneous pronouncements over an extended period of time.

The heart of the book is the eight visions:

Vision 1. Riders on colored horses through a grove of trees. This is interpreted as pronouncing judgment on the nations, with God being the rider of the main horse. Israel is to be comforted in three ways: The Temple was to be built, the city of Jerusalem was to be rebuilt, and the outlying districts were to overflow with prosperity.

Vision 2. Four horns that scattered Jerusalem. The four horns were four kingdoms (Assyria, Babylon, Egypt, and Medo-Persia), all of which would fall in recompense for having destroyed Jerusalem.

Vision 3. A young man with a tape measure to measure Jerusalem. This was an encouraging vision about safety in Jerusalem. The young man is forced to stop measuring the city for the rebuilding of its walls, because God would be a wall of fire around it to guard it from the surrounding nations.

Vision 4. Joshua the High Priest in rags before the Lord. This is a graphic vision depicting the grace of God. Joshua is not fit to stand before God wearing the rags of his own self-worth. Satan accused him, only to be silenced by God who provides clothes fit for the divine presence. The point is clear. Only God can make us presentable in the courts of heaven, by an act of grace and mercy. The coming Messiah is referred to in 3:8 as "the Branch."

Vision 5. Two trees feeding oil into a central bowl supplying seven lamps. This is a complicated vision of great significance. Basically, it shows the never-failing supply of strength from God (the trees), the agent of supply (the Holy Spirit), the human agents used by God (Joshua and Zerubbabel), and the fact that the job gets done. The key verse in this vision is 4:6. "Not by might nor by power, but by my Spirit, says the Lord Almighty." This has been paraphrased in our own day in these words: God's work done in God's way will never lack God's supply.

Vision 6. A flying scroll. This is a public declaration that the sins of Israel will be punished. It shows that even in the restored community sin was still a problem and needed to be dealt with.

Vision 7. A flying bushel basket. This is basically the same as vision 6. The basket, when opened, reveals the sins of the nation. They are removed when two stork-winged women carry the basket away. This shows both the presence of sin in the community and the fact that God can forgive it, removing it forever.

Vision 8. Four chariots between two copper mountains. This obscure vision speaks of the certainty of God's will being done. The mountains represent the strength of God's decrees and the chariots represent the divine agencies through which God accomplishes his purposes.

The collection of miscellaneous visions is important because they refer to the coming Messiah as the Good Shepherd, rejected by his people, sold for 30 pieces of silver, riding into Jerusalem in triumph on a donkey, and ultimately mourned for as an only son. The New Testament sees all this as having been fulfilled by Jesus Christ.

Theological Themes

The basic message of Zechariah concerns the accomplishment of God's will. God, the Lord of hosts, is in absolute control of life and history. By symbol, vision, image, and statement, Zechariah hammered home the point that we need never fear if we are doing God's will. God knows what he is doing and is in complete control. The Messiah (Jesus Christ) will come to represent God and will do God's will. First he comes in weakness, but later as sovereign Judge.

Outline

1. Introduction   *1:1–6*
2. A series of eight visions   *1:7–6:15*
3. Miscellaneous oracles   *7:1–14:21*

Malachi
Author: Malachi
Date: between 450 B.C. & 425 B.C.

Content

This book, like the prophecies of Haggai and Zechariah, was addressed to the restored community of Israel, but came considerably later. Another wave of refugees had come, and such notable figures as Ezra and Nehemiah were also on the scene.

All was not well in the nation of Israel. Pagan and other questionable practices were common in the land. There was religious unconcern, greed, corruption in governmental circles, and marriages to foreign women (which meant introducing foreign gods back into the land). The priesthood especially was a problem. Religious matters had become routine, lacking any real significance, either for the priests or for the people of the land. The lack of concern here was called nothing less than robbery of God.

The book consists of two sections. The first deals with the sins of Israel and the second with promised blessings and judgments. It is set up as a series of questions and answers, much like a courtroom scene, with Israel asking rhetorical (and often self-justifying) questions and God answering. The questions are as follows: How have you loved us (1:2)? How have we despised your name (1:6)? How have we defiled you (1:7)? Why do we profane the covenant of our fathers by breaking faith with one another (2:10)? How have we wearied him (God) (2:17)?

Theological Themes

Malachi singled out the clergy (priests) for judgment. They of all people knew what God required. The sacrifices were unworthy, there was no sincerity in their service, their duties were performed in a lazy manner, and they had no real commitment to God. If the religious leaders go wrong, why should the people be any different? Second, Malachi said, the people had not learned the lesson of the exile. They had gone into captivity because of their sins and had returned bent on following their old ways. Judgment would come again, as it had of old, if the nation continued to reject God. Third, a message of hope was proclaimed for the future. The day of the Lord was coming, a day of judgment, but on it the Lord would purify the priests and the Temple, would redeem the righteous, and would usher in the reign of God. All this would be preceded by a messenger who would prepare the way of the Lord. The New Testament understands this messenger to be John the Baptist.

Outline
1. The sins of Israel itemized   *1:1–2:17*
2. Promised blessings and judgments   *3:1–4:6*

This statue of a menorah in Jerusalem reminds us of the Feast of Lights (Hanukah), which began in 167 B.C. (J. Jennings)

Apocrypha

The Apocrypha is a collection of books and additions to Old Testament books written sometime between 500 B.C. and A.D. 100. These books were included, in whole or in part, in the Greek versions of the Old Testament, but were excluded from the Hebrew versions and their inclusion in the Old Testament Scripture was explicitly rejected by the Jews at the great council held at Jamnia in A.D. 90. The status of the apocrypha was ambiguous in the early days of the church, and views about it differ widely to this day, ranging from outright rejection (most evangelical Protestant denominations), to allowance for devotional use (the Church of England), to acceptance as Scripture (the Roman Catholic Church).

A study of history does little to help settle the issue. The New Testament does not explicitly quote any apocryphal book, providing good reason for some to be suspicious of the biblical nature of the books. Early theologians (second and third century) did quote apocryphal books, but they quoted many other books as well. Augustine was inclined to acknowledge their authentic nature, but Jerome, who translated the Latin Vulgate, rejected them as canonical Scripture. All of this tends to argue against the Apocrypha's status as genuine Scripture. Arguing for the Apocrypha is the fact that many of the books were found alongside the Old Testament books in manuscripts of the Bible, and some theologians did in fact use them as Scripture.

At the Reformation, the Protestant reformers and denominations rejected the Apocrypha as Scripture, but in some instances allowed devotional use of it. The Council of Trent (1545–63) settled the issue for Roman Catholics by proclaiming the books Scripture and pronouncing an anathema on those who disagree. The first Vatican Council (1870) reiterated what Trent had

said, although many Catholic writers speak today c
the apocrypha's deutero-canonical status, rather tha
canonical status.

The books themselves are extremely interesting an
valuable historical documents that range from sobe
historical narrative to pious fiction.

1 Esdras

This historical narrative parallels three Old Testamen
books, 2 Chronicles, Ezra, and Nehemiah. In 1 Esdras
long section not found in the Old Testament concerns de
termining what is the strongest force in the world (3:1
5:6). The forces defended are wine, the King, women, an
truth, with truth being declared the most powerful force i
the universe. The rest of the material in 1 Esdras does no
differ significantly from the Old Testament.

2 Esdras

This composite work is essentially a Jewish apocalyptic
book (in some ways similar to parts of Daniel) with Chris
tian additions. The heart of the book consists of seven vi
sions experienced by Ezra and more or less explained tc
him by Uriel the angel. The visions deal variously with Is
rael, the end of the age, the dawn of the age of salvation
the afterlife, election, Jerusalem, Rome, the Messiah
judgment, and eternity. The constant theme of 2 Esdras is
that God is in control of history and human destiny, anc
therefore we should not look on appearances but pene
trate through to the inner realities that truly govern our
existence. Doing this we will never despair, because we
know that God is Sovereign Lord of all.

Tobit

This is a rather fanciful short story that depicts the care of
God for individual human beings. The tale takes place
during the Captivity and concerns Tobit, who has been ac
cidentally blinded, and his son Tobias. Tobias prays that

he may die, while simultaneously a maiden named Sarah
prays for deliverance from the demon Asmodaeus who
has successfully slain seven men, each on the night she
was to have married him. God responds to both prayers by
sending the angel Raphael, who takes human form as a
man named Azariah. Tobias links up with Azariah on a trip
and, following Azariah's advice, preserves the heart, liver,
and gallbladder of a fish caught in the Tigris River. Tobias
later marries Sarah, burning the heart and liver of the fish
on their wedding night to drive away the demon Asmodaeus. On returning home, Tobias anoints his father's
eyes with the gallbladder from the fish, restoring Tobit's
sight. The point is that God cares and answers prayer.

Judith

Judith is the fictional account of a heroine's action saving
her country. After Nebuchadnezzar's army advances on Israel, Judith makes her way into Nebuchadnezzar's camp
offering to give away some military secrets. She manages
to gain his confidence by charm and wit and beheads him
at a private banquet. The enemy army (misnamed Assyrian) retreats, while Judith and the Jews rejoice in praise to
God.

Additions to Esther

This is a collection of six passages that significantly enlarge the book of Esther. Most scholars consider the additions to be material written later to supplement Esther,
but some Roman Catholics consider the enlarged version
to be original, with the present book of Esther a shortened
version. The additional material contains Mordecai's
dream, the king's edict, prayers of Esther and Mordecai,
Esther's talk with the king, permission given for Jewish
self-defense, and the interpretation of Mordecai's dream.

The Wisdom of Solomon

This is a genuinely significant book composed of a collec-

Figure 17   Jewish Feast Days (see also the Jewish Calendar, p. 26)

Feast	Commemorates	Description
Rosh Hashanah Lev. 23:24–25	God as king, judge, and redeemer	On this two-day New Year celebration the Israelites prepared themselves for Yom Kippur which comes ten days later. In this celebration they extolled God as the one whose standard men have failed to meet and recounted His greatness, love, and mercy.
Yom Kippur Lev. 23:26–32	atonement for sins of the nation	The people spent Yom Kippur (the day of atonement) away from the world, praying in the house of God while the priests offered sacrifices for the nation's sins. Recognizing this day as the holiest of feast days, Jews neither ate nor drank for 24 hours.
Sukkot Lev. 23:33–43 John 7:2	Israel's wanderings in the wilderness	During the seven-day celebration of Sukkot (the feast of tabernacles or booths) the people gave thanks for divine protection and harvest blessings. For seven days they lived in shelters made of branches, demonstrating their vulnerability to external elements yet confidence in God's care.
Hanukah Maccabees John 10:22	rededication of the temple in 164 B.C.	On Hanukah (the festival of lights) Jews celebrated their victory over the Syrians and their rededication of the temple which the Syrians had desecrated. Through lighting a new candle each day for eight days, the Jews commemorated the miracle of the temple's holy candelabrum: for the rededication they had only one day's worth of consecrated oil but it burnt for eight full days, the time needed to consecrate more oil.
Purim Esther 9	the failure of Haman's plot to destroy the Jews	During Purim (the feast of Esther) the people expressed their faith in the working of an invisible God behind the scenes of human events. It was a time of feasting and merriment.
Passover and Unleavened Bread Lev. 23:4–8 Matt. 26:17	Israel's deliverance from Egypt	Known to the Jews as Pessah, Passover feast was the Independence Day of the Israelites. Each family symbolically reenacted the first Passover as they ate their own Passover meal. The celebration continued for seven days as they commemorated the Exodus and wilderness wanderings by eating unleavened bread and doing no work.
Pentecost Lev. 23:9–22 Acts 2:1	celebration of harvest	On Pentecost (the feast of weeks) the Jews celebrated the ingathering of the first fruits of the wheat harvest. This was a time of feasting and thanking God for harvest and daily bread.

ion of Jewish proverbial wisdom. It draws on Old Testament thought, but also on Greek philosophy, and includes Platonic and Stoic terminology. Essentially the book is an appeal to seek wisdom with the promise of great reward for those who find it. It breaks easily into three sections: section 1 (1–5) deals with the search after wisdom; section 2 (6–9) offers praise to wisdom, which is likened to God's highest creature; and section 3 (10–19) reviews Israel's history, showing how wisdom has guided the footsteps of the fathers. The Wisdom of Solomon is a powerful book that has many true things to say and it would be helpful to anyone willing to ponder its message.

Ecclesiasticus

Like the Wisdom of Solomon, Ecclesiasticus, or the wisdom of Joshua (Jesus) ben Sira, is a collection of proverbial sayings aimed at improving life. There are two major sections (1–23; 24–50) with a concluding chapter (51) to round off the book. The first collection speaks at length about the fear of the Lord and the observance of the law. It extols such actions as telling the truth, exercising self-control, acknowledging God, living in humility, and being a friend. The second collection is a catalog of famous and exemplary men, telling how each one lived according to wisdom's precepts. In many ways the book of Ecclesiasticus is like Proverbs in the Old Testament, offering sage advice concerning many topics in a practical down-to-earth way.

Baruch

This book is attributed to Baruch, the secretary of the prophet Jeremiah. It consists of short addresses, prayers, confessions, comfort, encouragement, and laments, purportedly from the Exile of the sixth century B.C. Standing out in the whole book is a deep faith in God that allows a person to rejoice even during the darkest hours of captivity.

The Letter of Jeremiah

This short book is supposedly a letter written by the prophet Jeremiah to the exiles in Babylon during the sixth century B.C. The letter denounces idolatry and stresses the need for true worship of God.

Additions to Daniel

The Prayer of Azariah and The Song of the Three Young Men are inserted into the book of Daniel between 3:23 and 3:24. In spite of the fact that fire was surrounding him as he prayed, Azariah's prayer extols God who is worthy of all praise. The prayer of the three is an extended hymn of praise, blessing God for all he has done and urging all of creation to bless his name. Reminiscent of some of the Psalms, these short prayers are moving and powerful.

Susanna

This is the story of a beautiful young woman who is falsely accused of adultery by two evil elders whose advances she has rejected. The two men engineer a trial that results in Susanna's death sentence. While she is being led to execution, Daniel, under the inspiration of God, demands a second trial and confounds the false accusers. These two are then executed and Susanna is exonerated. The book's point is to show that lust causes people to do crazy things, that virtue will be rewarded, and that God takes care of his own.

Bel and the Dragon

These two tales concern the prophet Daniel. The first tells how Daniel exposes the fraud of the priests of the god Bel. The priests had been eating the food brought to Bel's idol and claiming the god had eaten it. The point of this tale is to hold up idolatry to ridicule. The second story tells how Daniel kills a dragon and is thrown into a lion's den, only to be preserved by God and visited miraculously by the

Ruins of the monastery at Qumran, in use about 130 B.C. (J. Jennings)

prophet Habakkuk. The point of this tale is to show God's miraculous power over all things and his protection of his own.

The Prayer of Manasseh

This short prayer, purported to be the one mentioned in 2 Chronicles 33:18–19, gives praise to God, confesses sin, and calls on God for mercy.

1 and 2 Maccabees

Both of these books are historical narratives that deal with the period between the Old Testament and the New Testament. 1 Maccabees deals specifically with 175–134 B.C. and the fierce struggles that took place between the Jews and the Syrians. In particular, the battles with Syrian ruler Antiochus Epiphanes, whose outrageous behavior caused the war, are described. The name of the book is derived from the Jewish ruler Judas Maccabees, "the Hammer," who hammered the Syrians into submission.

1 Maccabees also covers the wars engaged in when the Maccabean family ruled, and ends with the death of John Hyrcanus, nephew of Judas.

2 Maccabees covers much the same territory as 1 Maccabees, but viewed from a different angle and drawn from a different source, probably Jason of Cyrene. The two books disagree on a number of details.

The point of both books is that God controls the destiny of nations and that God is yet working through Israel.

An Arab couple in Jerusalem. *The New Testament reveals how God extended his promises beyond the Jews to believers of all nationalities. (R. Nowitz)*

New Testament

In the Old Testament, God promised Israel that someday he would make a new covenant (or testament) with his people (Jeremiah 31:31–34). At that time he would "write the law upon their hearts" instead of on stone tablets (like the Ten Commandments). Jesus established that "new testament" with his life, death, and resurrection, and therefore the writings that relate to him and his church are called the *New Testament.* It has four sections: the Gospels, Acts, Epistles (or letters), and the Revelation. (See the N.T. chronology on p. 262.)

Gospels

The first section of the New Testament, called the Gospels, consists of four accounts of the life of Jesus. (The word *gospel* means "good news.") The first three Gospels have been given the title "synoptic" because they look at Jesus' life from a similar point of view.

Figure 18 Chronology of New Testament Books

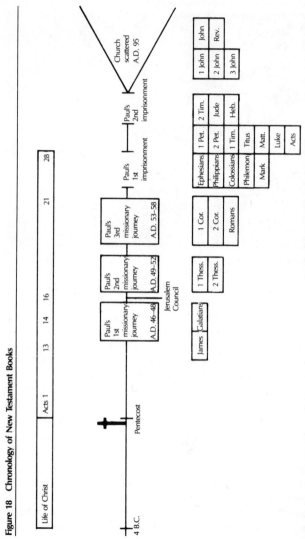

This church, built on a hill called the Mount of Beatitudes, commemorates Jesus' "Sermon on the Mount," Matthew 5–7. (H. Vos)

Matthew

Author: Matthew
Date: between A.D. 60 & A.D. 80

Content

The Gospel of Matthew has been one of the favorite books of the church throughout its history for several reasons. It is the most detailed regarding Jesus' life; it contains the famous "Sermon on the Mount," a collection of teaching that even nonbelievers hold in high regard; it is richest in detail about the birth of Jesus, a traditionally interesting event because of our celebration of Christmas; and it includes a large collection of parables for which Jesus is remembered as a master teacher.

Opinion differs as to when this Gospel was written. Those who put it earlier (c. A.D. 60) point to Jesus' predictions about the destruction of Jerusalem (which took place in A.D. 70) and argue that they are regarded as

Map 12 Geographical Features of Palestine

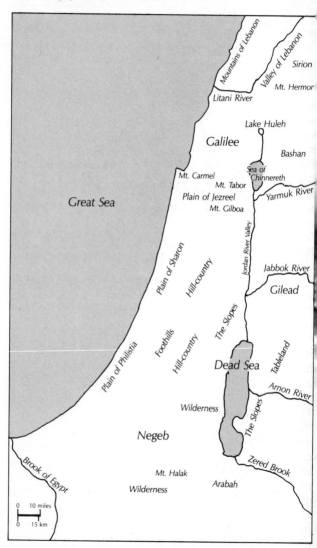

future. Those who make it later (c. A.D. 80) say it has all the appearance of being a later document, reflecting a more developed situation. The book has no author's name attached to it, but very early in its history Matthew was regarded as the author and there is no reason to doubt that this is true.

The Gospel of Matthew was written for a number of reasons, some practical, some theological. Practically, there was a need for more information about Jesus. As people were becoming believers, questions were being asked that needed answers. It simply wasn't possible to travel to Jerusalem and ask the apostles, but a book dealing with the basic facts could be sent to each congregation. There was also a need for accurate information. Jesus' enemies were spreading lies about him. Others, who were trying to get personal gain from the new movement, were altering the facts to suit their own purposes. Followers of Jesus, like Matthew, wanted to set the record straight. The death of some of the apostles also made it necessary to put this valuable material in writing. If all those who knew Jesus were gone, who would be around to tell the story? Had Matthew (and the other three Gospel writers) not done this, Christianity might never have been more than a local, ancient phenomenon. God had a hand in this documentation, guiding selected people to preserve the truth for future generations. So the book of Matthew functioned as something of a handbook for believers.

Theological Themes

Matthew had other reasons to write than just the practical needs of the church. He was trying to confront some special problems and to stress particular things in his writing. First, he realized the importance of Old Testament prophecy and how it was fulfilled in Jesus' life. The church did not arise by accident, nor was it unplanned for by God. Throughout the whole Old Testament the days that had now arrived had been predicted. Matthew showed how virtually all the events of Jesus' life were foreseen by the prophets: his birth, events surrounding his early life, healings, teachings, arrest, death, and resurrection.

Second, Matthew was concerned to show to his Jewish readers that Jesus was the fulfillment of their history and dreams. He was, in fact, the Messiah who was to come. The very first verse of the book shows this: Jesus was "the son of David, the son of Abraham."

Third, Matthew was concerned to show that although Jesus came *from* the Jews, he came *for* all people, Gentiles included. Consequently, emphasis is placed on the coming of the Magi (Wise Men) to acknowledge Jesus' birth, the inclusion of the Gentiles in the kingdom, and the command to go into all the world to preach the gospel to every creature.

Fourth, Matthew specifically mentioned the founding of the church and how certain problems should be handled.

Finally, Jesus' teachings are prominent in Matthew's Gospel as a guide for believers. Large sections are devoted to what Jesus said about basic circumstances of life (5:3–7:27; 10:5–42; 13:3–52; 18:3–35; 24:4–25:46).

Outline

1. Jesus' early life   *1:1–4:25*
2. Sermon on the Mount   *5:1–7:29*
3. Jesus' ministry: events and teachings   *8:1–12:50*
4. Parables of Jesus   *13:1–52*
5. Jesus' ministry: further events and teachings   *13:53–19:30*
6. Jesus in Jerusalem   *20:1–25:46*
7. Jesus' death, burial, and resurrection   *26:1–28:20*

Modern fishing boats and nets at Tyre. (H. Vos)

Mark
Author: Mark
Date: c. A.D. 60

Content

The Gospel of Mark was probably the first Gospel written, forming the base, in one way or another, for both Matthew and Luke. The three together are called "Synoptics" because they view the life of Jesus from roughly the same angle. The Gospel of John takes a different tack, and hence is usually discussed by itself. Mark has all the appearances of being written early in the church's history, certainly before the fall of Jerusalem in A.D. 70.

There are two basic theories regarding authorship. A modern view suggests that the book arose over a period of time, being added to, edited, altered, and rearranged according to the current needs of the church. Although some passages in this Gospel look as though they have been reworked, such a wholesale revamping is unlikely. The church would hardly have felt it right to alter the life of Jesus so drastically that little description of the actual events would be found. The traditional theory that John Mark, the companion of the apostle Peter, took down Peter's recollections and later wrote them up as a Gospel is to be preferred. That view has the support of all the early writers in the church as well as accounting for the facts of the Gospel quite satisfactorily.

Mark probably wrote his Gospel in Rome sometime before the civil war that took place there in A.D. 68–69. It was a difficult time for the church. Persecution had taken the lives of many prominent Christians, including the apostles Peter and Paul. No doubt Mark felt the time had arrived to put his material into a more permanent form. The style of writing has the appearance of being hastily done, without a lot of editing to smooth out the rough places. This gives the book a feeling of immediacy. Vivid detail, fast action, violent conflict, all are present in abundance. Mark used a literary device (the word *immediately*) to give this feeling of fast-paced activity. It occurs over 40 times.

Theological Themes

The purposes for Mark's writing are not hard to find. First, and in this case foremost, is to show us what the *gospel* is, namely, Jesus' life, death, and resurrection. The church was preaching a message of salvation in abbreviated form and Mark wanted to show what the message was all about. It was the story of Jesus, the incarnate Son of God, who died for our sins, was buried, and rose again. Mark spends no time at all on Jesus' birth, early years, or secondary life events. The story begins with the preaching of John the Baptist, moves quickly to Jesus' confrontation with authorities, and concentrates on the events of the last week of his life. Ten chapters are used for the first 30 years of Jesus' life and six chapters are devoted to the last week. That gives an idea of what was important to Mark. It is not without reason that the church has chosen the cross as its symbol; the Gospel of Mark shows the reason why.

A second point that Mark wanted to make was that Jesus, Son of God though he was, was also human. Mark stressed the emotions of Jesus more than any other writer. Jesus is seen as one who was like us in every way, except for sin. Jesus got tired, hungry, weary, discouraged, was encouraged, strengthened, determined, and steadfast. All of us can identify with what Jesus went through because as human beings we have experienced similar feelings.

Third, Mark wrote to encourage Christians who were being persecuted. To see Jesus stand up in the face of opposition should give them the strength to do that too.

Finally, Mark wanted to show the power of Jesus. All through the Gospel we are able to see Jesus as he overcame demonic powers, disease, ignorance, enemies, and finally death. The Father stood by him and he accomplished the task God had for him to do.

Outline
1. Prologue   *1:1–13*
2. Jesus' early ministry   *1:14–9:1*
3. Transfiguration and trip to Jerusalem   *9:2–10:52*
4. Jesus' last week   *11:1–15:47*
5. Resurrection of Jesus   *16:1–8(20)*

Model of the palace Herod the Great built for himself in Jerusalem in 24 B.C. (G. Beers)

Luke
Author: Luke
Date: C.A.D. 65

Content

The third Gospel was written by an ancient medical doctor named Luke, a traveling companion of the apostle Paul. He put together what was evidently intended to be a history of the Christian movement from its beginnings up to his own day. It included the Gospel about Jesus of Nazareth as volume one; the book of Acts, which was about the work of the risen Jesus in the lives of his followers as volume two; and perhaps a volume three, which is either lost to us today or was never written because of the persecution that arose at that time (in which Luke may have died). Paul and Peter died at approximately that time so it is possible that Luke did too.

The first four verses of Luke's Gospel tell us what was going on historically at the time of writing, as well as how ancient writers went about doing their job. Luke pointed out that Christianity was of interest to a lot of people, so much so that "many" had begun writing histories of the movement (no doubt Mark was one of them). That was good in a way, but also worrisome. Luke was concerned that the truth might get lost in all that was being written if it were not carefully verified. Consequently, he decided to make a careful study of what had been said, checking the facts out with people who had been around since the early days of Jesus. The result of his research was this Gospel that bears his name. He directed the book to a Roman official named Theophilus, no doubt to convince him that Christianity was no threat to the empire, as well as being God's appointed way of salvation.

Theological Themes

Luke's Gospel has several characteristics. First, Luke made a special point of relating Jesus to world history. In his genealogy he traced Christ's ancestors all the way back to Adam, rather than just to David or Abraham, as Matthew did. That would have meant very little to a Gentile reader, but tracing Jesus to Adam makes him part of all history, including Gentile history.

Second, Luke was especially interested in Jesus' birth and infancy. Matthew saw it as a fulfillment of prophecy, Luke saw it as an extraordinary event that took place in the midst of secular history. He itemized six historical notes (3:1–2) intended to insure historical accuracy. The information is so precise in this section of the Gospel that Mary, the mother of Jesus, was probably the source of much of it.

Third, Luke was concerned to stress the relation of the kingdom of God to those in need. He showed that Jesus brought good news for the poor, oppressed, sick, downtrodden, and captive. Jesus came to set men and women free from bondage and oppression. It is a spiritual message that touches all parts of our lives, including the social dimension.

Fourth, Luke was interested in women and in social relationships. He described the place that women played among Jesus' followers with sympathy and interest. He also realized that Jesus' acceptance of women went against some of the rules of his day. Jesus was not afraid to set new standards, especially for those who were not being treated properly.

Finally, Luke was concerned to show the universal dimension of the gospel of Christ. Matthew was, too, but he spoke as a Jew. Luke spoke as a Gentile, showing that the gospel is for everyone—men, women, slaves, free, Jews, Gentiles—whoever is in need is invited to come to Jesus to be saved.

Outline

1. Prologue 1:1–4
2. Jesus' birth and early years 1:5–4:13
3. Jesus' Galilean ministry 4:14–9:50
4. Jesus' trip to Jerusalem 9:51–19:27
5. Triumphal entry and last week in Jerusalem 19:28–23:56
6. Resurrection and post-resurrection appearances of Jesus 24:1–53

Map 13 Distances of Key New Testament Cities from Jerusalem

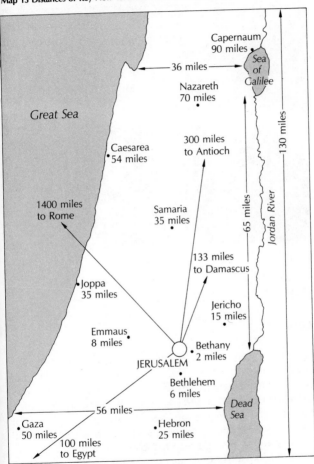

A scene in the Garden of Gethsemane, the place where Jesus agonized and prayed the night he was betrayed by Judas. (L. Shaw)

John
Author: John
Date: c. A.D. 95

Content

The Gospel of John does not have a name attached to it, but from earliest times it has been attributed to John the beloved apostle, one of the followers of Jesus. John had been a rather violent youth, getting a nickname somewhat akin to *Loudmouth*—"Son of Thunder," to be exact. His personal knowledge of Jesus, and the many years that had passed between Jesus' death and resurrection and the writing of his Gospel, had transformed him into an apostle of love. No one speaks with more understanding about that aspect of God's nature than does John. He asserted that "God is love" (1 John 4:8) and that God loved the world so much that he gave his only Son for it (3:16). It is all the more striking that John should stress this in the light of the turbulent years through which he lived. Ultinately, John was sent to live on a deserted island, there to die.

John began his Gospel with an unusual prologue that is in effect a cosmic genealogy. It takes us back before the dawn of time, when only God existed, and there we are told that Christ, identified as "the Word," also existed. He was with God and was God (1:1). That proposition creates the foundation for what Christians have asserted from the earliest days of their existence, that Jesus was no less than God himself. Jesus, before coming down to earth, was the possessor (and creator) of life, the one who conquered darkness (all forces of evil). He is the light that enlightens human minds (1:9) and opens the door to become children of God to those who take God at his word (1:12).

John continued his Gospel by recounting many of the facts also found in the other three Gospels, but with an extensive interpretation woven into it that draws out their inner meaning. He also recorded some incidents that were not mentioned by the others. There must have been a large number of stories circulating at that time, and John notes that if everything Jesus did was written down it would be hard to find room enough in the world for all the books about him (21:25).

One special section, chapters 14–17, in John's Gospel has no parallel in the other Gospels. Only John has the section known as the "upper room discourse." In it Jesus speaks in the most personal terms imaginable about life, spirituality, prayer, hope, comfort, God, heaven, and joy. It is one of the favorite sections of the Bible, containing such familiar words as "I am the way and the truth and the life (14:7), and "Greater love has no one than this, that one lay down his life for his friends" (15:13).

Theological Themes

By writing his Gospel, John was trying to accomplish several things in addition to giving us some basic facts of Jesus' life. First, he was trying to show that Jesus was God.

Many in his day (and in our own, too, for that matter) doubted this. It does seem to be an almost impossible thing to believe, but nothing less will do. Jesus was, and is, the eternal God of the universe, along with the Father and the Holy Spirit.

Second, John was stressing the human nature of Jesus. He was a man as well as God. He was born, lived in Palestine, drank water and ate food, grew weary with travel, suffered, and died. It was necessary for John to emphasize the humanity of Jesus because some thinkers in his day were looking on Jesus as merely passing through this world ghost-like, never really becoming a part of it. John was stressing that only a real human being could save humankind.

Third, the Gospel was written specifically so that we might believe in Jesus and "have life in his name" (20:31). John was concerned that those who heard of Jesus should benefit by that knowledge.

Finally, John wanted to emphasize the close relationship between Jesus and his followers. He is the good shepherd and we are his sheep; he is the door through which we enter life; he is the bread of life that feeds our souls; he is the water of life that cures our deepest thirst; he is the vine of which we are branches. All those figures of speech were intended to help us see that without Jesus we can do nothing. As we live in that realization, our joy will be complete (15:11).

Outline

1. Prologue *1:1–18*
2. Jesus' Galilean ministry *1:19–12:50*
3. Jesus in Jerusalem for the last time *13:1–38*
4. Upper room discourse *14:1–17:26*
5. Jesus' death, resurrection, and appearances to his disciples *18:1–21:25*

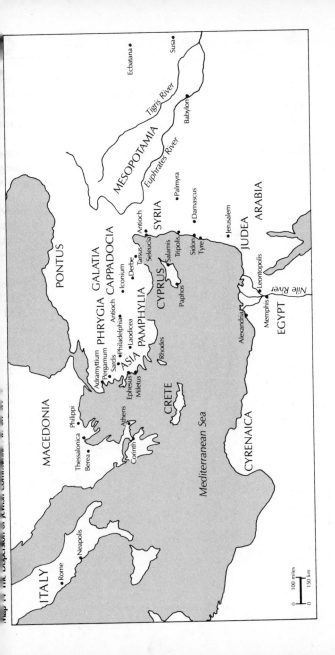

Acts

The second section of the New Testament is one book, the book of Acts. It contains the history of the early church from Jesus' ascension to the imprisonment of the apostle Paul in Rome. In Acts we have the story of the gospel going from Jerusalem to Judea to Samaria and then out to distant parts of the earth (Acts 1:8). Even today, Christians are called to continue that story of concern for the world and evangelistic outreach.

Map 15 Paul's First Missionary Journey

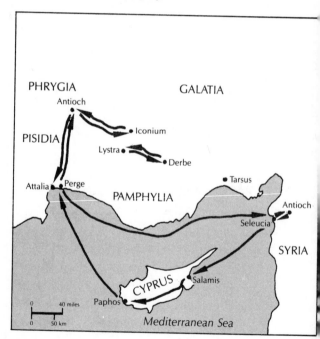

Map 16 Paul's Second Missionary Journey

Map 17 Paul's Third Missionary Journey

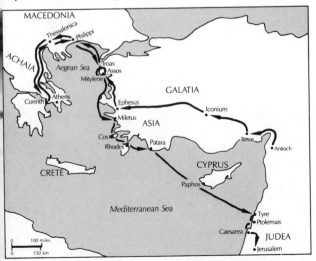

Map 18 Paul's Journey to Rome

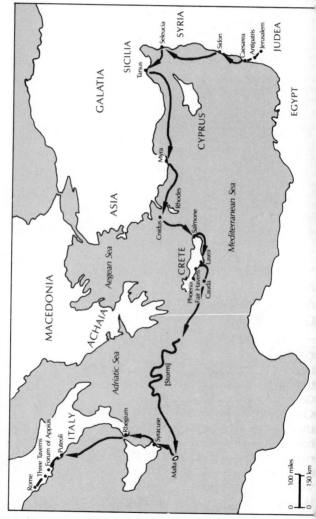

steps on the Areopagus at Athens, a meeting place of the Areopagus council. Paul's words to this council are found in Acts 17. (H. Vos)

Acts
Author: Luke
Date: c. A.D. 65

Content

Luke wrote the book of Acts as a continuation of his history of the church. Volume one, which we know as the Gospel of Luke, tells about Jesus and the establishment of Christianity by his death and resurrection. Volume two, the book of Acts, picks up with the ascension of Jesus back to heaven and the spread of the gospel out from Jerusalem, ultimately to Rome, where the book ends. It is not known whether or not Luke intended a volume three which would have gone to the end of the apostles' lives. It is possible that he never lived to complete the work, even if that was his intention.

The reasons Luke wrote the book of Acts are not hard to find. First, he wanted to present the facts about the new movement. Much was being said about it that was false and Luke wanted to correct any misimpressions that might have existed.

Second, he may have wanted to show Theophilus, to whom the book was dedicated, that as a Roman official he need not fear what Christianity might do. Granted when it went to some places trouble arose, but it was not the fault of the believers. They were trying to live peaceably, and within the law. It was usually the pagans who rose up in protest causing the difficulties.

Third, Luke wanted to show how the two primary leaders of the church, Peter and Paul, exercised their ministry. Because of some misunderstandings about the relations between the two, some people were trying to create separate churches. Luke tried to show that they were not in opposition to each other, but in fact, agreed on the basic point at issue, namely, whether a person needed to become a Jew in order to become a Christian. Both said that it was not necessary, and so did the rest of the church (15:1–21).

Finally, Luke wanted to chart the progress of the gospel from Jerusalem to Syria, to Asia Minor, to Macedonia and Greece (Europe), and finally to Rome. (See maps on pp. 278–280.) It was Paul's desire to see the gospel go to all people and this was a fulfillment of his dreams. It is ironic that he went as a prisoner, rather than free, but he saw God's hand in it. He wanted to make it to Rome, one way or another, and this was how God decided to do it. So Paul, the prisoner, preached freedom in Christ.

The book divides easily into two sections, the first half dealing with events in and around Jerusalem (1:1–12:25), and the second half with the spread of the gospel out from there (13:1–28:31).

Modern Antioch in Syria. Each of Paul's three missionary journeys began in this town. (H. Vos)

Theological Themes

The first half of the Acts stresses some important theological points. The message is rooted in the Old Testament, as would be expected, because the preaching was primarily to Jews. There was also a strong emphasis on the death and resurrection of Jesus. This point could be made forcefully because it was in the very place where those events took place and many people there remembered it well. There was also a special focus on coming judgment and the end of the age. The judgment was to come sooner than most expected it, with the fall of Jerusalem in A.D. 70. Finally, there was an urgent call to repentance and faith.

In the second half of the book, new theological insights are added to what is found in the first part. Because the gospel had gone beyond the bounds of Palestine, follow-up was stressed. That was necessary if the church was to grow. It isn't enough to preach the gospel and leave; one must make sure that the church's continuing needs are met. Also, the organizational structure of the church must be attended to. The church is not a place where any one can be anything or one person rules like a despot. It i a place where the Spirit of God directs life and worship i an orderly manner through proper organizational struc tures.

Finally, new ways of expressing the message wer needed. Because most of the converts outside Palestin were Gentiles, they would not be familiar with the Old Tes tament or its ideas. Ways to communicate to them, with out changing the essential nature of the gospel, had to be found. What was done by the early missionaries in the book of Acts sets a pattern for all of us to follow.

Outline

1. Early days of the church   *1:1–2:47*
2. The gospel in Jerusalem   *3:1–7:60*
3. Spread of the gospel to Samaria, Joppa, Caesarea, and Anti och   *8:1–12:25*
4. Missionary journeys of Paul   *13:1–21:16*
5. Arrest of Paul and journey to Rome   *21:17–28:31*

Epistles (Letters)

The third section of the New Testament contains the letters of apostolic writers. The largest number were written by the apostle Paul (Romans–Philemon). His writings have been subgrouped into letters (Romans, 1 and 2 Corinthians, Galatians, 1 and 2 Thessalonians); prison letters (Ephesians, Philippians, Colossians, Philemon); and pastoral letters (1 and 2 Timothy, Titus). Hebrews is considered by some scholars to have been written by Paul as well. The remaining letters, James–Jude, are called general or *catholic* letters because most of them except 2 and 3 John, were written to the church at large (generally) as opposed to individual churches or people.

Latin inscription at Corinth probably referring to Paul's friend Erastus, identified as that city's treasurer in Romans 16:23. (L. Shaw)

Romans

Author: Paul

Date: c. A.D. 58

Content

The book of Romans is one of the most important, carefully-put-together, and theological books in the New Testament. The apostle Paul was evidently thinking about the great city of the ancient world, Rome, and although he had never been there he wanted to explain the nature of the Christian movement to them. He wrote in sweeping terms, covering the span of history and thought from Adam to the end of the age.

Theological Themes

Paul believed that God created the world and the first human beings as a kind of representative for all humanity. From Adam came the human race—but, alas, not as perfect, but imperfect, subject to sin and death. Sin and death are also our own choices, showing that we are truly our father's children. This fact has made the world a difficult place in which to live. Some people have sunk to extraordinary depths, giving up worship of God for worship of animals, snakes, or idols. No doubt Paul was reflecting on what he saw in many cities through which he had traveled, where such things were common. Not only had some individuals debased worship, they also debased human relationships, giving in to violent and unnamable passions toward one another. Paul saw this as essentially unthankfulness to God, who made us for glory and virtue. We *prefer* our degraded abuse of one another and of creation rather than the glory of God. Not every one has fallen that low, but all are sinful nonetheless. Paul summed this up by saying, "all have sinned and fall short of the glory of God" (3:23).

In spite of our desperate situation, God has not aban

loned us. Two things stand out. First, God can still be known by sinful human beings; God still speaks to us. There is evidence of God to be seen in creation, as well as a law written within our hearts that speaks to us of higher things. Second, God has done the seemingly impossible for us; he has made salvation available in Christ. Jesus died for us, who did not deserve it, so that we might be brought back to God—and all without compromise on God's part.

To benefit by this salvation offered to us, all we need to do is accept it. Paul thus says that the gospel is the power of God unto salvation to everyone who believes (1:16). To the one who does not "work" (for salvation) but who believes what God has done in Christ, his or her faith is accepted as righteousness (4:5). If we confess that Jesus is our Lord, believing that God raised him from the dead, we will be saved (10:9–10). Paul believed this strongly because earlier, when he was practicing his Jewish religion, he had tried to earn his salvation but had failed. Martin Luther later found out the same thing when he tried to earn salvation by following monastic rules. Rules, whether Jewish, pagan, or Christian, don't save; only God saves.

Paul followed those insights with a lengthy discussion on the benefits of the Christian life and how to live it. The benefits are beautifully described in chapter 8 in detail. Let two points suffice to summarize the whole. First, God never ceases to love us. Nothing in all of creation can separate us from the ruler of creation (8:37–39). Second, God is able to work good for us in all things (8:28). It is not possible to explain exactly how God can do this, but because he is God, he can, and we become aware that he does this as we trust him. There is also a discussion of how to work out our Christian life in practical ways (chapters 12–15).

An important part of the book of Romans is Paul's discussion of Israel and the church (chapters 9–11). He was trying to show that God was at work all through history, but especially in Israel. That brought up the problem of why God seemed to set certain people aside. Paul showed

that this is only an apparent dilemma. In actual fact, onl
the *believers* in Israel were really Israel, and the believer
in Jesus now continue as the spiritual Israel. But that di
not mean that Israel as a nation was set aside utterly.
some mysterious way, when God's dealings with the Ge
tiles are over, all Israel will be saved (11:25-26).

The book of Romans is a theological and practical guid
for the believer. To learn its secrets is to learn the essen
of being a Christian.

Outline

1. Greeting   *1:1-7*
2. All the world is sinful   *1:8-3:20*
3. The fact of salvation   *3:21-5:21*
4. Salvation applied   *6:1-8:39*
5. Israel and the church   *9:1-11:36*
6. Guidelines for the believer   *12:1-15:33*
7. Closing greetings   *16:1-27*

uins at Corinth. In the background are doric columns of the Temple of Apollo.
). Birkey)

1 Corinthians
Author: Paul
Date: C. A.D. 56

Content

Paul traveled to Corinth on his second missionary journey
(see map on p. 279), and spent some time there establishing the church. It was a difficult task, not only because of
the opposition that he met, but because of the city itself.
Corinth was notorious even in ancient times for being a
city of great evil. As a seaport, it attracted all kinds of people who would work their evil, depart without being held
accountable, and leave behind misery and distress. When
people in that setting became Christians, they were transformed into new creations in Christ. But regrettably, some
brought along many of their old habits.

Theological Themes

It is important to remember that when we believe we are not usually transformed instantly into something totally other than what we were before. We are new creations, but we need to "grow in grace" with the power that God gives us. It is the power of God that makes the difference and it is there if we will avail ourselves of it. Some of the Corinthian Christians did, but many did not.

A large portion of this book is devoted to Paul's responding to questions put to him by representatives from Corinth. They cover a spectrum of theological and practical problems. First, Paul dealt with the relationship of faith to life, showing that faith is the essence of Christian existence. It might seem foolish to some, but it is in fact the only way to live a life that is pleasing to God. Paul continued by discussing how we are then to work this out and what rewards we will receive. In a metaphorical description of judgment (3:10–15), Paul showed that some of our acts will not survive the test. But some will, and, like precious stones, will shine forever. A very important passage about living non-judgmentally opens chapter 4. We are not to pass judgment on each other; only God can do that. Paul then took up a series of problems—lawsuits, personal grievances, immorality, issues related to marriage, eating food that had been sacrificed to idols, human freedom to act as we please; then he went on to discuss the Lord's supper, spiritual gifts, and the doctrine of the resurrection.

Paul's discussion of spiritual gifts is especially important. Three chapters outline how our gifts are to be exercised (chapters 12–14). Here is a partial list of the gifts that the Spirit distributes among believers and the constructive use of them. Paul stressed the motive that should underlie the use of anything God gives us: love (chapter 13). If we possessed all the brilliance or strength in the world, and did not live lovingly, we would be nothing at all.

. The discussion on the resurrection (chapter 15) is equally important. It is not just today that people are inclined to doubt the truth of what Christians say about Jesus' coming back from the dead. It was also true in Paul's day. He found it necessary to defend the doctrine of Christ's bodily resurrection. It is the foundation of the Christian faith that Jesus died and rose again. Based on that, we have eternal hope.

Paul concluded his letter with a series of greetings and an exhortation to make a contribution to the church in Jerusalem. That might sound like a small matter, but in fact it was very important to Paul. He wanted the early Christians to recognize their dependence on one another. The gospel had come from Jerusalem and had been a spiritual benefit to the Corinthians. They, in turn, were to accept some responsibility for those who were suffering there. In that way both groups would recognize the oneness they had in Christ. If more of this spirit were evident today, we would have far fewer problems.

Outline

St. Paul's Bay, Malta. Paul was shipwrecked here on his voyage to Rome. (Malta Government Tourist Board)

2 Corinthians
Author: Paul
Date: c. A.D. 57

Content

This letter was written by the apostle Paul shortly after he wrote 1 Corinthians. He had received word from Corinth about how the first letter had been received and was responding to that. It is probably the most personal and emotional of his letters.

The first thing he wanted to do was to reestablish his place as apostle to the Corinthians. Some persons were attacking his authority; others were fragmenting the church. Paul wanted them to realize that he had nothing personal to gain by preaching to them; what he was doing was for their good. Not only that, he did it at great cost to himself. He listed some of the things he had gone through (6:3–10; 11:23–29), including beatings and imprisonments. His desire to have authority was not for his sake, but theirs. They needed someone to lead them through the darkness into the light. As for those who were splitting the church, a simple look at the results would show they were on the wrong track. Strife and discord are never the result of the work of God's Spirit, only of selfish people.

Theological Themes

Paul made a special point of emphasizing Christ's death for us and the glory of salvation. Our helpless condition resulted in God's sending his Son to save us. It was God's love that moved him to help us and that moved Paul to preach the gospel (5:14). The work that Christ did on the cross was world-changing. He did not die simply to be an example of dedication to a cause, but to reconcile the world to God. We had gone astray in error and sin. It required that a drastic step be taken to bring us back, and that was taken by Jesus as he died for our sins (5:19). Now, if we believe in him, we may become part of the new creation, renewed in Christ (5:17). The offer has been made; the right moment to accept it is the moment it is understood; later might be too late (6:1-2).

A good part of this letter is devoted to living the Christian life. This material is not found in one place, as is the case in some of Paul's other letters, but is scattered throughout. Paul again made mention of sexual irregularities and the necessity to keep ourselves only for God's use; that means solely for our marriage partners. Our bodies are temples of the Holy Spirit and ought not to be abused (6:14-7:1). We are also to support those who minister to us. Paul had earlier used an ox grinding out the grain as an example. The Old Testament forbade the muzzling of an ox while it was working, because it needed the nourishment to continue. If God cares for oxen, does he not also care for human beings who give unselfishly of themselves for the benefit of others?

Finally, Paul spoke of some of his own struggles. He hinted at his physical problems only in one other place

(Gal. 4:12–15), but here he went into some detail, explain
ing how he had begged God for healing but did not receive
it (12:1–10). He did receive something even more impor
tant, however—a meeting with God that made him a
stronger person. He learned how to achieve *through* suf
fering, rather than flee the suffering and live apart from it.
There is a great mystery in this, but it is often only when
we willingly accept our burden, whatever it is, that we
grow to maturity and overcome it in the end. Paul learned
that our weakness is the opportunity for God's strength to
manifest itself.

Outline
1. Salutation   *1:1–11*
2. Paul's plea to the Corinthians   *1:12–3:18*
3. The nature of Paul's ministry   *4:1–7:16*
4. Responsibility to those who serve   *8:1–9:15*
5. Defense of apostleship and concluding remarks   *10:1–
   13:14*

Jewish men in a synagogue in Israel. Paul wrote Galatians to counter claims by Jewish Christians that we are saved by faith plus legalism. (R. Nowitz)

Galatians
Author: Paul
Date: c. A.D. 48

Content

The letter to the Galatians is probably the first letter the apostle Paul wrote. He had made a missionary trip to the churches in that region (Galatia), which was described by Luke in Acts 13–14 (see map on p. 278). The major cities Paul preached at were Antioch, Lystra, Iconium, and Derbe, important centers of population and trade. Paul felt it important to preach the gospel to such strategic crossroads. That way travelers could be reached who would carry the gospel back to their own countries. Paul was not received well by those cities, however. The Jews listened at first because Paul was also a Jew, but their willingness to listen changed when Paul began speaking about Jesus as the Messiah. The Gentiles became hostile when Paul rejected their paganism. At Lystra Paul was savagely attacked and left for dead. In spite of that, a number of people believed and the church was established in the region of Galatia.

A serious problem arose, prompting the writing of this letter. Some strong-minded Jewish Christians had arrived in Galatia to undermine Paul's authority. They were of the opinion that a person could not be saved if he were not circumcised according to Jewish custom. They said that Paul was arrogant, a liar, had not told the Galatians the whole truth, was weak and sickly, and a coward. The Galatians were beginning to waver in their allegiance to Paul and in their acceptance of his gospel preaching. Because of those circumstances, Paul wrote the letter now titled "Galatians."

Theological Themes

The central message of the letter to the Galatians is that a person is saved by faith alone; being saved means being free. Being saved by faith alone is the heart of the gospel. Paul made his case by showing that Abraham was saved by faith (a good example because the Jews considered Abraham the father of their nation). This is the way God has established the salvation of humankind. Jesus died so that we would not have to earn our own salvation—which we could not do even if we wanted to. To deny that we can be saved by faith is to deny God himself.

When a person believes, that person becomes free—free from the penalty of sin, from useless rules, from the law, from evil powers, from himself or herself. It is a message that opens the door to meaningful life and joy. The Holy Spirit enters, bringing "love, joy, peace, patience, kind-

ness, goodness, faithfulness, gentleness, and self-control"
5:22–23). A person can then live for others, loving them
and bearing their burdens. Freedom to be what God wants
and to serve others is the heart of the Christian life.

Paul defended his point that we are saved by faith, and
made free, by an elaborate set of arguments. He showed
that his apostleship entitled him to speak with authority,
that the risen Jesus had revealed the truth to him, that
the other apostles in Jerusalem agreed, that the Old Testament taught what he was teaching, that the Holy Spirit affirmed the truth of his message by working miracles, and
that this gospel worked in life. Anyone who did not agree
should be careful so as not to be fighting against God.
Whatever persons sow, that will they reap. A life of faith
brings life. A life of self-seeking and evil brings death. The
choice is always before us, and Paul urges that we choose
life.

Outline

Remains of the splendid marble Arkadiane Way of Ephesus. This street led from the theater to the city's harbor. (J. Jennings)

Ephesians
Author: Paul
Date: *c.* A.D. 60 or 61

Content

The city of Ephesus, one of the great cities of antiquity, was located on the western coast of Asia Minor, in present-day Turkey. It is no longer of any consequence. All that remains are some magnificent ruins, now being excavated by numerous organizations from around the world. Because the main roads, buildings, temples, houses, and amphitheater are more or less intact, one may get the feel of what it must have been like to live in Roman times by wandering among those extraordinary remains of a past civilization.

Paul traveled to Ephesus on his second journey and left Priscilla and Aquila there to engage in ministry (Acts 18:18–19). They must have done a good job because when Paul arrived later, to stay for almost three years, he found a growing Christian community (Act 19:1–10) (see maps on p. 279). Paul was forced to leave the city after a violent uprising of the people because of loss of money for the local temple of Artemis (Diana), which was blamed on his having said that idols were nothing and ought not to be supported. The temple, one of the great monuments of antiquity, must have brought an enormous amount of money into Ephesus by the worshipers of Artemis. A touching sermon is recorded in Acts 20:17–38, in which Paul encouraged the Ephesian elders to remain in the ways of the Lord. It is also a beautiful portrait of Paul the missionary and his love for the church.

The letter to the Ephesians was written by Paul near the end of his life while he was in prison in Rome. It is important to keep the serenity and peace of the letter in mind. Paul's sense of calm came from the presence of the Lord, not from his external circumstances. The letter was probably intended as a circular letter to be passed on from church to church for everyone's instruction.

Theological Themes

The book of Ephesians makes numerous important theological points, mainly dealing with the nature of salvation and the Christian life. The first chapter stresses the comprehensive nature of salvation. In one of the longest sentences of the Bible (1:3–14; see KJV—other versions divide it up), Paul spoke of the eternal purpose of God. God planned, executed, sustains, and directs our salvation. The only reason given for God's electing some to be saved is his love. From the depth of God's being there poured forth compassion and grace that resulted in the salvation of those who believe. Chapter 2 continues this theme, broadening it to explain how Jew and Gentile are now made one in Christ. No barriers should keep human beings apart; all are alike in God's eyes. Love does not discriminate but freely blesses the object of its affection. Chapter 3 continues with an emphasis on Paul's gospel and how it related to the overall mystery of God. The riches of Christ, which are past finding out, are made available to us if we will reach out and take them. When one does this he or she enters into the love of Christ, with knowledge that goes beyond words and experience. To know it is enough. Chapters 4 through 6 contain teachings about Christian living. Paul touches on marriage, family, temptation, anger, service, and spiritual conflict. In all of this the solution is to know Christ better in practical experience. Prayer becomes a key to winning the victory over sin, evil, Satan, and our own wayward selves.

Outline

1. The glorious nature of salvation   *1:1–23*
2. The unity of all who believe in Christ   *2:1–22*
3. The mystery of the love of Christ   *3:1–21*
4. The nature of the Christian life   *4:1–6:24*

Part of the Egnation Way near Philippi. Paul used this major Roman road during his missionary travels in Greece. (H. Vos)

Philippians
Author: Paul
Date: *c.* A.D. 60 or 61

Content
Paul wrote the letter to the Philippians while in prison in Rome. He had visited the city on his second missionary journey as described in Acts 16:11–40 (see map on p. 279). Paul had been fairly well received there until he cast the demon out of a slave girl who made money for her

owner by foretelling the future. Paul and his companion Silas were then beaten and thrown into prison. An earthquake opened the doors but they did not escape. As a result the jailor was converted when he heard the gospel. Paul made use of his Roman citizenship to gain his freedom on the following day.

Theological Themes

The letter Paul wrote to his friends at Philippi is one of the most personal in the New Testament. It does not begin with the usual assertion of authority (Paul, an apostle...), but rather, "Paul and Timothy, servants of Christ Jesus." The theme of the book is that of rejoicing in the Lord. No fewer than eight times does Paul speak about how we are to rejoice in spite of our circumstances (1:18; 2:17; 2:18; 2:28; 3:1; 4:4). It must be remembered that Paul was in prison at the time with little hope of release, virtually alone, weary from his labors of preaching the gospel, and without funds. How remarkable that Paul should stress the gratitude and joy we ought to have. He was able to do that because he had learned the secret of rejoicing, namely, we are to rejoice *in the Lord.* Because God does not change and is our loving heavenly Father, we need not fear. God has everything under control, so whether we are in abundance or in want, we may be content (4:1–12).

Paul also stressed his certainty that God who began the work in each believer would bring it to completion. If it were left up to us, it would be in great doubt. But because God will never fail us or push us beyond what we are able to bear, we will be able to see life through (1:6). This does not mean that we are to sit down and do nothing. We are to work out our own salvation with fear and trembling (2:12), pressing toward the goal of the upward call of God in Christ (3:14).

Another point that Paul made is that heaven awaits the believer upon death. Paul was not being morbid about it, but he realized that we all must face death sooner or later. For the believer death should hold no terrors (1:21). To die is gain because we will be entering into the presence of Jesus who loved us and gave himself for us. Paul did not know it at the time but within a few years he was to die in the city of Rome. Paul used the life of Jesus as the model for believers to follow (2:5–11). Though he was in glory with the Father he left it to die on the cross for all who would believe in him. Because of that, someday every knee will bow and every tongue confess that Jesus Christ is Lord.

The value of prayer was stressed by Paul as the way to have true freedom from anxiety (4:4–7). The peace of God will be given to those who offer themselves to God in simple commitment. Paul gave up everything else, he said, in order to know Christ, the power of his resurrection, and the fellowship of his suffering and death (3:10).

Outline

The theater at Pergamum. As in Colosse, the church at Pergamum was an indirect result of Paul's missionary travels in Asia Minor. (J. Jennings)

Colossians
Author: Paul
Date: c. A.D. 60 or 61

Content

Paul wrote this letter while he was in prison in Rome. It is part of a group of letters called "the prison letters" (Philippians, Ephesians, and Philemon). There is no evidence that Paul had ever been to Colosse, but he obviously knew people there. Probably they were converted in Ephesus, a nearby city, when Paul was ministering there on his third missionary journey (see map on p. 279). He had been there for about two and a half years, and Luke records that all the residents of Asia (Asia Minor, which includes Colosse) heard the word of the Lord (Acts 19:10). The letter itself is not as personal as some of Paul's other letters, and understandably so. He does mention a special messenger, Epaphras, who is the link between him and the church there (1:7), as well as a series of other people whom he knew (4:10–17).

As is true with many of Paul's letters, Colossians may be divided into two major sections, the first doctrinal and the second practical. It is significant that Paul's letters are often arranged this way, with doctrine coming first. Correct teaching must always be the foundation for correct action. Doctrine or teaching alone would lead to narrowness and self-righteousness. Practice or action alone would lead to conflict and error. Together, with correct doctrine as the foundation, it is possible to lead a life that is pleasing to God, ourselves, and others.

Theological Themes

The main emphasis in the doctrinal section of this letter is on what theologians call Christology, or the doctrine of Christ. Paul wanted to emphasize the unique nature of Jesus. Jesus was the image, or express reflection, of the invisible God. He was involved in the creation of the world and of all things in it. He is also party to sustaining it in existence. Nothing exists apart from Christ. He is also the head or ruler of the church. Paul was stressing that the eternal, divine qualities of God, which might have been hidden forever from us, have been made known in Jesus, who became one of us. But two things need to be said about his coming to earth.

First, it was not in the way that most pious Jews expected. He came to conquer evil in all its forms, but he came as a servant of God who was willing to die. It was, in fact, the death of Jesus that was the undoing of evil (2:13–15). To those who are capable of believing it, the truth is there. If we would forget ourselves and live for God and others, we would find true life. Jesus pointed the way by dying for our sins and rising again.

Second, Jesus' self-sacrifice was not simply for us to look at and think about. It was designed by God to make us better people. As believers in Christ, we have everything we need to live our lives. He freed us from all evil forces, he is seated at God's right hand for us, and we are to set our minds on things above, not on things below (3:1–4).

The practical material follows this doctrinal material and in some cases is mixed in with it. It deals with how we are to live our Christian lives; how to have personal peace; comments about parents, wives, husbands, and children; matters of prayer, personal purity, and Christian freedom.

Outline

1. Opening salutation and prayer *1:1–12*
2. Christological teaching *1:13–2:15*
3. Practical implications of Christology *2:16–4:6*
4. Closing remarks and greetings *4:7–18*

Exterior of the Roman Colosseum, built in A.D. 80. In this structure more than 40,000 people could gather to watch gladiator fights. (H. Vos)

1 Thessalonians
Author: Paul
Date: c. A.D. 50–51

Content

Paul wrote this letter to the Thessalonians from Corinth a short time after preaching there on his second missionary journey (see map on p. 279). There had been a great deal of persecution of the believers that began while Paul was still there. Apparently a group of violent men had decided that it was their responsibility to destroy this new movement. They were, in actuality, afraid of it and how it might change their evil lives. It is often the case that opposition is based on fear and misunderstanding, rather than on reason. Had these men thought about it, it would have been to their advantage as well as to the advantage of their city to have Christianity there. At any rate, Paul had traveled on, having been run off from Thessalonica, and ended up in Corinth. Then he sent Timothy back to find out how things were going. The good news that all was well was a great relief to him, prompting him to write. He thanked them for their concern for him and went on to straighten out some misunderstandings over doctrine that had arisen.

Theological Themes

Paul began his letter by commending the church for their spiritual activity and witness. What they were doing was being talked about in other places and was a good example for others to follow. In this they were following Paul's good example, who in turn, was following the Lord. Paul was aware of how difficult it is to remain faithful, especially in the midst of heavy persecution, and was deeply thankful to God for the way they were continuing in their commitment. He reminded them that Jesus not only delivered us from our sins, but will deliver us from all evil when he returns again.

Paul continued this theme by speaking about his own ministry and how it was for him. He, too, had been persecuted so he understood what they were going through. Others, too, had suffered for Christ, notably, the believers in Judea (the land of Israel). It had never been easy to be a Christian, and Paul wanted to share his confidence with these new followers of the Lord. He spoke in a very personal way, telling them that his care for them was like that of a nurse for her children or a father for his sons. In all of this there was the practical intent of helping the Thessalonians live a better life.

A special problem regarding marriage and personal holiness had arisen, so Paul dealt specially with that. The ancient world was notoriously lax in such matters, creating severe problems for those who were trying to keep everything in the proper place in their lives. With the grace and strength of God, Paul said, they would be able to overcome those temptations and obstacles to Christian growth.

Paul spent the last part of his letter discussing a serious misunderstanding that had arisen about the second coming of Jesus. It is difficult to know exactly what the problem was, but it evidently took two forms. First, some people were confused about who would benefit by Christ's return, assuming that only the *living* would be included. Those who died before Jesus came back would simply be left out. Second, others were worried about *when* Christ would come back, to the point of no longer working; they became a burden on the rest of the church. Paul set those two problems straight and went on to stress the *fact* of Christ's return and what that should mean to us. It is a certainty that will terminate this age, bringing comfort to believers and judgment to unbelievers. We are to live expectantly, joyfully, and courageously in the light of its near occurrence.

Outline

Emperor Augustus' Altar of Peace in Rome shows the kind of clothing worn by Roman citizens in the time of Paul. (H. Vos)

2 Thessalonians
Author: Paul
Date: c. A.D. 51

Content

After Paul had written his first letter to the Thessalonians he received word that further confusion had arisen in the church there about the doctrine of the second coming of Christ. Seemingly it was reported that Paul himself had sent the information, or at least was the source of it. In addition to that, some people were thinking that the coming of Christ was so near that it was no longer necessary to support one's self or one's family. Why work if Christ is about to end the world? To deal with those issues, as well as to encourage believers, Paul wrote a second letter, probably within a few months of having written his first letter.

Theological Themes

Paul began by encouraging the Thessalonians in the midst of their persecutions. He pointed out that they were called to be worthy of the kingdom of God for which they were currently suffering. If they bore up under it, when Christ returned they would be comforted and their persecutors would feel the judging hand of God. On the day when Christ returns he will be glorified among his saints and will banish from his presence all who have rejected the gospel (1:5–12).

Paul went on to say that the coming of Christ would not take place without some other events happening first. It is a mistake, Paul said, to imagine that the second coming can happen without relation to the rest of the plan of God. Christ's return must be preceded by a general falling away (or apostasy); the unveiling of a "man of lawlessness," usually called the Antichrist, and his attempts at universal domination. The Antichrist is already at work in spirit, but he must be manifested as such before the end can come. After these things take place, the Lord Jesus will return to destroy him (2:8).

Paul followed this explanation with ethical exhortations of a practical sort. The doctrine of Christ's coming is not to make us lazy, arrogant, or immoral, but busy, humble, and pure. We are not to be weary in well-doing (3:6–13).

Outline

1. The glorious coming of Christ reaffirmed   *1:1–12*
2. The events that must precede Christ's coming   *2:1–17*
3. Exhortations to holy living in the light of Christ's return   *3:1–18*

Ornate arch of the Temple of Hadrian at Ephesus (c. A.D. 117–138). Timothy was living in this city when Paul wrote him this first letter. (J. Jennings)

1 Timothy
Author: Paul
Date: c. A.D. 64

Content

After Paul's release from prison in 62 A.D., he spent about two years traveling (some early sources say as far as Spain), both preaching the gospel and encouraging the churches that were in existence. He was rearrested in 64 and probably died in that year. Sometime between his two imprisonments Paul wrote three letters (1, 2 Timothy, and Titus) called the "pastoral letters" to his associates in Ephesus and on the island of Crete. Timothy seems to have been the younger of the two men and with a single church; Titus appears to have been an ambassador of some sort whose job it was to appoint elders and oversee the affairs of many churches.

Paul's first letter is basically practical, dealing with matters related to living a Christian life. There is also important doctrinal material. False views were developing. Some individuals wanted to establish little empires for themselves independently of the established churches.

Theological Themes

In a short summary of who Jesus was, Paul outlined some essentials of the faith (3:16). Christian faith is a profound mystery; God alone knows all there is to know. Our job is to trust God and not worry about things over which we have no control. Christ's incarnation and resurrection are at the heart of what we believe. Jesus could have remained forever one with the Father in all his eternal glory, but that would have meant our eternal loss. But because of his love for us, he was willing to leave all that temporarily behind so that he might bring us to salvation. Paul's short doctrinal abstract ends with an emphasis on Christ's ascension and the preaching of the gospel to the world.

Paul also reiterated other theological points such as the place of prayer, the resurrection, the nature of God, and the benefits of the death of Christ.

The practical material in this letter covers two areas, public church life and private existence. The material about church life should be studied carefully by anyone who aspires to be a church officer. Paul listed the requirements for those who want to serve as bishops (or elders) and deacons. There are some differences in the requirements but basically they require that a person be wholly committed in life and heart. There is also a leader designated to look after the widows, an unusually large category of women in antiquity. The fact that there are church officers indicates that we all have a need for order and regularity. Just as a household or a business cannot run well without leaders and regulations, so the church must have its officers, guided by the Spirit and answerable to God and the people.

The material devoted to practical Christian living covers human relationships and actions. There is material for children, parents, husbands, wives, and servants. There is also a stress on freedom properly exercised. Evidently there were some who wanted to run the lives of others but Paul would not allow that. We are to make up our own minds about what to eat or drink, whether to marry and how to handle our affairs (4:1–10). Our basic human needs are not to be despised because God made us this way. But they are not to dominate us, turning us into gluttons, drunkards, or adulterers. Everything must be put in its proper place under the guidance of the Spirit and with an attitude of humility.

Outline
1. Greetings and charge to Timothy   *1:1–20*
2. Church officers and worship   *2:1–3:16*
3. General regulations   *4:1–16*
4. Specific regulations and instructions   *5:1–6:10*
5. Final charge to Timothy   *6:11–21*

These starting lanes for runners in the stadium of Delphi, Greece, remind us of Paul's comparison of the believer's life to a race (2 Tim. 2). (H. Vos)

2 Timothy
Author: Paul
Date: C. A.D. 64–66

Content
Paul's second letter to Timothy was probably the last one he wrote. He had been rearrested and was in prison (4:6), knowing that the end was at hand. It is a letter filled with courage and strength, showing us what kind of person Paul really was—or, better, what kind of person God can help us to be if we trust in him. The letter consists basically of four charges directed to Timothy from the aged Paul.

Theological Themes
In the first charge, Paul reminded Timothy of his godly heritage. His grandmother and mother had set a wonderful example and Timothy was to follow it. It is impossible to overestimate the influence of our homes and parents. As parents and others live a godly life, so the younger

ones absorb that atmosphere and become like that themselves. When we are parents our task is to continue that
pattern so our children will live before the Lord as well. It
is significant that Paul singled out the two women for
commendation, whether because the father was an unbe-
liever or deceased. In any case, by the grace of God, one
parent can do it if necessary.

That charge continues with Paul reminding Timothy to
rekindle his gift. We have all been given endowments by
God, but they must be used. If they are not, they will
wither and die, like an unused muscle. If we exercise our
gifts, they will grow and be strengthened. In Timothy's
case this included defending the faith against error.

The second charge is in essence a command to be
strong in God's grace. Paul used a marvelous collection of
metaphors to describe the Christian life. A Christian is like
a soldier whose task it is to do his commander's will. No
soldier would dare go off on his own in the midst of battle,
nor would a faithful Christian desert his post when engaged in fighting evil. Paul had used this metaphor before, describing it as the armor of God that we are to wear
as we stand against the evil of our day (Eph. 6:1–17). The
Christian is also like an athlete who prepares for the race,
runs hard, and goes by the rules. We too must remember
that, as Christians, discipline and honesty count for a
great deal if we are to succeed. Finally, the Christian is like
a farmer who breaks up the stubborn earth to bring out
the best that is in it. A farmer's life is never easy, but the
rewards are worth it. So too, for a Christian, we put our
hand to the plow and do not turn back. In all of those figures we have before us the example of Jesus Christ.

The third charge is to be watchful over the flock and vigilant concerning the world. God has all kinds of people in
his church and all must be cared for. As for ourselves we
are to shun evil passions, live with a pure heart, and avoid
controversies. The servant of God must not be quarrel-
some and bigoted. If one is, that is a sure sign that God is
not there. With respect to the world, God's servant must

be aware of its evil and refuse to be a part of it. In the world there will be greed, arrogance, hatred, and indecency. Those sins must be kept out of the life of the church and of Christians. The tragedy is that sometimes these very things are to be found even among believers. When that happens, they must be compassionately but firmly dealt with.

Paul's fourth charge is to preach the word and be an example to the congregation. We are to be ready at all times to do whatever needs to be done to accomplish God's will. Paul closed this section with the memorable words, "I have fought the good fight, I have finished the race, I have kept the faith" (4:7). Timothy was to remember that he was not alone. Others had gone before him, setting an example for him.

Outline

1. Greetings *1:1–5*
2. First charge: Remember your part; rekindle your gift *1:6–18*
3. Second charge: Be strong in the grace of God *2:1–19*
4. Third charge: Be watchful *2:20–3:17*
5. Fourth charge: Preach the word *4:1–8*
6. Concluding greetings *4:9–22*

Baker's shop at Pompeii from the New Testament era. (H. Vos)

Titus
Author: Paul
Date: C. A.D. 64–66

Content
Between Paul's two imprisonments in the early A.D. 60s, he traveled throughout the Mediterranean area. He went at least once to the important island of Crete but was appalled by what he found there. The church was weak, disorganized, corrupt, and under the influence of the society around it. After he left, Paul wanted to stay in touch. His letter is short, personal, and filled with practical advice.

Theological Themes
One of the fundamental problems facing the church concerned authority. It simply did not work when there was no reasonable organization. As a result, Titus needed to ex-

plain to the congregation how elders were to be chosen and how they were to function. But it was not just the church elders who needed instruction. All those whose lives had an impact on the church were in need of correction, from older adults to young people. To be a Christian means that Christ has changed our lives. Those changes ought to be evident by our actions and attitudes.

Paul continued his exhortation by stressing that Christians are to be good citizens. We are not to give in to evil rulers, but we are to be willing to live according to the laws of whatever land we live in. Not to do this is to bring discredit on the gospel.

Paul concluded with a series of ethical exhortations in the light of Jesus' coming again. He came once to provide salvation for the world; he will come again to bless his people and judge the world. In the light of this, we are to be pure and zealous for good works (2:11–14). We have been saved by God's mercy, not according to our deeds, but in order to do good deeds. The order is important. We do not live Christian lives in order to be saved, but when we are saved, we live godly lives.

Outline

1. Greetings *1:1–4*
2. Qualities required of an elder *1:5–9*
3. Qualities required of others *1:10–2:15*
4. General instructions for all believers *3:1–15*

Philemon
Author: Paul
Date: c. A.D. 61

Content

Philemon was a friend of the apostle Paul who lived at Colosse, was a fellow worker in the gospel, and had a church in his house. He was a wealthy man who owned at least one slave, Onesimus. Onesimus had escaped from Philemon and after making his way to Rome was converted by the ministry of Paul. There is no need to speculate on how he met Paul. Probably, friendless and alone in a foreign city, he sought out the only person whose name he knew, Paul. At any rate, Onesimus was now going back, bearing this brief letter from Paul to Philemon, asking forgiveness and reinstatement. Paul expressed his desire that Onesimus now be truly *useful*—a play on words, because the name Onesimus means "useful," something he had hardly been in the past (v. 11).

The letter is important for at least two reasons. First, it shows how the preaching of the gospel changes lives. Paul, Philemon, Onesimus, Apphia, Archippus, Timothy, Epaphras, Mark, and Aristarchus, all mentioned by name, had been brought to new life in Christ. Where would these people have been without the Lord? Where would any of us be without the Lord? It is easy to forget that many great saints of the church were once pagan blasphemers who reviled the name of Christ. But in the mercy of God they came to a true knowledge of the risen Christ, who saved them and gave them new life.

Second, the basis for vast social change is implicit in the gospel of Christ. When Paul says "[take] him back for good—no longer a slave, but better than a slave, as a dear brother" (vv. 15–16), the deep human prejudices are forced to give way. In Christ there is "neither Jew nor Greek, slave nor free, male nor female" (Gal. 3:28; Col.

3:11). All are one in the eyes of God and in the eyes of the gospel. It is out of the question that some are better than others. All must come in exactly the same way, in humility. All are saved to serve God in the same way, with total commitment to him and others no matter who they are.

Outline
1. Salutation and thanksgiving   *1:1–7*
2. Paul's appeal for Onesimus   *1:8–21*
3. Concluding greetings   *1:22–25*

On this panel from the Arch of Titus, temple treasures are paraded after Rome's destruction of Jerusalem in A.D. 70. (H. Vos)

Hebrews
Author: unknown, possibly Paul or Apollos
Date: between A.D. 60 & A.D. 70

Content
The key event in the last half of the first century as far as the church was concerned was the destruction of Jerusalem in A.D. 70. It had been predicted by Jesus, and when it happened, it marked the end of Christianity's dependence

on Judaism and the old order of things. Not that Christians did not recognize their Jewish heritage. They kept the Old Testament, modeled their worship after the synagogue, worshiped the God of Israel, thought of themselves as the fulfillment of prophecy, acknowledged Jesus as the Messiah, and described themselves as the inheritors of the "new covenant" promised to Israel. But nonetheless they realized that the old order was over. The end of the age had arrived. They could experience the power of the new age in the present through the salvation offered by Christ. They also recognized that divisions of race did not matter any more; all are free to come to Christ exactly the same way, by faith in Jesus, God's Son.

To some of the Jewish believers this created a problem. Their Jewishness meant more to them than it should have and they were tempted to revert to the old order, abandoning their new-found faith in Christ. They wanted things to be as they had always been. But that could never be. The city of Jerusalem was gone, the temple destroyed, the priesthood disbanded. The nation was in shambles. The writer to the Hebrews was trying to point out that it is impossible to turn the clock back. We must press on in the new plan of God because the future is our goal, not the dead past.

It is not clear who wrote this book. Numerous people have been suggested, including Paul, Apollos, and Priscilla. After studying the problem, the church father Origen said that only God knows who wrote the letter to the Hebrews. It doesn't really matter. Whoever wrote it understood the situation well and was dealing with an important problem.

Theological Themes
Several themes can be found in this book. First, there is an emphasis on the superiority of Christ. To those Jewish believers who were wavering in their faith, the writer wanted to point out that there is no where else to go. Where can one find anything better than Jesus, who is the express

image of God, better than Moses, better than Aaron, better than angels, better than anything? Jesus the Messiah is what they needed.

Second, the obsolete nature of the old covenant and the establishment of the new covenant is stressed. The old is gone and the new has come. How could anyone want to go back to what God did not plan to keep? The old order served its purpose, and served it well, but its time is over. Now people are to come to Christ wherever they are, not by way of "Jerusalem"—except perhaps in a figurative way, through the heavenly Jerusalem.

Third, the writer speaks of the present glorious priesthood of Jesus in contrast to the defunct priesthood of Jerusalem. Jesus is now at the right hand of God eternally pleading our case. He knows what it is like to be human, so he can plead with understanding. We may go boldly to the throne of grace, there to find help in time of need.

Fourth, the book of Hebrews stresses the need for perseverance. It is easy to quit and fall in the wilderness like the fathers of old. That ought never to happen again, and won't, if God's people do not lose heart.

Fifth, the writer extols the glories of faith and those who have exercised it. Chapter 11 is a marvelous sermon on those who endured, strengthened by their faith in the living God.

Finally, instructions for practical Christian living are given in chapters 12 and 13.

All of this together presents a complete defense of the Christian faith against its detractors and those who would look for salvation elsewhere.

Outline

Head of Claudius, Roman emperor A.D. 41–54. He was in power at the time James wrote his epistle. (H. Vos)

James
Author: James
Date: c. A.D. 45–48

Content

The book of James was written by the half-brother of Jesus. Evidently James had been unsure about the claims of Jesus during Jesus' lifetime, but following his resurrection became one of his most ardent followers. James was elected ruler of the church in Jerusalem and was well liked by all, even the Jews who were opponents of Christianity. According to tradition, he had the nickname "the camel-kneed," because of the calluses on his knees from time spent in prayer. This was deeply respected by the Jews of antiquity as a sign of reverence and spirituality.

James wrote in a style reminiscent of Jesus and the Sermon on the Mount. Similarities can be found in about a dozen places, as well as other hints that what Jesus said was in the back of James's mind. The book is practical, straightforward, forceful, aimed at correcting errors, and without compromise. To read it is to be stricken in conscience because many of the problems addressed by James still exist in the church today. In essence the book is in the "wisdom tradition" that goes back to the Old Testament, in particular the book of Proverbs. Over 50 commandments are given in this short homily.

Theological Themes

James was comparing true and false spirituality, the former called by him "pure" religion (1:27). It must come from the heart, be filled with understanding, and will issue forth in positive action. True spirituality is a life of faith in action. To be a hearer of the word and not a doer is to deceive ourselves (1:22). We must couple our profession of faith with overt evidence that we are changed people. James spent a lot of time (chapter 2) dealing with this problem. It is easy to *say* we have faith; the true test of faith is not our words, but our works. If someone knocks on our door and asks for help, what do we do? If we say "I wish you well" and shut him out, that is a sure sign of unbelief. If we offer him help, that is a sign of belief. Some people find this emphasis disturbing because it seems to oppose what Paul said; it seems to imply that we are saved by our good works. We need to remember that Paul, too, stressed that faith must work (Gal. 5:6), we must bear one another's burdens (Gal. 6:2), and God has foreordained that those who are saved by faith will walk in good works (Eph. 2:10). James, on the other hand, was well aware that "every good and perfect gift" comes from God and is not earned (1:16–17). Their views are not contradictory.

True spirituality knows how to keep its mouth shut. Another section deals with the effects of evil speech (chapter 3). Too many people want to be heard, even when their minds are empty or filled with jealousy and ambition. When such a person speaks, discord abounds. A storm of evil is unleashed, and the suffering that results is enormous. True wisdom is good, peaceable and meek (3:13). Just as Jesus was wise among us, a servant of all, so must we be wise in good works, decency, and humility.

True spirituality is unselfish, generous, impartial, and patient. All of this is emphasized in 4:1–5:7. We are not to look out for ourselves alone, but must learn what it means to love in deed as well as in theory.

Finally, true spirituality looks to God in prayer in all the events of life. God is able to help and he values prayer. Prayer is always heard, and his answer is always the right one, no matter what it is, because he knows best.

Outline

Coin with Nero's image. According to tradition, Peter was martyred in Rome during Nero's rule. (G. Archer)

1 Peter
Author: Peter
Date: c. A.D. 64

Content

Along with Paul, Peter was a leading figure in early church history. Peter was among the first converts to Jesus, leaving his home to travel to the Jordan River while John the Baptist was still preaching. He returned to his home on the sea of Galilee, there to await Jesus' call to active ministry. He was with Jesus during his entire three years of preaching and became one of the leading apostles, along with James and John. When the three are listed in the Gospels, Peter is always listed first, because of his preeminence in the group. He was singled out by Jesus as one who would be foundational to the church (Matt. 16:16–19). The church, *in fact*, is founded on Christ (1 Cor. 3:11). But it was Peter who preached on Pentecost, was instrumental in the spread of the gospel, opened the door to the Gentiles with his witness to Cornelius, and gave strong support from the beginning. Peter was clearly a rock on which the growth of the church depended. Peter was not always a rock, however, and his denial of the Lord at his crucifixion and his altercation with Paul (Gal. 2:11–14) show that his zeal could run hot and cold. After Jesus' death and resurrection, Peter exercised his ministry in Jerusalem, was then forced to travel, and ended up in Rome where he was martyred during the reign of Nero, sometime between A.D. 64 and A.D. 68. Peter probably wrote this letter during those difficult days.

Theological Themes

Several themes run through the book of 1 Peter. First, Peter wanted his readers to reflect on the greatness of salvation. We have an inheritance reserved in heaven for us. It is unfading, unchanging, and protected by God. If we are asked to give up our earthly lives, it does not matter by comparison with the glory that will be ours. If we are not asked to die for our faith, it is worth living for.

Second, Peter emphasized the need for spiritual growth. When we become believers we are like infants in need of simple nourishment. As we grow, we need more substantial food. Believers grow by nourishing themselves on prayer, meditation, reading God's Word, and fellowship. It would be great if we could all attain instant perfection, but such is not to be. Growth means effort, time, and patience.

Third, Peter spent a great deal of time talking about living the Christian life. We must realize that our time on earth is short; our lives are like grass that withers away. In light of that, we must stand firm against evil and refuse to conform to the destructive patterns of the age in which we live. It is so easy to become like everybody else, but we must resist that temptation. When persecutions arise, we must be ready to suffer, just as Jesus did. He left an example for us to follow (2:21–25). When Satan attacks we must resist him in faith, knowing that if we reject his offer he will depart from us (5:8–9). We must cast all our care and anxiety on the One who cares for us.

Fourth, Peter included specific instructions to husbands, wives, servants, and believers as citizens. His words revolve around commitment in love to one another, with a view to making life better for all. Finally, Peter singled out the leaders for admonition. Those who have oversight should realize that they are under the authority of God. No one should lord it over someone else; we are all under God. We are all to be clothed with humility, because God resists the proud and gives grace to the humble.

Outline

2 Peter
Author: Peter
Date: c. A.D. 64

Content
Peter wrote his second letter to the church at large rather than to the specific churches in upper Asia Minor. Some theologians dispute that Peter actually wrote this letter, but there are no compelling reasons to doubt that he was actually the author.

Theological Themes
This short book has three basic themes. First, Peter wanted to encourage the believers in their Christian life. God's divine power has provided us with all that we need to live for him, but it remains up to us to make use of that

power. Peter said that we actually "participate in the divine nature" (1:4). This probably means roughly what Paul meant when he spoke about Christians' being the body of Christ and united to him. The concrete way that we make use of God's power is by our exercise of spiritual virtues: faith, virtue, knowledge, self-control, steadfastness, godliness, brotherly affection, and love. When these are found in our lives we may have assurance that our calling and election are real.

A second theme in this book is a description of those who reject the gospel. They are depicted in a long series of statements that are none too flattering (2:1–22). Peter is probably using a bit of polemical material that was more or less traditional at that time, because it reappears in the book of Jude in much the same form.

A third theme concerns the second coming of Christ. Some were beginning to grow weary in waiting and were being taunted by those who disbelieved. Peter wanted to reassure his friends that Jesus is indeed coming back, at which time this world order will be renovated. The old order will dissolve and be replaced by a new heaven and new earth in which righteousness dwells.

Outline

1. Living the Christian life   *1:1–21*
2. The nature of ungodliness   *2:1–22*
3. The sure return of Jesus Christ   *3:1–18*

Figure 19   Rulers Named in the New Testament

Ruler	Reference	Title	Relation to biblical narrative
Roman Empire			
Octavianus Augustus 31 B.C.– A.D. 14	Luke 2:1	Caesar	Ruled through the first half of Jesus' life.
Tiberius A.D. 14–37	Luke 3:1	Caesar	Ruled through the second half of Jesus' life.
Claudius A.D. 41–54	Acts 11:28; 18:2	Caesar	Ordered all Jews to leave Rome.

Ruler	Reference	Title	Relation to biblical narrative
Nero A.D. 54–68	Acts 25:21–25; 27:1; 28:19	Caesar	Was the ruler Paul appealed to during his imprisonment by Felix and Festus. Beheaded Paul and crucified Peter.
Palestine Herod the Great 40 B.C.–4 B.C.	Matt. 2:1–22; Luke 1:5	King	Attempted to kill the baby Jesus by killing all the male children two years old or younger in Bethlehem.
Archelaus 4 B.C.– A.D. 6*	Matt. 2:22	1st Procurator of Judea & Samaria	
Herod Antipas 4 B.C.– A.D. 39*	Matt. 14:1–10 Mark 6:14–28 Luke 3:1,19; 9:7–9; 13:31; 23; Acts 4:27; 13:1	1st Tetrarch of Galilee and Perea	Beheaded John the Baptist. Pilate sent Jesus to Antipas for trial but Jesus stood before him in silence.
Philip II 4 B.C.– A.D. 34*	Luke 3:1	1st Tetrarch of Iturea	
Pontius Pilate A.D. 26–36	Matt. 27:11–62 Mark 15 Luke 3:1; 13:1; 23 John 18–19 1 Tim. 6:13	6th Procurator of Judea & Samaria	Stood as judge at trial of Jesus.
Agrippa I A.D. 37–44	Acts 12	King	Beheaded the apostle James. Arrested Peter but he escaped with the help of an angel.
Antonius Felix A.D. 52–58	Acts 23–24	12th Procurator of Judea & Samaria	Arrested and imprisoned Paul.
Porcius Festus A.D. 58–62	Acts 24:27; 25–26	13th Procurator of Judea & Samaria	As successor of Felix, Festus kept Paul a prisoner and finally sent him to Rome.
Agrippa II A.D. 52–70	Acts 25–26	4th Tetrarch of Galilee, Perea, and Iturea	Heard Paul's defense while Paul was imprisoned by Festus.

Key: *Caesar*—emperor of the Roman Empire; *Procurator*—the governor of a territory (e.g. Judea) not having the status of a province; *Tetrarch*—the ruler of a province (originally the province being 1/4 of the whole);

*When Herod died in 4 B.C. Palestine was divided among three of Herod's sons by Augustus.

Ruins of the palace of Domitian (A.D. 81–96) at Rome. This emperor banished the apostle John to Patmos. (H. Vos)

1, 2, 3 John
Author: John
Date: c. A.D. 90–95

Content

These three letters are best taken together because they were written at the same time to the same church by the same author, the apostle John. John had been an early follower of Jesus, even during the days of John the Baptist. He was a fisherman and had a volatile temperament, with the nickname "son of thunder." He was deeply attached to the Christian movement and became one of three disciples in the inner circle, along with Peter and James. At the crucifixion, Jesus asked John to take care of his mother Mary, indicating the confidence that Jesus had in him. John wrote the marvelous life of Jesus, or Gospel, that is the fourth book of the New Testament. Association with Jesus changed John's temperament from being overly aggressive and loud to being serene and loving. He lived in Ephesus for most of the rest of his life, but was at one point exiled to the island of Patmos where he received the visions written down in the book of Revelation.

Theological Themes

Toward the end of the first century, false theories had arisen that needed combatting, in particular, one that denied that Jesus really was a human being. It is interesting to note that the first christological error (false teaching about Jesus) was not a denial that he was God, but that he was a man. In our day the opposite is the case. People have no problem seeing Jesus as human, but sometimes struggle with the idea that he could be God incarnate. John stressed that Jesus was indeed human. He was seen, touched, and heard. John himself knew Jesus intimately as a human being.

In this first letter, the longest of the three, John spent a lot of time discussing the need for Christian living and how that works out in practice. We are to recognize that we need God's grace; are to keep his commandments; love other human beings; resist the allures of the world, the flesh, and the devil; refrain from sinning; and test out anyone's claims to truth. John emphasized the importance of love. God is love and those who know how to love rightly know God truly. True love is liberating and healing. God sent Jesus to earth to embody and exhibit that love, so that as we believe in him we may have a similar love as our assurance that God is ours.

John also wanted Christians to be aware of the dangers that lurk around us. So much is anti-Christian. If we are not aware of this we might be taken in by it. To know it is to resist the devil and his attempts to take control of our lives.

Finally, John wanted Christians to have confidence in God and his work in our lives. We are not to be overcome by doubt, despair, anxiety, or fear. God is in control and can be trusted. We may be certain of our eternal life because we are certain about God. That knowledge should allow us to live freely and with strength in the face of opposition.

The second letter of John is written to an unnamed person called "the chosen lady." John said basically two things to her. First, he emphasized the need for love in the Christian life. Without love we do not know God. Second, he stressed the need for correct doctrine and the necessity to be on guard against those who reject the truth.

John's third letter is to an elder named Gaius. It is basically a practical exhortation to practice hospitality, follow the truth, imitate what is good, and stand against what is wrong.

Outlines
1 John
1. Living the Christian life   *1:1–2:2*
2. Living in fellowship with God   *2:3–29*
3. Living apart from sinfulness   *3:1–24*
4. Living in love   *4:1–21*
5. Living in confidence in God   *5:1–21*

2 John
1. Greetings   *1:1–3*
2. Remarks concerning love and right doctrine   *1:4–11*
3. Concluding remarks   *1:12–13*

3 John
1. Greetings   *1:1–4*
2. Exhortations to Christian living   *1:5–12*
3. Concluding remarks   *1:13–14*

Jude
Author: Jude
Date: c. A.D. 64–70

Content
Jude, one of Jesus' half-brothers (Matt. 13:55), was considered the writer of this letter throughout most of the history of the church. Recently, doubts have been cast upon this, but there is no compelling reason to doubt his authorship.

Theological Themes
Three basic themes run through this short book. First, Jude wanted to warn believers against evil persons who were trying to use the gospel for their own ends. Those people found it easy to prey on the openness and sincerity of the believers, using them for immoral purposes. Jude warned Christians not to listen to everyone but to be certain when they committed themselves to anyone that that person was worthy of trust. Second, Jude wanted the believers to realize that they must take responsibility for the gospel and defend it when necessary. This does not mean that they are to go out of their way to be offensive, but when the necessity arises they are to be able to state with knowledge and conviction what they believe. If they do not do this, the wrong people will win out in the end. Finally, Jude gave a series of practical exhortations related to the Christian life. They are to build themselves up in the faith; pray in the Holy Spirit; live in God's love; wait for the mercy of Jesus to manifest itself; and refuse to take part in the immorality of their age. All this can be accomplished because Jesus is able to keep them from falling. He is our Lord and Savior, possessing divine glory, dominion, majesty, and authority, and able to protect us from all harm.

Outline

1. Greetings *1:1–2*
2. Defend the faith *1:3–4*
3. The evil detractors of the gospel *1:5–16*
4. Practical instructions *1:17–25*

Revelation

The fourth section of the New Testament consists of one book, Revelation, which is also called the Apocalypse. It stands by itself as a book of prophecy depicting the eventual course of history, both on earth and beyond this life. Here we find a picture of heaven and the promise of being forever with the Lord.

First or second century A.D. Roman aqueduct in Smyrna, one of the seven cities addressed by John in Revelation. (H. Vos)

Revelation

Author: John
Date: c. A.D. 95

Content

The book of Revelation consists of seven letters written by John the apostle to churches in Asia Minor, along with a complex series of visions that deal with world history, cosmic struggle, and the end of the age. It is the most difficult book in the Bible to understand, and varied interpretations abound. In general, there are four points of view: one sees the book as dealing with John's day only (preterist); another sees it as dealing with the end of the age only (futurist); a third, as referring to the whole church age (historicist); and a fourth, as depicting the triumph of good over evil (poetic or mythological). There are also subvarieties of these views and combinations of them. Probably a combination is the best way to understand the book.

After the seven letters at the beginning, there follow the visions. John first sees a complex picture of God on his throne, surrounded by elders, angels, creatures, the Lamb, and violent noises. It is an awesome experience that prepares John for a series of three sets of visions consisting of seals of a scroll opened, trumpets blown, and bowls of judgment poured out. The seals represent war, slaughter, famine, death, martyrdom, and the end of the age. The trumpets represent various plagues, judgments, sufferings, war, and death, ending again with the end of the age. The bowls represent disease, plagues, judgments, demonic spirits, destruction, and general mayhem. Scattered through this set of three complex visions are interludes that deal with world government, spiritual struggle, heaven, worship, angels, and false religion. The book ends with a glorious picture of heaven, where all tears are wiped away and God is all in all.

Theological Themes

John wrote down these visions at the command of God. Believers needed encouragement in a time of great persecution. To show them God in heaven and the saints surrounding him was intended to strengthen them to endure so that they too might take their place there. It was also to prepare the church for what was to take place during its history and especially before the end of the age. Written in veiled terms, the way things will go is depicted. The Revelation was also written to show the triumph of good over evil and the certainty of Satan's defeat. We should never forget that evil survives because we choose to let it rule over us. We must resist it on every hand, using the power that God gives us. Finally, the book was written to show how victory is won through the power of the slain Lamb of God who appears as a triumphant Lion devouring his foes.

The principal actor in the book is the figure of the Lamb, who is dead yet living, and also a Lion. It is hard to imagine how all this appeared to John throughout the course of his visions, but that is how he describes it. He has only human words to picture what was an ineffable experience. As slain, the Lamb receives honor, glory, and blessing because his blood cleanses the Christians from their sins. He, the light of heaven, prepares a banquet for those who have believed in him and endured sufferings in his name. He sits on the throne of heaven, sharing the glory of God forever. As Lion, the Lamb defends his own with a rod of iron; he has authority to open the scroll holding the wrath of God. He himself pours out wrath on those who have persecuted Christians. He defeats Satan and his forces, establishing righteousness forever.

The end of the book is a high note of comfort and encouragement. After darkness comes dawn; after suffering comes peace; after labor comes rest; after tears comes joy forevermore. It is marvelous to realize that life has meaning and is worth it. That realization gives us courage to carry on, no matter what.

Outline

1. Seven letters   *1:1–3:22*
2. The course of world events leading to Christ's return   *4:1–19:21*
3. The last judgment   *20:1–15*
4. The new heaven and new earth   *21:1–22:21*

Figure 20 New Testament Authors

Name	Nationality	Occupation	Writings	How they died
Matthew	Jew	tax collector	Gospel of Matthew	Tradition: died a martyr's death in Ethiopia
Mark	Jew		Gospel of Mark	Tradition: died a martyr's death
Luke	Greek	physician	Gospel of Luke Acts of the Apostles	Tradition: died a martyr's death in Greece
John	Jew	fisherman	Gospel of John 1,2,3 John Revelation	Banished to Patmos A.D. 95 then released Tradition: died a natural death
Paul	Jew	Pharisee/tentmaker	Romans 1 & 2 Corinthians Galatians Ephesians Philippians Colossians 1 & 2 Thessalonians 1 & 2 Timothy Titus Philemon (maybe Hebrews)	Tradition: beheaded at Rome on Nero's order A.D. 67 or 68
James	Jew		Book of James	Tradition: died a martyr's death A.D. 62
Peter	Jew	fisherman	1 & 2 Peter	Tradition: crucified up-side-down by Nero at Rome A.D. 67 or 68
Jude	Jew		Book of Jude	Tradition: died a martyr's death

Exploring
the Bible

5 / Exploring the Bible

Glossary of Important Biblical Words
by Leon Morris

Certain words and ideas are found over and over again in the Bible because they refer to significant concepts that governed the lives of God's people. These words have come down through the centuries as aspects of church life and thought and, today also, reflect the essence of what Christians believe. The entries here are the most important words to be found in the Bible and in Christian theology. If a person really understood what each of these ideas meant, in theory and in life, he or she would be on the way to becoming a mature believer. Each idea is defined, and a few references are given to the biblical context. For in-depth study look up the word in a concordance and trace how it has been used throughout the biblical revelation.

Hikers exploring the Sinai. (R. Nowitz)

Adoption

The process through which a person who does not belong to a given family is formally brought into it and made a full, legal family member with the rights and responsibilities of that position. The practice of adoption was not common among the Jews, but was more widespread in the Greek and Roman world. The apostle Paul used the term to illustrate the truth that believers have been given the status of "sonship" in the heavenly family; they can call God "Father" (Rom. 8:15; Gal. 4:6). Adoption makes it clear that our sonship is conferred on us, in distinction from Christ's, which is inherent.

Apostle

"Someone who is sent," often "a messenger." In the New Testament the word refers particularly to twelve men whom Jesus selected to be with him and whom he sent out to preach and to cast out demons (Mark 3:14–15). Other individuals than the Twelve bore that title—for example, Paul and Barnabas (Acts 14:14). Apostles were important figures in the early church (1 Cor. 12:28). They were appointed by Christ, not by men (Gal. 1:1), and they gave authoritative witness to what God had done in Christ (Acts 1:22).

Assurance

Certainty of salvation, because of the promises of God and the effectiveness of Christ's atonement (1 John 5:13). The word does not occur often in the Bible, but the idea is more frequent. It is basic that people do not deserve their salvation because of their own efforts; that would leave them always uncertain, never knowing whether they had been good enough. But Christ did all that was needed, and we can rely on his perfect work. Further, believers have evidence of God's power in their lives (1 John 2:3–5; 3:19–21). Our assurance rests on the certainty that what God has begun he will complete (Phil. 1:6).

Atonement

Literally "at-one-ment," the making at one of those who have been separated. The word is used of Christ's dying to bring God and sinners together. Sin had separated them (Isa. 59:2) and made them enemies (Col. 1:21); it was thus a very serious matter. A many-sided act was required to remove that sin; words like *redemption* and *reconciliation* bring out significant aspects of Christ's saving work. Whatever had to be done about sin, Christ's death did, and thus opened up salvation for sinners.

Christ

English form of a Greek word meaning "anointed"; "Messiah" is the English form of the Hebrew word with the same meaning. In Old Testament days God anointed people for special service, especially the king (2 Sam. 1:14; 23:1) and the priest (Lev. 4:3). Eventually the understanding developed that an outstanding "anointed one" would appear, who would do God's will in a very special way (Dan. 9:25–26). This great One is often referred to without the use of the term *anointed* (Isa. 9:6–7; 11:1–9). The New Testament shows that Jesus was this chosen One, God's Messiah (John 4:25–26; cf. Matt. 23:10; Mark 9:41).

Conversion

The decisive act in which a sinner turns away from sin in genuine repentance and accepts the salvation that Christ offers. The imagery in conversion is that of turning. A person is going along a road and realizes that he or she is on the wrong track. They will never reach the destination if they continue in that direction. So the person "turns," or "is converted." He or she ceases to go in the wrong direction and begins going in the right one. Conversion changes the direction of one's course of life from the wrong way to the right way, the way that God wants.

Covenant

A solemn agreement, such as the pact between Jacob and
Laban (Gen. 31:44). God's love and grace are shown in his
readiness to make covenants with people. When God
promised Noah that he would not again destroy the world
with a flood, he made a covenant with him (Gen. 6:18;
9:9–17). A very important covenant existed between God
and Israel (Exod. 24:1–8), which is pictured in the book of
Hebrews as the "old covenant." When the people repeatedly broke that covenant, God promised a new covenant
based on forgiveness and the writing of his law on people's hearts (Jer. 31:31–34). Jesus inaugurated this new
covenant with his blood (Mark 14:24; 1 Cor. 11:25).

Typical bedouin tents in Jordan. (J. Jennings)

Disciple

In Bible times, a student. Whereas a student today studies
a subject (law, architecture, or whatever), a disciple in
olden days learned from a teacher. Attachment to a specific teacher was the essence of discipleship. The Phari-

sees and John the Baptist had disciples (Mark 2:18). The Jews saw themselves as disciples of Moses (John 9:28). The term is used often in the Gospels and Acts of the followers of Jesus. They learned from him and attached themselves wholeheartedly to him. It meant putting Christ before family and possessions. It meant taking up the cross (Luke 14:26–33). Today, too, to be a disciple of Jesus means total commitment.

Doctrine

"Teaching"; used of the content rather than the act of teaching. The Greek word may be used of the doctrines of men (Matt. 15:9), but, more important, refers to the teaching of Jesus (Matt. 7:28) and later the teaching of his followers. "My teaching," Jesus said, "is not my own. It comes from him who sent me" (John 7:16; i.e., it is from God). The word was used of Christian doctrine (Acts 2:42), to which believers are to be wholeheartedly committed (Rom. 6:17). It is important to "continue" in the doctrine (2 John 9) and to be able both to teach it and to refute those who oppose it (Titus 1:9).

Election

Chosen by God. The idea of election goes back to Abraham (Gen. 12:1–3). God chose to make a nation of that patriarch's descendants. He chose Israel to be his people. He worked his purposes out through that one nation and in due course sent his Messiah as a Jew. After that, God continued to choose, or elect, people in accordance with his purpose (Rom. 9:11), grace (Rom. 11:5), love (1 Thess. 1:4), and foreknowledge (1 Pet. 1:2). The "elect" can rely on God's concern for them (Luke 18:7) and on their sure salvation (Rom. 8:33). They are to live lives befitting their status (Col. 3:12–14). Mystery is inherent in the concept of election, because we also know that God desires the salvation of all persons (1 Tim. 2:4).

Expiation
See Propitiation.

Faith
Relying on what God has done rather than on one's own efforts. In the Old Testament, *faith* is rarely mentioned. The word *trust* is used frequently, and verbs like *believe* and *rely* are used to express the right attitude to God. The classic example is Abraham, whose faith was reckoned as righteousness (Gen. 15:6). At the heart of the Christian message is the story of the cross: Christ's dying to bring salvation. Faith is an attitude of trust in which a believer receives God's good gift of salvation (Acts 16:30–31) and lives in that awareness thereafter (Gal. 2:20; cf. Heb. 11:1).

Gospel
"Good news." Our word *gospel* comes from two Old English words. There is no good news like the good news that God sent his Son to die on a cross to get rid of our sins. 1 Corinthians 15:1–11 summarizes the good news, or gospel, that the apostle Paul preached. The term emphasizes the truth that salvation is entirely of grace. From its use for the central Christian message, the word came to be used as the title of each of the four books (Matthew, Mark, Luke, John) that tell the story of Jesus' life and atoning death.

Grace
God's unmerited favor. The Greek words for *joy* and *grace* are related; grace causes joy. In the Christian understanding, nothing brings joy like the good news of what God has done in Christ to bring us salvation. Salvation by grace is "through faith—and this not from yourselves, it is the gift of God—not by works . . . " (Eph. 2:8–9). God's

grace also brings about qualities of conduct in the believer (2 Cor. 9:8; 12:9; Eph. 4:7). The word *grace* came to be used as a kind of prayer ("grace to you") in Christian greetings at the beginning and end of some of the New Testament letters (2 Cor. 1:2; 13:14).

Heaven

The abode of God (1 Kings 8:30) and of the angels (Mark 13:32); believers will be there in due course (1 Pet. 1:4). The New Testament uses striking imagery to bring out the wonder and loveliness of heaven (gates of pearl and a street of gold—Rev. 21:21). Heaven means eternal joy in the presence of God.

Hell

The abode of Satan and his angels (Matt. 25:41), described in the Bible with the imagery of eternal fire, outer darkness, being lost, perishing, and the like. It is impossible to envisage a state that can be described in so many different ways. Clearly it is horrible and is to be avoided at all costs (Mark 9:43).

Incarnation

Literally, "en-flesh-ment" (Latin *carnis*—"flesh"); the doctrine that the Son of God became human (John 1:14). Jesus did not play at becoming a man but took on our flesh with all its problems and weaknesses. Incarnation, in the Christian understanding, means that Christ was both God and human.

Justification

Legal term meaning "acquittal," a declaration that someone is in the right. Sinners are in the wrong before God. They have broken his laws, they deserve punishment, but on the cross Christ took their place. Now, when they put their trust in Christ, they are declared to be in the right, acquitted, justified. The cross shows God to be just, not simply in the fact that he forgives, but in the way he forgives. To pass over sins would show mercy, but it would not show justice. Forgiveness by the way of the cross shows both (Rom. 3:25–26).

Cultivated papyrus. Papyrus "paper" was made by layering strips of the inner stem together and pounding the layers with mallets. (H. Vos)

Kingdom of God

An expression first used by Jesus, although the idea that God reigns is everywhere in the Old Testament. The coming of the kingdom of God was the most frequent topic in the teaching of Jesus (Mark 1:15). It expresses the truth that God is a great God who does what he wills in human affairs. Specifically he wills to save people through the life, death, resurrection, and ascension of Jesus. In one sense the kingdom of God is a present reality. People enter it now (Matt. 21:31). In another sense it is future (Matt. 16:28). God's control is plain in both aspects, and in the end his sovereign will will be perfectly done (1 Cor. 15:28).

Last Judgment

The evaluation of all humankind on the basis of works at Christ's return (Matt. 25:31–32). The wicked will be condemned because of their evil deeds. Salvation is by grace and through faith (Eph. 2:8); the last judgment will test what believers have done with their lives (1 Cor. 3:13–15). Some will be rewarded (Luke 19:16–19). Thus, although our salvation depends on what Christ has done, our eternal reward is related to the use we have made of God's gifts to us.

Love

God's benevolent concern for humankind. All religions have some idea of the importance of love. Christian theology stresses the importance of love because God has revealed that he is love (1 John 4:8, 16). Love is both what God is and what he has done; God always acts in love.

Love is a transitive reality—that is, it requires an object. In the Bible, love is described as personal (between persons) and selfless (desiring the best for others). Christians see God's love in sending his Son to die on the cross to save sinners (Rom. 5:8; John 3:16; 1 John 4:10). Christians are to be known by the fact that they love God and others (John 13:34–35). Their love is not to be like the love the world has (Luke 6:32, 35). Love is best seen in actions and in most cases is to be identified with what we do—in our compassion and commitment to those around us, regardless of the object's virtue (1 John 4:19). Our loving attitudes and behavior are to reflect God's love. Jesus said that only two commands are needed to govern our lives: love of God and love of neighbor. If such love is demonstrated, all the law and prophets are fulfilled.

Messiah
See Christ.

Predestination
God's sovereign working out of his purposes in the affairs of nations and in individual lives. God predestines those who are saved (Rom. 8:28–29; Eph. 1:4–5). He does not stand on the sidelines, a helpless spectator (so to speak), until we, with our repentance and conversion, give him permission to do something. Unless our names were written "in the book of life from the creation of the world" (Rev. 17:8) we would not even make the motion of turning from sin. Predestination means that our salvation, from first to last, is God's work. See also *Election*.

Propitiation / Expiation
Offering whatever will turn away anger; paying the penalty. Propitiation has to do with persons, expiation with things. Sin arouses the wrath of God; if people are to be forgiven, something must be done about his anger. Jesus' death on the cross brought about a process of propitiation; it was the means by which divine anger was averted from sinners.

Redemption
Originally, the payment of a price to secure the release of a prisoner of war. The word came to be used also of the release of a slave, and sometimes of a person under sentence of death (Exod. 21:28–30). Redemption always means the payment of a price to secure release. People who sin become slaves of sin (John 8:34); they cannot free themselves from that slavery. Christ's death on the cross was the payment of a ransom price (Mark 10:45) by which sinners are set free. Now that they are redeemed they must live as free people (1 Cor. 6:19–20; Gal. 5:1).

Regeneration

Being reborn; the subject of Jesus' discourse with Nicodemus in John 3 (cf. Titus 3:5). This word is not found often in Scripture, but the idea is important. Regeneration is seen to be the work of the Holy Spirit (John 3:5–8). The "natural man" always thinks of salvation (however understood) as resting in one's own hands, but Jesus taught that it is necessary for a divine work to take place if anyone is to be saved. Sinners must be reborn spiritually.

Remnant

Something remaining. In the Old Testament some passages refer to total destruction of a nation (e.g., the Babylonians in Jer. 50:26). When God brings judgment on his people, however, he does not destroy the faithful with the wicked, but leaves a remnant (Ezek. 6:8; Mic. 2:12). The concept of a remnant stood for that part of the nation who were faithful even though most people rejected the ways of God (Isa. 4:2–4). The fact of the existence of a remnant is said to be due to God himself (Isa. 1:9; Zeph. 3:12). The remnant, then, is the real people of God, a concept we also find in the New Testament, "a remnant chosen by grace" (Rom. 11:5).

Repentance

Sorrowing over and forsaking sin, a wholehearted turning away from all that is evil. This is more than regret or remorse, attitudes that point to sorrow over sin but no more. Repentance was looked for in Old Testament times (Ezek. 14:6; 18:30). It was the first item in the preaching of John the Baptist (Matt. 3:1–2), Jesus (Matt. 4:17), and the apostles (Mark 6:12; cf. Acts 2:38). Beyond repentance, faith is needed. But repentance is indispensable. Sin must be forsaken decisively.

Resurrection

The raising and transformation of a person who has died. Resuscitation means the bringing back of people to this life after they have left it, for example, the raising of the son of the widow of Nain (Luke 7:11–15) or of Lazarus (John 11). Resurrection is more than that. Jesus rose on the third day after he died, but his new body was transformed. It was not subject to the limitations of his former earthly life (Luke 24:16, 31; John 20:19). Jesus' resurrection, following his atoning death, is central to the Christian faith (1 Cor. 15:14–19). Believers, too, will be resurrected (1 Thess. 4:16; 1 Cor. 15:42–57).

Revelation

Uncovering, making plain what was not known before. The word may be used of something God makes known during a church service (1 Cor. 14:26), but more usually it has to do with something on a larger scale, like God's righteousness, wrath (Rom. 1:17–18), or righteous judgment (Rom. 2:5). It may be used to describe a book (Rev. 1:1). God reveals things through the Spirit (1 Cor. 2:10). The gospel is not something people have made up but has been revealed by Christ (Gal. 1:11–12). The fullness of revelation awaits the return of Christ (2 Thess. 1:7; 1 Pet. 1:13).

Righteousness

Right standing, specifically before God. Among the Greeks, righteousness was an ethical virtue. Among the Hebrews it was a legal concept; the righteous man was the one who got the verdict of acceptability when tried at the bar of God's justice. Christ's death took away our sins and made it possible for sinners to have "the righteousness of God," i.e., right standing before God (Rom. 1:16–17; 3:22; 5:17). That gift of righteousness is to be followed by upright living (Rom. 6:13–14).

This cave was created by wind and water erosion in the sandstone region of the Sinai. (R. Nowitz)

Salvation

Deliverance of various kinds, for example, deliverance from the enemy (Exod. 14:13). In the Bible it is God who brings salvation from temporal as well as spiritual ills. Thus in the Gospels, referring to his miraculous healings, Jesus sometimes says, "Your faith has saved you," meaning "healed you" (Luke 18:42 KJV). Characteristically, the term refers to salvation from sin (Rom. 1:16; 1 Thess. 5:9). Salvation means the decisive defeat of sin on the cross, but also victory over evil in a believer's daily life. Its full content will be realized only in the life to come (Heb. 9:28; 1 Pet. 1:5).

Sanctification

The process of developing holiness. God said to Israel, "Be holy, because I am holy" (Lev. 11:44–45). Because God wants us to become like him, it is necessary that his people be a special kind of people, holy men and women. The basic idea in sanctification is "being set apart for God"; those thus set apart live in a way that is pleasing to God. They have no power of their own to do that, but God enables them (2 Cor. 3:17–18). Sanctification is not an option. God requires it of all his people (1 Thess. 4:3).

Second Coming

Christ's return at the end of the world to establish God's kingdom (1 Cor. 15:23–25). The New Testament does not use this expression; it refers simply to "the coming" (*parousia*), also called a "reveal(ing)" of Jesus (1 Cor. 1:7), or an "appearing" (Titus 2:13). There is dispute about the relationship of Christ's second coming to the thousand years, or millennium (Rev. 20:4), but none as to the fact that it will be God's decisive and indispensable intervention. Christ's coming to destroy all evil will be the culmination of his redemptive work.

Drawing water from a cistern at Arad. With its long dry season and inadequate rainfall, Palestine depends heavily on cisterns and wells. (J. Jennings)

Sin

Anything that fails to conform to the law of God. Evil is a complex phenomenon in the Scriptures. The idea of sin is conveyed by a variety of expressions with meanings like missing the mark, rebelling, going astray, transgressing, stumbling, etc. Basically "sin is lawlessness" (1 John 3:4), referring to an inward attitude as well as to the breaking of written commandments. All people commit sin (1 Kings 8:46; Rom. 3:23). To deny that we have sinned is to make God a liar (1 John 1:10); all his dealings with humanity are on the basis that we are sinners. But the blood of Jesus cleanses from all sin (1 John 1:7).

Sovereignty

Term used to describe the fact that God is the supreme ruler of everything. God created the world and all that is in it. He sustains the entire created order in existence. He guides the affairs of human beings and nations. He providentially interacts with all that takes place. He works for the good of the world and finally will bring all things to a satisfactory conclusion. Because he is God, he has the absolute right to work his will. Sometimes sovereignty is misunderstood to mean that God forces his will on people and that we are not free to choose. That is false. God's sovereignty includes the free choices of human beings. What makes God's sovereignty effective is that his will is ultimately done—sometimes along with, sometimes in spite of our free choices.

Spiritual Gifts

Special gifts of the Spirit (*charismata*; e.g., Rom. 12:6–8; 1 Cor. 12:4–11, 28–31). There is some dispute as to whether these gifts were all meant as permanent endowments of the Christian church or as gifts only for its early days. In modern times, charismatics claim to exercise particular gifts, especially "tongues," "healing," and "prophecy." Other believers emphasize the fruit of the Spirit more than spiritual gifts (Gal. 5:22-23).

Tithe

Word meaning "tenth," used of the offering of a tenth for religious purposes. Abraham gave a tenth to Melchizedek, the priest-king (Gen. 14:18-20). The Israelites were required to give a tithe to the Levites (Num. 18:21, 24), and the Levites in turn were to give a tithe of the tithe to the priests (Num. 18:25-28). The tithe was taken from things like grain, fruits, and animals (Lev. 27:30-32). There is no command to tithe in the New Testament (cf. 1 Cor. 16:2), but many Christians believe that the concept is a useful guide in their giving.

Contemporary Bethlehem, town of Jesus' birth. (H. Vos)

Tongues

Speaking in a language one has not learned. Luke wrote of a gift of tongues on the day of Pentecost (Acts 2:4–6), when everybody understood what was being said. Elsewhere we read of the Spirit's enabling people to speak in words that neither they nor anyone else understood unless they had another gift, that of interpretation (1 Cor. 12:10, 28). The possessor of the gift of tongues used it to speak about God, but edified nobody but himself, Paul said (1 Cor. 14:2–4). His mind was not active (1 Cor. 14:14). Paul did not forbid the use of the gift, however; he spoke in tongues himself (1 Cor. 14:18). But he regulated its use (1 Cor. 14:27–28) and saw edification as a more important consideration (1 Cor. 14:4–5).

Wrath of God

In Scripture, God's strong and vigorous opposition to everything evil. There is a Greek verb that can be used both of anger and of the swelling of buds as the sap rises. It points to the kind of anger that results from a settled and consistent disposition, and not to a losing of one's temper. God's wrath is like that, rather than like human anger on a grand scale. With us, wrath always has elements of passion, lack of self-control, and irrationality. The wrath of God does not.

Messianic Prophecy in the Bible

One of the extraordinary things about the Bible is that it talks about events before they happened. This was part of the prophet's ministry, along with his commission to preach repentance and faith to his own generation. There is a special group of prophecies, unique to the Bible, that relate to the coming of God's redeemer, called the Messiah. In every other collection of religious literature, the leader or chief figure of the group is talked about after he appeared, sometimes many centuries later, and in terms of rather fantastic myth or legend. In the Bible, however, Jesus Christ is talked about long before he came to earth and in such exact terms that no one should have missed his appearing. As we look back on this set of prophecies and fulfillments, it only confirms our faith in the God who knew the end from the beginning and prepared the stage for the sending of his Son to redeem the world. Following is only a selection of the many such prophecies.

Prophecy	Fulfillment
An important ruler would come from the little town of Bethlehem, one whose origins were in the "days of eternity." *Micah 5:2*	Jesus was born in Bethlehem. *Luke 2:4–7*
A virgin would bear a son, whose name would mean "God with us." This would be a sign from the Lord. *Isaiah 7:14*	Mary, a virgin, was told by an angel that she would conceive a child, by the power of the Holy Spirit, whose name was to be Jesus ("Savior"). *Luke 1:26–35; Matthew 1:18–25*

The Lord would send a special messenger to prepare the way for his own coming. *Malachi 3:1*	John the Baptist came to preach and prepare the way for one greater than himself. *Luke 3:15-18; 7:24-27*
The Lord would raise up a prophet in Israel to whom they should pay attention. *Deuteronomy 18:15*	The apostles saw Jesus as this prophet: the Christ. *Acts 3:18-23*
The Lord God would anoint a liberator, one who would preach good news to the poor, the brokenhearted, the captive, and the mourning. *Isaiah 61:1-3*	Jesus began his ministry by explaining that he was the person referred to in Isaiah's prophecy. *Luke 4:16-20*
The special Servant of the Lord would suffer and be rejected. *Isaiah 53:3*	Jesus was rejected and put to death for being who he was and saying what he said. *Luke 23:13-25; John 1:10-11*
The coming righteous King/Redeemer would come to his people riding on a young donkey. *Zechariah 9:9*	The last week of his life on earth, Jesus rode into Jerusalem on a donkey. *Mark 11:1-11*

The special Servant of the Lord would remain silent when cruelly treated. *Isaiah 53:7*	Jesus refused to answer the false charges made to Pilate against him. *Mark 15:3–5*
The special Servant of the Lord would suffer on behalf of others. *Isaiah 53:5*	The heart of the gospel is the good news that Christ died for our sins. *Romans 5:6–8*
The Messiah would be mocked and insulted because his God was not delivering him in his time of anguish. *Psalm 22:7–8*	Bystanders sneered at Jesus on the cross because God had not saved him from death by crucifixion. *Luke 23:35*
The Messiah would be given gall and vinegar. *Psalm 69:21*	After carrying his cross to Golgotha, Jesus was given wine vinegar mixed with gall (bad tasting) for his thirst. *Matthew 27:34*
The Messiah's love for his people would be met with hostility, but his response would be to pray for them. *Psalm 109:4*	Jesus prayed that God would forgive those who crucified him, because they did not realize what they were doing. *Luke 23:34*

The Messiah's clothing would be divided up by lot. *Psalm 22:18*	After crucifying him, the Roman soldiers divided up Jesus' clothes by casting lots. *Matthew 27:35*
The Messiah's bones would not be broken. *Psalm 34:20*	The Roman soldiers didn't break Jesus' legs after the crucifixion, as they ordinarily did to people punished in this way, because Jesus had already died. *John 19:32–33, 36*
The Messiah would be pierced. *Zechariah 12:10*	Jesus' side was pierced by a Roman soldier. *John 19:34*
God would redeem his Holy One (the Messiah) from the grave; his body would not decay. *Psalm 16:10; 49:15*	God raised Jesus from the dead. Without the resurrection, the hopes of Christianity would be only wishful thinking. *Mark 16:6–7;* *1 Corinthians 15:16–19*

Key Verses for the Christian Life

One of the features of God's Word, the Bible, is that it is a guidebook for Christians who want to live God's way. By meditating on Scripture verses and learning them from memory, you can carry parts of this guidebook with you all the time.

Following is a list of key verses for Christian living, in three categories: Understanding God, Understanding My Relationship to God, and Understanding My Relationships with Others. From these lists, choose verses that help you where you are right now in your Christian life, and begin to memorize them one at a time.

The verses here are taken from the following translations of the Bible: the *Good News Bible* (GNB), *Jerusalem Bible* (JB), *New English Bible* (NEB), *New International Version* (NIV), *The New Testament in Modern English* translated by J.B. Phillips *(Phillips)*, *The Revised Standard Version* (RSV), *The Living Bible* (TLB). You may memorize the verses in the version printed or you may look them up in another translation that is more meaningful to you. (It's a good idea to look up any verse you memorize and read it in its context for better understanding.)

You'll find that memorizing comes quickly and easily when you read the verse several times a day. Copy it on a notecard and tape it where you will see it often—the dashboard of your car, your notebook, your mirror, your desk, your refrigerator. And remember, this short list of verses is just to get you started as you make the Bible an important part of your life through memorization.

Understanding God

God is our shelter and strength, always ready to help in times of trouble. So we will not be afraid, even if the earth is shaken and mountains fall into the ocean depths. *Psalm 46:1–2 (GNB)*

Know and believe me and understand that I am He. Before me no god was formed, nor shall there be any after me. *Isaiah 43:10 (RSV)*

He saved us—not because we were good enough to be saved, but because of his kindness and pity—by washing away our sins and giving us the new joy of the indwelling Holy Spirit whom he poured out upon us with wonderful fullness—and all because of what Jesus Christ our Savior did. *Titus 3:5–6 (TLB)*

Our mouths were filled with laughter, our tongues with songs of joy. Then it was said among the nations, "The Lord has done great things for them." The Lord has done great things for us, and we are filled with joy. *Psalm 126:2–3 (NIV)*

Blessed be the God and Father of our Lord Jesus Christ, a gentle Father and the God of all consolation who comforts us in all our sorrows, so that we can offer others, in their sorrows, the consolation that we have received from God ourselves. *2 Corinthians 1:3, 4 (JB)*

The Lord does not look at the things man looks at. Man looks at the outward appearance, but the Lord looks at the heart. *1 Samuel 16:7 (NIV)*

I have told you all this so that you may find peace in me. In the world you will have trouble, but be brave: I have conquered the world. *John 16:33 (JB)*

Christ is the visible likeness of the invisible God. He is the firstborn Son, superior to all created things. For through him God created everything in heaven and on earth, the seen and the unseen things, including spiritual powers, lords, rulers, and authorities. God created the whole universe through him and for him. Christ existed before all things, and in union with him all things have their proper place.   *Colossians 1:15–17 (GNB)*

Yours, O Lord, is the greatness and the power and the glory and the majesty and the splendor, for everything in heaven and earth is yours. Yours, O Lord, is the kingdom; you are exalted as head over all. Wealth and honor come from you; you are the ruler of all things. In your hands are strength and power to exalt and give strength to all. *1 Chronicles 29:11–12 (NIV)*

He who did not hesitate to spare his own Son but gave him up for us all—can we not trust such a God to give us, with him, everything else that we can need?   *Romans 8:32 (Phillips)*

Understanding My Relationship to God
God loved the world so much that he gave his only Son, that everyone who has faith in him may not die but have eternal life.   *John 3:16 (NEB)*

I am convinced that neither death nor life, neither angels nor demons, neither the present nor the future, nor any powers, neither height nor depth, nor anything else in all creation, will be able to separate us from the love of God that is in Christ Jesus our Lord.   *Romans 8:38–39 (NIV)*

If we confess our sins, he is faithful and just and will forgive us our sins and purify us from all unrighteousness. *1 John 1:9 (NIV)*

When the Holy Spirit controls our lives he will produce this kind of fruit in us: love, joy, peace, patience, kindness, goodness, faithfulness, gentleness and self-control. *Galatians 5:22 (TLB)*

Every test that you have experienced is the kind that normally comes to people. But God keeps his promise, and he will not allow you to be tested beyond your power to remain firm; at the time you are put to the test he will give you the strength to endure it, and so provide you with a way out.   *1 Corinthians 10:13 (GNB)*

Do not be anxious about anything, but in everything by prayer and petition, with thanksgiving, present your requests to God. And the peace of God, which transcends all understanding, will guard your hearts and your minds in Christ Jesus.   *Philippians 4:6–7 (NIV)*

Offer yourselves as a living sacrifice to God, dedicated to his service and pleasing to him. This is the true worship that you should offer.   *Romans 12:1 (GNB)*

We know that to those who love God, who are called according to his plan, everything that happens fits into a pattern for good.   *Romans 8:28 (Phillips)*

What does the Lord your God ask of you but to fear the Lord your God, to walk in all his ways, to love him, to serve the Lord your God with all your heart and with all your soul, and to observe the Lord's commands and decrees. *Deuteronomy 10:12–13 (NIV)*

I will always guide you and satisfy you with good things. I will keep you strong and well. You will be like a garden that has plenty of water, like a spring of water that never runs dry.   *Isaiah 58:11 (GNB)*

Understanding My Relationships with Others

You should try to become like God, for you are his children and he loves you. Live your lives in love—the same sort of love which Christ gave us and which he perfectly expressed when he gave himself up for us as an offering and a sacrifice well-pleasing to God.   *Ephesians 5:1–2 (Phillips)*

Cheerfully share your home with those who need a meal or a place to stay for the night. God has given each of you some special abilities; be sure to use them to help each other, passing on to others God's many kinds of blessings.   *1 Peter 4:9–10 (TLB)*

Thoughtless words can wound as deeply as any sword, but wisely spoken words can heal.   *Proverbs 12:18 (GNB)*

Obey your masters in everything; and do it, not only when their eye is on you and to win their favor, but with sincerity of heart and reverence for the Lord. Whatever you do, work at it with all your heart, as working for the Lord, not for men, since you know that you will receive an inheritance from the Lord as a reward. It is the Lord Christ you are serving.   *Colossians 3:22–24 (NIV)*

Be ready at all times to answer anyone who asks you to explain the hope you have in you, but do it with gentleness and respect. Keep your conscience clear, so that when you are insulted, those who speak evil of your good conduct as followers of Christ will be ashamed of what they say.   *1 Peter 3:15–16 (GNB)*

You should be clothed in sincere compassion, in kindness and humility, gentleness and patience. Bear with one another; forgive each other as soon as a quarrel begins. The Lord has forgiven you; now you must do the same.   *Colossians 3:12–13 (JB)*

Honor your father and your mother, as the Lord your God has commanded you, so that you may live long and that it may go well with you in the land the Lord your God is giving you.   *Deuteronomy 5:16 (NIV)*

May God who gives patience, steadiness, and encouragement help you to live in complete harmony with each other—each with the attitude of Christ toward the other. And then all of us can praise the Lord together with one voice.   *Romans 15:5–6 (TLB)*

If you pour yourself out for the hungry and satisfy the desire of the afflicted, then shall your light rise in the darkness and your gloom be as the noonday.   *Isaiah 58:10 (RSV)*

Love your enemies, do good to them, and lend to them without expecting to get anything back. Then your reward will be great, and you will be sons of the Most High.   *Luke 6:35 (NIV)*

Figure 21 The Bible at a Glance

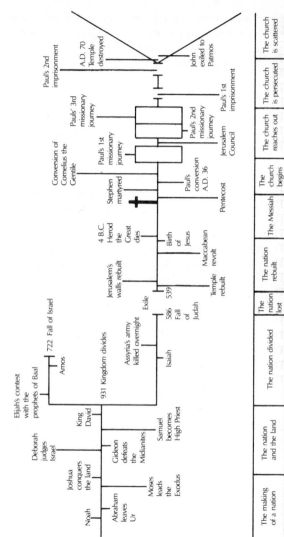

Key Bible Passages

The Creation Story *Genesis 1:1–2:7*
The Fall of Man *Genesis 3:6–24*
The Flood *Genesis 6:1–9:17*
The Call of Abraham *Genesis 12:1–9*
The Ten Commandments *Exodus 20:1–17*
The Shepherd's Psalm *Psalm 23*
The Birth of Christ *Matthew 1:18–2:23;*
  Luke 1:26–2:40
The Golden Rule *Luke 6:31*
The Sermon on the Mount *Matthew 5–7*
The Beatitudes *Matthew 5:3–11*
The Lord's Prayer *Luke 11:2–4*
The Prodigal Son *Luke 15:11–32*
The Good Samaritan *Luke 10:29–37*
The Last Supper *Matthew 26:20–25; Mark 14:12–26*
The Death of Christ *Luke 23:26–56; John 19:16–42*
The Resurrection of Christ *Matthew 28; Luke 24;*
  John 20
The Ascension *Acts 1:1–12*
The Advent of the Holy Spirit *Acts 2:1–21*
The Conversion of Paul *Acts 9:1–31*
The Love Chapter *1 Corinthians 13*
The Faith Chapter *Hebrews 11*

This sycamore tree at Jericho reminds us of the story of Zacchaeus and Jesus in the Gospels. (H. Vos)

Interesting Bible Facts

The Bible is a book full of treasures for those willing to look for them. It offers historical information, God's gift of salvation, advice for living pure lives, moving poetry, comfort and encouragement for suffering people, and much more. This section is a partial list of some of the interesting facts found in the Bible.

The Bible Itself
The Bible has 66 books, 39 in the Old Testament and 27 in the New Testament. It is composed of the writings of more than 30 different authors, who wrote during a time span of approximately 1500 years. The total number of verses in both Testaments is 30,442.

The Twelve Tribes of Israel
Reuben	Judah	Dan	Naphtali
Simeon	Zebulun	Gad	Joseph
Levi	Issachar	Asher	Benjamin

The Ten Commandments

You shall have no other gods besides me.

You shall not worship any idol.

You shall not misuse the name of the Lord your God.

Remember the Sabbath day by keeping it holy.

Honor your father and your mother.

You shall not murder.

You shall not commit adultery.

You shall not steal.

You shall not give false testimony.

You shall not covet anything that is your neighbor's.

(Paraphrased from Exodus 20:3–17)

Eight Women Prophets of the Bible

Miriam (Exod. 15:20)

Deborah (Judg. 4:4)

Huldah (2 Kings 22:14–20)

Anna (Luke 2:36–38)

Four daughters of Philip (Acts 21:8–9)

Musical Instruments in the Bible

harp (Gen. 4:21)

flute (Gen. 4:21)

ram's horn trumpets (Josh. 6:4)

tambourines (1 Sam. 18:6)

lutes (1 Sam. 18:6)

lyres (1 Chron. 16:5)

cymbals (1 Chron. 16:5)

stringed instruments (dedications to psalms such as 4, 6 and 55)

horn (Dan. 3:5)

zither (Dan. 3:5)

pipes (Dan. 3:5)

Animals in the Bible

donkeys (Gen. 12:16)
cattle (Gen. 12:16)
goats (Gen. 27:9)
horses (Gen. 47:17)
sea cow (Exod. 25:5)
rabbit (Lev. 11:6)
pig (Lev. 11:7)
bat (Lev. 11:19)
weasel (Lev. 11:29)
rat (Lev. 11:29)
gazelle (Deut. 12:15)
deer (Deut. 12:15)
ox (Deut. 14:4)
roe deer (Deut. 14:5)
ibex (Deut. 14:5)
wild goat (Deut. 14:5)
antelope (Deut. 14:5)

coney or rock badger
   (Deut. 14:7)
lion (Judg. 14:5-6)
sheep (1 Sam. 16:11)
bear (1 Sam. 17:34-36)
dog (1 Sam. 17:43)
mule (1 Kings 1:33)
apes (2 Chron. 9:21)
baboons (2 Chron. 9:21)
camels (Job 1:3)
behemoth—hippo or
   elephant (Job 40:15)
boar (Ps. 80:13)
foxes (Song of Sol. 2:15)
jackals (Isa. 34:13)
hyenas (Isa. 34:14)
leopard (Jer. 13:23)
wolves (Matt. 7:15)

Palestinian donkey. Jesus fulfilled messianic prophecy when he came to his people riding on a donkey. (H. Vos)

Birds in the Bible

raven (Gen. 8:7)
dove (Gen. 8:8)
quail (Exod. 16:13)
eagle (Lev. 1:13)
vulture (Lev. 11:13)
red kite (Lev. 11:14)
black kite (Lev. 11:14)
horned owl (Lev. 11:16)
gull (Lev. 11:16)
hawk (Lev. 11:16)
owl (Lev. 11:17)
cormorant (Lev. 11:17)
great owl (Lev. 11:17)
white owl (Lev. 11:18)
desert owl (Lev. 11:18)

osprey (Lev. 11:18)
stork (Lev. 11:19)
heron (Lev. 11:19)
hoopoe (Lev. 11:19)
falcon (Deut. 14:13)
sparrow (Ps. 84:3)
swallow (Ps. 84:3)
screech owl (Isa. 34:11)
swift (Isa. 38:14)
thrush (Isa. 38:14)
partridge (Jer. 17:11)
hen & chicks (Matt. 23:37)
rooster (Matt. 26:34)
pigeons (Luke 2:24)

Rivers, Lakes, & Seas in the Bible

Abana, River
Arnon, River
Chebar, River (Canal)
Cherith, Brook
Egypt, River of or Brook of
Egypt, Stream of (Nile River)
Euphrates, River
Gihon, River
Hiddekel, River
Jabbok, River
Jordan, River
Kanah, River or Brook
Kidron, Brook

Kishon, River
Pharpar, River
Pison, River
Zared, Brook
Sea of Galilee
   or Sea of Chinnereth
   or Sea of Chinneroth
   or Lake of Gennesaret
   or Lake of Tiberias
Great Sea (Mediterranean Sea)
Salt Sea (Dead Sea)
   or Sea of the Arabah
   or Sea of the Plain
East Sea
The Sea

Figure 22   Sects & Parties in New Testament Palestine

Name	Description
Religious	
Pharisees	The Jewish sect holding the religious power in Palestine during Christ's ministry. These "separated ones" believed that their detailed descriptions of how to obey the law were equal in authority to the Mosaic law and that their meticulous adherence to these traditions made them the only righteous Jews alive.
Sadducees	A Jewish sect consisting mainly of priests. These "righteous ones" believed that the Mosaic law was the supreme authority and that no oral law or traditions could be considered equal to Scripture. In contrast to the Pharisees, they did not believe in resurrection or angels and spirits (Acts 23:8).
Essenes	A Jewish sect whose members lived a life analogous to monastic life in the Middle Ages. In their isolated communities, these "pious" or "saintly" ones sought ideal purity and divine communion through practicing self-denial, temperance, labor (farming), and contemplation.
Political	
Herodians	A sect consisting of Jews who agreed to be subject to Roman rule and practice. These Jews believed that Herod and his descendants were the last hope for Israel to maintain any semblance of a national government of their own.
Zealots	A strongly nationalistic sect whose battle cry was "No Lord but Jehovah; no tax but that of the Temple; no friend but the Zealots." They combined religious practices of the Pharisees with a strong hatred for any Gentile government.
Galileans	A sect whose members believed that foreign control of Israel was unscriptural, and therefore refused to acknowledge or pray for foreign princes. Because of their strong similarity politically to the Zealots, the Galileans were eventually absorbed into that sect.
Social	
Scribes	A class of men who copied, taught, and explained the law. Like the Pharisees, they held to the authority of oral traditions. As teachers of the law they maintained an important place in Jewish society, and also served as judges or lawyers, making judgments in light of the law they knew so well.
Nazarites	Jews who took a vow of separation either for a limited time or for life. Recognizable to others because they vowed never to cut their hair, Nazarites separated themselves by their lifestyle for closeness to God and as a testimony about the sinful condition of the nation.
Proselytes	A non-Jew who had been converted to Judaism. By being circumcized such a person was thought to be grafted into the family of Abraham and therefore was expected to follow the law.
Publicans	Jews who worked for the Roman government collecting taxes. Their willingness to work in the government was seen as a lack of loyalty to Israel and a willingness to have commerce with Gentiles.

The Twelve Apostles

Peter	Matthew
James	James (son of Alphaeus)
John	Simon Zelotes
Andrew	Lebbaeus Thaddaeus (Judas, brother of
Philip	James)
Thomas	Judas Iscariot
Bartholomew	

Ten Biblical Records of People Raised from the Dead

Zarephath widow's son (1 Kings 17:17–24)
Shunammite woman's son (2 Kings 4:32–37)
Man whose body touched Elisha's bones
　(2 Kings 13:20–21)
Saints at Jesus' death (Matt. 27:50–53)
Jesus (Matt. 28:5–8; Mark 16:6; Luke 24:5–7)
Son of the widow of Nain (Luke 7:11–15)
Jairus' daughter (Luke 8:41–42, 49–55)
Lazarus (John 11:1–44)
Dorcas (Acts 9:36–42)
Eutychus (Acts 20:9–10)

Jesus' Seven Last Sayings on the Cross

"Father, forgive them, for they do not know what they are
　doing." (Luke 23:34)
"I tell you the truth, today you will be with me in para-
　dise." (Luke 23:43)
"Dear woman, here is your son. Here is your mother."
　(John 19:26-27)
"My God, my God, why have you forsaken me?" (Mark
　15:34)
"I am thirsty." (John 19:28)
"It is finished." (John 19:30)
"Father, into your hands I commit my spirit." (Luke 23:46)

Visions of God by Biblical People

Jacob dreamed of "a stairway resting on the earth, with its top reaching to heaven, and the angels of God . . . ascending and descending on it." Above the ladder stood the Lord. (Gen. 28:12–13)

"Moses and Aaron, Nadab and Abihu, and the seventy elders of Israel went up and saw the God of Israel." (Exod. 24:9–10)

Moses saw the back of God. (Exod. 33:23)

Micaiah saw "the Lord sitting on his throne with all the host of heaven standing on his right and on his left." (2 Chron. 18:18)

Isaiah saw "the Lord seated on a throne, high and exalted." (Isa. 6:1)

Ezekiel saw "what looked like a throne of sapphire, and high above on the throne . . . a figure like that of a man." (Ezek. 1:26)

In Daniel's vision "thrones were set in place, and the Ancient of Days took his seat. His clothing was as white as snow; the hair of his head was white like wool. His throne was flaming with fire." (Dan. 7:9)

"Stephen . . . looked up to heaven and saw the glory of God, and Jesus standing at the right hand of God." (Acts 7:55)

Paul wrote "I know a man in Christ who . . . was caught up to the third heaven." (2 Cor. 12:2)

John wrote "I was in the Spirit, and there before me was a throne in heaven with someone sitting on it." (Rev. 4:2)

Important Biblical Names

Aaron *enlightened*

Abel *breath, a meadow*

Abigail *father of joy, father's joy*

Abraham *father of a multitude*

Absalom *father of friendship or of peace*

Adam *man*

Agrippa *causing pain at birth*

Ahaz *possessor*

Amos *burden, one with a burden*

Andrew *a man, manly*

Anna *grace, gracious*

Apollos *belonging to Apollo*

Aquila *an eagle*

Balaam *foreigner, Lord of the people*

Barnabas *son of consolation*

Bartholomew *son of Ptolemy*

Bathsheba *daughter of an oath or of seven*

Benjamin *son of the right hand*

Bernice *bringer of victory*

Boaz *fleetness, strength*

Cain *acquisition, possession*

Caleb *a barker, a dog*

Cephas *a stone, rock*

Clement *mild, gentle*

Cornelius *of a horn*

Cyrus *sun, splendor*

Dan *judge*

Daniel *God is my judge, God's judge*

David *dear, beloved*

Deborah *a bee*

Delilah *weak, tender, unhappy*

Ehud *the only*

Eleazar *God my helper*

Eli *lifting up*

Elijah *Jehovah my God*

Elisabeth *oath of God*

Elisha *God as a Savior*

Enoch *dedicated, consecrated*

Esau *hairy*

Esther *a star*

Eve *life, living*

Ezekiel *strength of God, or God will strengthen*

Ezra *help*

Felix *happy*

Festus *joyful*

Gabriel *man of God*

Gad *good fortune, fortunate*

Gaius *of the earth*

Gideon *a hewer, tree-feller*

Goliath *expulsion, expeller*

Habakkuk *clasper of the hands, embrace*

Haggai *festive*

Ham *hot, black*

Hannah *grace, prayer*

Hazael   *sight of, seen by God*

Herod   *glory of the skin*

Hezekiah   *might of Jehovah*

Hosea   *deliverance, salvation*

Immanuel   *God with us*

Isaac   *laughter*

Isaiah   *salvation of Jehovah*

Ishmael   *whom God hears*

Israel   *soldier of God*

Jacob   *supplanter*

James   *supplanter*

Jason   *healer*

Jehoiakim   *set up by Jehovah*

Jehoshaphat   *Jehovah judges*

Jehovah   *the eternally existing*

Jehu   *Jehovah is He*

Jeremiah   *exalted by God*

Jesse   *wealth, firm*

Jesus   *healer, savior*

Jethro   *preeminent*

Jezebel   *without cohabitation, chaste*

Joab   *Jehovah is father*

Job   *the much injured, afflicted*

Joel   *whose God is Jehovah*

John   *God's gift, grace*

Jonah   *a dove*

Jonathan   *Jehovah's gift, Jehovah is gracious*

Joseph   *he shall add*

Joshua   *Jehovah is salvation*

Josiah   *God is healer*

Jotham   *Jehovah is upright*

Judah   *praised*

Judas   *praised*

Jude   *praised*

Judith   *Jewess*

Laban   *white, beautiful*

Lazarus   *God my helper*

Leah   *weary*

Levi   *crowned, crown*

Lot   *covering, veil*

Lucifer   *light-bringer*

Luke   *light-giver*

Lydia   *contention*

Malachi   *one sent, messenger of Jehovah*

Manasseh   *forgetting, one who makes to forget*

Mark   *polite*

Martha   *lady*

Mary   *resistance, rebellion*

Matthew   *gift of Jehovah*

Melchizedek   *king of righteousness*

Methuselah   *man of a dark, of offspring*

Micah   *who is like God?*

Michael   *who is like God?*

Miriam   *resistance, rebellion*

Moab   *the desirable land*

Mordecai   *consecrated to Merodach*

Moses   *drawn out of the water*

Nahum   *consolation, sympathy, comforter*

Naomi   *gracious, comely, pleasant*

Nathan   *gift (of God)*

Nathanael   *gift of God*

Nebuchadnezzar   *prince of the god Nebo*

Nehemiah   *consolation from God*

Nicodemus   *conqueror of the people*

Noah   *rest*

Obadiah   *servant of Jehovah*

Othniel   *lion of God*

Paul   *little*

Peter   *a rock, stone*

Philemon   *affectionate*

Philip   *lover of horses*

Priscilla   *ancient*

Rachel   *a ewe*

Rahab   *roomy, gracious*

Rebecca   *a fetter, fettering cord*

Reuben   *lo! a son, Jehovah has seen, God's mercy*

Ruth   *a friend*

Samson   *like the sun*

Samuel   *name of God, placed by God, heard of God*

Sarah   *princess*

Satan   *adversary*

Saul   *asked for*

Seth   *sprout*

Simeon   *one heard*

Simon   *one heard*

Solomon   *peaceful*

Stephen   *a crown*

Thaddaeus   *man of heart*

Thomas   *twin*

Timothy   *honored by God, honoring God*

Titus   *honorable*

Uriah   *light of Jehovah, Jehovah is my light*

Uzziah   *power of Jehovah, strength of Jehovah*

Zachariah   *remembered by Jehovah*

Zedekiah   *justice of Jehovah*

Zephaniah   *treasure of Jehovah, Jehovah hides*

Names of Jesus

Alpha and Omega
(Rev. 1:8)
Anointed One (Ps. 2:2)
Author of Life (Acts 3:15)
Branch (Zech. 6:12)
Bright and Morning Star
(Rev. 22:16)
Christ (Matt. 1:16)
Daystar (2 Pet. 1:19)
Everlasting Father (Isa. 9:6)
Gate (John 10:9)
Good Shepherd
(John 10:14)
Holy and Righteous One
(Acts 3:14)
I Am (John 8:58)
Immanuel (Isa. 7:14)
King of Kings (Rev. 19:16)
Lamb (Rev 5:6-13)
Lamb of God (John 1:29)

Lion of Judah (Rev. 5:5)
Lord of Lords (Rev. 19:16)
Mighty God (Isa. 9:6)
Nazarene (Matt. 2:23)
Prince of Peace (Isa. 9:6)
Rabbi (John 1:38)
Root of David (Rev. 5:5)
Root of Jesse (Isa. 11:10)
Son of David (Matt. 15:22)
Son of God (Mark 1:1)
Son of Man (Matt. 8:20)
True Vine (John 15:1)
Wonderful Counselor
(Isa. 9:6)
Word (John 1:1)
Word of God (Rev. 19:13)

Eleven Benedictions in the Bible

"The Lord bless you and keep you; the Lord make his face shine upon you and be gracious to you; the Lord turn his face toward you and give you peace." (Num. 6:24–26)

"Grace and peace to you from God our Father and from the Lord Jesus Christ." (Rom. 1:7)

"The God of peace be with you all. Amen." (Rom. 15:33)

"Peace to the brothers, and love with faith from God the Father and the Lord Jesus Christ. Grace to all who love our Lord Jesus Christ with an undying love." (Eph. 6:23–24)

"Now may the Lord of peace himself give you peace at all times and in every way. The Lord be with all of you." (2 Thess. 3:16)

"Grace, mercy and peace from God the Father and Christ Jesus our Lord." (1 Tim. 1:2)

"The Lord be with your spirit. Grace be with you." (2 Tim. 4:22)

"May the God of peace, who through the blood of the eternal covenant brought back from the dead our Lord Jesus, that great Shepherd of the sheep, equip you with everything good for doing his will, and may he work in us what is pleasing to him, through Jesus Christ, to whom be glory for ever and ever. Amen." (Heb. 13:20–21)

"Peace to all of you who are in Christ." (1 Pet. 5:14)

"Grace and peace be yours in abundance through the knowledge of God and of Jesus our Lord." (2 Pet. 1:2)

"Grace and peace to you from him who is, and who was, and who is to come, and from the seven spirits before his throne, and from Jesus Christ, who is the faithful witness, the first born from the dead, and the ruler of the kings of the earth." (Rev. 1:4–5)

Figure 23   Miracles of Jesus

Miracle	Matthew	Mark	Luke	John
Jesus passes through angry crowd			4:28–30	
Demon-possessed man cured in synagogue		1:23–26	4:33–35	
Peter's mother-in-law healed	8:14–15	1:30–31	4:38–39	
Catch of fish			5:1–11	
Leper healed	8:2–3	1:40–42	5:12–13	
Paralyzed man healed	9:2–7	2:3–12	5:18–25	
Man's withered hand healed	12:10–13	3:1–5	6:6–10	
Centurion's servant healed	8:5–13		7:1–10	
Widow's son raised from the dead			7:11–15	
Calming of the storm	8:23–27	4:37–41	8:22–25	
Demon-possessed man healed	8:28–34	5:1–15	8:27–35	
Jairus' daughter raised from dead	9:18–25	5:22–42	8:41–56	
Hemorrhaging woman healed	9:20–22	5:25–29	8:43–48	
Five thousand people fed	14:15–21	6:35–44	9:12–17	6:5–13
Demon-possessed boy healed	17:14–18	9:17–29	9:38–43	
Blind, dumb, and demon-possessed man healed	12:22		11:14	
Woman with a bent back healed			13:11–13	
Man with dropsy healed			14:1–4	
Ten lepers healed			17:11–19	
Bartimaeus & another blind man healed	20:29–34	10:46–52	18:35–43	
Malchus' ear healed			22:50–51	
Two blind men healed	9:27–31			
Dumb and possessed man healed	9:32–33			
Money found in fish's mouth	17:24–27			
Deaf and dumb man healed		7:31–37		
Blind man healed		8:22–26		
Water turned into wine				2:1–11
Nobleman's son healed of fever				4:46–54
Invalid man at Pool of Bethesda healed				5:1–9

Miracle	Matthew	Mark	Luke	John
Man born blind is healed				9:1–41
Lazarus raised from the dead				11:1–44
Second catch of fish				21:1–11
Walking on water	14:25	6:48–51		6:19–21
Canaanite woman's daughter healed	15:21–28	7:24–30		
Four thousand people fed	15:32–38	8:1–9		
Fig tree withers	21:18–22	11:12–26		

A round tombstone such as this one was rolled into place at the entrance to Jesus' tomb. (L. Shaw)

Figure 24   Parables in the Bible

Parable	Reference		
Old Testament			
The ewe lamb	2 Samuel 12:1–4		
The widow and her two sons	2 Samuel 14:1–11		
Escaped captive	1 Kings 20:35–40		
Vineyard and grapes	Isaiah 5:1–7		
Eagles and the vine	Ezekiel 17:3–10		
The lion's whelps	Ezekiel 19:2–9		
The boiling pot	Ezekiel 24:3–14		
Parables of Jesus	*Matthew*	*Mark*	*Luke*
New cloth on an old garment	9:16	2:21	5:36
New wine in old wineskins	9:17	2:22	5:37–38
Houses on rock and on sand	7:24–27		6:47–49
The two debtors			7:41–43
The sower and the soil	13:3–8	4:3–8	8:5–8
Lamp under a bushel	5:14–15	4:21–22	8:16; 11:33
The good Samaritan			10:30–37
The persistent friend			11:5–8
The rich fool			12:16–21
Servants watching for their master			12:35–40
The faithful steward			12:42–48
A fig tree without figs			13:6–9
The mustard seed	13:31–32	4:30–32	13:18–19
Leaven	13:33		13:20–21
Places of honor			14:7–14
The great banquet & reluctant guests			14:16–24
Counting the cost			14:28–33
The lost sheep	18:12–13		15:4–6
The lost coin			15:8–10
The prodigal son			15:11–32
The dishonest manager			16:1–8
The rich man and Lazarus			16:19–31
Servants and their duty			17:7–10
The unjust judge & the persistent widow			18:2–5
The Pharisee & the tax collector			18:10–14

Parable	Matthew	Mark	Luke
Talents (or pounds)	25:14-30		19:12-27
The wicked tenants	21:33-41	12:1-9	20:9-16
Leaves on the fig trees	24:32-33	13:28-29	21:29-31
Return of the houseowner		13:34-36	
The growing seed		4:26-29	
Tares	13:24-30		
The hidden treasure	13:44		
Pearl of great value	13:45-46		
The fisherman's net	13:47-48		
The unforgiving debtor	18:23-34		
Laborers in the vineyard	20:1-16		
The two sons	21:28-31		
The wedding banquet	22:2-14		
Ten virgins	25:1-13		
The sheep and the goats	25:31-36		

Suggested Reading List

If you would like to learn more about the Bible or look more closely at a specific subject covered in *The Shaw Pocket Bible Handbook,* here is a list of titles for you to consider. Under each heading the books are arranged in order from the simpler to the more complicated works.

General

Stott, J.R.W. *Understanding the Bible.* Grand Rapids: Zondervan, 1982.

Watson, D. *Is Anyone There?* Wheaton, Ill.: Shaw, 1979.

Chapman, C. *The Case for Christianity.* Grand Rapids: Eerdmans, 1981.

Bruce, F.F. *The English Bible.* New York: Oxford, 1961.

Douglas, J.D., ed. *The New Bible Dictionary.* Grand Rapids: Eerdmans, 1971.

Howley, G.C.D., Bruce, F.F., and Ellison, H.L., eds. *The New Layman's Bible: Commentary in One Volume.* Grand Rapids: Zondervan, 1979.

Archer, G.L. *The Encyclopedia of Bible Difficulties.* Grand Rapids: Zondervan, 1982.

Old Testament

Bush, F.W., and Hubbard, D.A. *Old Testament Survey: The Message, Form, and Background of the Old Testament.* Grand Rapids: Eerdmans, 1982.

Unger, M.F., and White, W., eds. *Nelson's Expository Dictionary of the Old Testament.* Nashville: Nelson, 1980.

Bruce, F.F., ed. *Israel and the Nations.* Grand Rapids: Eerdmans, 1963.

Harrison, R.K., *Old Testament Times.* Grand Rapids: Eerdmans, 1970.

Harrison, R.K., *Introduction to the Old Testament.* Grand Rapids: Eerdmans, 1969.

New Testament

Gundry, R. *A Survey of the New Testament*. Grand Rapids: Zondervan, 1982.

Hunter, A.M. *The Work and Words of Jesus*. Philadelphia: Westminster, 1973.

Hunter, A.M. *Introducing the New Testament*. Philadelphia: Westminster, 1973.

Hunter, A.M. *Introducing New Testament Theology*. Philadelphia: Westminster, 1957.

Ladd, G.E. *A Theology of the New Testament*. Grand Rapids: Eerdmans, 1974.

Guthrie, D. *New Testament Theology*. Downers Grove, Ill.: Inter-Varsity, 1981.

Theology

Stott, J.R.W. *Basic Christianity*. Downers Grove, Ill.: Inter-Varsity, 1969.

Lewis, C.S. *Mere Christianity*. New York: Macmillan, 1964.

McDonald, H.D. *Salvation*. Westchester, Ill.: Crossway, 1981.

Blamires, H. *The Christian Mind*. Ann Arbor: Servant, 1978.

Blamires, H. *On Christian Truth*. Ann Arbor: Servant, 1983.

Ryle, J.C. *Holiness*. Old Tappan, N.J.: Revell, 1980.

Elwell, W.A., ed. *Evangelical Dictionary of Theology*. Grand Rapids: Baker, 1984.

Culture, Archaeology

Daniel-Rops, H. *Daily Life in the Time of Jesus*. Ann Arbor: Servant, 1981.

Free, J.P. *Archaeology and Bible History*. Wheaton, Ill.: Scripture Press, 1956.

Yamauchi, E.M. *The Stones and the Scriptures*. Grand Rapids: Baker, 1981.

Vos, H.F. *An Introduction to Bible Archaeology*. Chicago: Moody, 1983.

Thompson, J.A. *The Bible and Archaeology*. Grand Rapids: Eerdmans, 1962.

Subject Index

Illustration Credits

Cover photos: *V. Gilbert Beers*
V. Gilbert Beers: p. 270
Donna Birkey: pp. 22, 84, 100, 140, 227, 289
British Library, London: p. 128
E.G. Howland: p. 182 *(from Agnes Scott College)*
Israel Office of Information: pp. 82, 91
James Jennings: pp. 35, 36, 48, 49, 53, 57, 60, 67, 108, 127, 162, 164, 167, 170, 173, 202, 213, 230, 238, 252, 259, 298, 304, 312, 348, 358
William Sanford LaSor: p. 327 (from Gleason Archer)
Malta Government Tourist Board: p. 292
National Aeronautics and Space Administration (NASA): p. 63
Richard T. Nowitz: pp. 18, 25, 80, 136, 144, 186, 190, 261, 295, 344, 357
The Oriental Institute of the University of Chicago (ORINST): pp. 20, 71 (from the British Museum), 219, 232, 245, 247
Harold Shaw: pp. 193, 207
Luci Shaw: pp. 28, 33, 42, 54, 70, 92, 138, 199, 241, 274, 285, 381, 388
David Singer: pp. 118, 124
University of Michigan Library, Department of Rare Books and Special Collections: p. 121
Howard F. Vos: pp. 30, 46, 51, 59 (from The Louvre), 68, 73, 74, 86, 95, 98, 103, 110, 114, 147 (from the British Museum), 154, 188, 196, 205, 210, 216, 222, 225, 263, 267, 281, 283, 301, 307, 310, 315, 318, 321, 324 (from The Louvre), 332, 337, 352 (from the Cairo Museum), 360, 374, 376

The Tabernacle drawing (p.156) is from *Lectures on the Tabernacle* by Samuel Ridout and is used by permission of the publisher, Loizeaux Brothers, Inc.

Charts prepared by *Richard J. Voyles*